From Tim
Christmas 1986

W9-CAM-720

Passage

VANCOUVER 100 c
city of the century

The publishers greatly appreciate the recognition of this book by
the 1986 Vancouver Centennial Commission.

Passage

FROM SAIL TO STEAM
CAPTAIN L.R.W. BEAVIS

Edited by M.S. Kline

DOCUMENTARY
BOOK PUBLISHERS
CORPORATION

BELLEVUE, WASHINGTON

In Cooperation With

Vancouver Maritime Museum

*Library of Congress Catalog Card
Number: 86-070175
Beavis, L. R. W. 1864—1940
Passage: from Sail to Steam
Includes index.
I. Kline, Mary Stiles, editor, 1953 -
II. Title.*

ISBN 0-935503-04-8

Distributed by the University of Washington Press, Seattle and London

Book design by Barry Provorse

Cover design by Dia Calhoun/Word Design

TABLE OF CONTENTS

ZIPPORA

Acamson, Rothesay

HAWAIIAN ISLES (later STAR OF GREENLAND)

In memory of
Peggy Elizabeth Beavis
and
Kenneth Allen Richardson

FOREWORD

Those who have served from apprentice to commander in square-rig sailing ships are growing fewer every day, and thus these memoirs of Captain Beavis possess an historical value.

A sailor's life is kaleidoscopic in its variety, and queer characters, out-of-the-way places and strange seas, added to a never-ending battle with the forces of nature, cannot help but make a sailor's reminiscences exciting reading. But there is something more; besides human characters there are the characters of that most beautiful of all men's handiworks, the sailing ship. In his ships Captain Beavis has been especially lucky, for besides serving his time in the famous jute clipper STAR OF FRANCE, and being employed as second mate, mate, and master of Colonel Goffey's well-known vessels MICRONESIA and EURASIA, he had the luck also to gain the second mate's berth in the old tea clipper TITANIA, when she was commanded by Captain Dandy Dunn and made those remarkable passages round the Horn to British Columbia under the flag of the Hudson's Bay Company.

In some sailors' memoirs one has to complain that ships' names are disguised or even not mentioned, but this is far from being the case in these reminiscences. Like all old-time sailors Captain Beavis has never forgotten a ship, and the names and characters of dozens of famous or notorious ships will be found recorded by the old captain.

When at length, through force of circumstances (due chiefly to the unfortunate burning of the MICRONESIA), he had to go into steam, the contrast between life in sail and life in steam is made very apparent. Yet for all that the last part of this book is by no means the least interesting, for steam has its adventures and its strenuous moments just as much as sail.

To those attracted by business ventures in new places Captain Beavis's account of the Hudson's Bay Company's attempt to gain a footing in Siberia after the Great War should be of very great interest.

Reading between the lines of this narrative one cannot help being struck by the breezy, virile sailor's attitude towards life which takes both the rough and the smooth with the same cheerful, indomitable spirit.

That this log of an old sea captain will be appreciated by all those who love the sea and its ships is the confident hope of Basil Lubbock.

By *Basil Lubbock* 1938

Many have lived through great events and significant eras but it is not a simple task to record history when you have lived it. My introduction to the work of a man who did occured one afternoon in 1979 when his granddaughter, Elizabeth Richardson, phoned my office. I listened with interest as she described this family collection of sailing ship photographs, numbering nearly 2000. She perceptively felt that they needed attention. Visiting her home, I glanced through the manuscript and became fascinated with this man, long since dead, and the experiences he was attempting to share through his writings.

As the executive director of Northwest Seaport, I was keenly interested in the primary sources of maritime history. My office was located on the passenger deck of the 1922 steam-powered ferry SAN MATEO which attracted its fair share of salty retirees. Along with others, I was committed to saving historic ships of the Northwest—the 1889 tugboat ARTHUR FOSS, a steam-driven lightship, and the last sailing schooner in the North-

MOSHULU at Victoria, B. C.

J. Genge

west, the WAWONA. My responsibilities included collecting and cataloging the Seaport's archives and photography, and deciphering many old colorful logs and journals depicting life at sea. An associate, George Bayless, and I were actively collecting and researching documents which eventually lead to my first book, *Ferryboats, A Legend on Puget Sound.*

The Beavis manuscript was a jigsaw puzzle. It was obvious that it was valuable but how could it best be used? Did it deserve more than a fire-proof cabinet and an occasional visitor? How could I make this photography and these recollections available to readers? Was it a story of wider appeal than to just those who have an interest in maritime matters? Much of my historical research is corroborated by eyewitness accounts and personal insights given me by people I interview. I call it "conversational history." It was obvious that this was an entertaining account of life at sea but unfortunately, the author was no longer around to help verify dates, places and contributing incidents. He was not pre-

sent to interpret foggy phrases or inferences. Few, if any, of his friends would be living 40 years after his death. I knew this project would be a real challenge and an education.

Time not occupied by the activities of the Seaport or the responsibilities of caring for a young family, or writing a definitive history of one of the largest ferry fleets in the world, was dedicated to getting acquainted with the Captain's manuscript. I wanted to know his character, imagine the way he thought through his problems, place myself in his shoes. I grew to recall incidents of his life as frequently as those of my own. I had to know the man in order to tackle the readability of his writing.

Here was a man of great accomplishment early in his life. He had command of a sailing ship by his mid-twenties, and it was a ship he had served aboard as a young officer on its maiden voyage. Following the vessel's total loss to a nitrate fire, Beavis's life went on the skids. Family pressure pushed him into steam, and once again he chose adventure over shoreside comforts. He knew very little about steamships, he cared even less for the lifestyle they offered. Beavis seemed to feel that his long streak of good fortune had vanished and his writing reflected this. The manuscript which had begun with a happy-go-lucky school boy attitude became entangled with the frustrations of maturity and experience. I was in a dilemma. My choices were to write a story based on the Captain's accounts and concern myself more with the reader's cheerful response to the memoirs, or I could simply reorganize and edit the work but let the Captain tell his own story. I chose to edit, hoping the reader, too, would appreciate this real-life drama.

I spent fleeting moments and concentrated hours reading this manuscript. I carried it with me on planes around the U.S. and used it as an mental escape after I sent another book, *STEAMBOAT Virginia V,* to the printer. This more leisurely approach gave me an opportunity to be objective about the Captain's writing and the chance to study his style. I concluded that though he was not a professional historian or a polished writer, his recollections were accurate and personable. Life had placed him in many interesting situations of history. He had witnessed royal parades and a Brazilian revolution, mayorial elections and plagues in the South Pacific, rescues and wars. He watched small communities burgeon into modern cities, while other ports with promise simply faded away. As a "CONWAY boy" who rose to captaincy, he was an experienced authority on the rigors of shipboard life. He knew the trials of strong winds and lingering doldrums, sickness and starvation, accidents at sea. He liked the comradeship of his shipmates and frequently remarked on the best clubs in ports. He had a grand sense of humor, a healthy taste for lust, and other sailor traits.

The Captain had a genuine ego, but the manuscript was not written to glorify his role in life. It was clearly intended as a conveyance of the meaningful activities he had witnessed. His text tells more than history, it imparts a *feeling* for life at sea. He lived each day as it happened, reacting quickly to the situation, whether as a youngster aboard a tall ship or as a pilot for trading voyages to Siberia. He had little appreciation for philosphy or fate. He lived for the next adventure and was sometimes disappointed when it did not arrive.

You can sense the excitement as another ship appears on the horizon. Races around the Horn were the highlight of every trip. Mail and messages were exchanged by gig. Captains and officers were invited to dinners and sometimes to dances. Provisions could be swapped during fleeting moments in the company of another ship. Captain Beavis described the ferocity of storms and the techniques used to survive them. He often noted the strengths of the ships he sailed, the skill of masters, and his pride in having been a part of that era.

After familiarizing myself with the story, I began to study the Captain's photography collection. He had had his own camera and eventually, a darkroom aboard ship. He exchanged photographs with others and by 1930, had assembled nearly 2000 images—some quite rare and valuable. Many of the photographs reflected the sailing ships he had passed at sea and in port. He had carefully catalogued the prints with statistics and names, collecting photos of ships by fleets and builders. I realized that there were photos of many of the ships he recalled in his story and they would serve as excellent illustrations. Each one has been credited as marked on the print, those without credits were not marked and are presumed to be Captain Beavis's originals.

After nearly five years of working with the manuscript and photos, I was finally confident about editing Captain Beavis's work and preserving his style. Most changes were made only when poor grammar,a choice of words, or disorganization interrupted the flow of the story. Many of the ports mentioned have new names, or depending upon nationality, they are spelled differently. Sometimes even the country's name has changed. In order to preserve the context of the story, I maintained most of the spellings used by Captain Beavis. The index of the book often gives the specific geographic location or indicates if it is an island, a point or other geographic information. I will admit that there were several references I could not decipher for locale. So much for not having the Captain at hand for confirmation...

The Captain's languauge reflects seafaring jargon and sometimes a Scotsman's dialect. In early days he often sailed with Scots who influenced his terminology. I traced some of his phrases to an 18th Century dictionary. This proved the influence of a mariner's isolation on lengthy voyages of sail. Definitions of the more unfamiliar seafaring terms have been footnoted. Rather than giving long, detailed explanations of historical accounts that led to events witnessed by the Captain, I chose to footnote in brevity only the specifics of history in which the Captain played a part. Excerpts from the Captain's original manuscript have been cited in quotes and italics in the footnotes when they were interesting but not particularly relevant to the organization of his story. Photo captions, too, have often been drawn from the text.

Credibility for Captain Beavis's story was found in his diaries and ship's journals kept from his earliest years at sea. He was also a frequent correspondant of Poet Laureate John Masefield, a CONWAY boy, and Basil Lubbock, distinquished marine historian. Their letters confirm facts and dates, and even a threatened lawsuit from Captain Jarvis, a subject of one of Beavis's vignettes.

Following the Captain's retirement from the sea in 1930, he concentrated his attention on the photographs which he had begun saving many years before. Each photo was carefully identified with as much information as he could provide. He contacted photographers in ports around the world, but primarily in the Pacific, and systematically organized the prints of vessels he had known and passed at sea or in port, their sister ships, and other ships of the owner's fleets. Several of the original photographer's collections have been lost. By 1930 Captain Beavis's private collection of sailing vessels was considered the second largest in the world. The largest known was then in Australia.

The Depression contributed to the failure of a magazine, *Sea Lore,* which he published at Vancouver, B.C. Following that misadventure but with strong encouragement from friends, readers, and the Vancouver City Museum, he moved to the tiny, remote island of Lasqueti, near Texada Island, in the Strait of Georgia. He had wanted to isolate himself with his journals and photos . . . to write. He, too, must have felt that the end of his life was anticlimatic. He had been sick, money was a problem, and death was near. Reading through those early diaries, he could feel the energy and inquisitiveness of youth, the powerful challenge of adventure, the lust for living he had once known. He felt on this island that he was once again at sea, but this time he was alone. I did not alter the ending of the book.

With the help of friends in the Vancouver Maritime Museum and the *Vancouver Sun,*

Elizabeth Richardson and I interviewed several former acquaintances of Captain Beavis. No one living had known him before the 1930s. I felt even more confident that my conclusions about Captain Beavis were correct.

He was an ordinary man. He recorded his personal reflections of an extraordinary lifestyle that ended shortly after the turn of the century. He was a witness to the impact of the age of technology and industry, and in many ways, it alterred his course. He described cargoes, ports, ships, traditions, disasters, geography, and changes that occured between 1876 and 1930. He was resentful of steam but he had spent half of his career in command of steamers and motorships. He never relinquished his love of sail. The aging Captain described people and the effects of change upon them and himself. He gave a taste of their emotions, their reactions, their humor and their thoughts. Conversations seemed simple but tangible.

Following the manuscript's completion, Captain Beavis submitted it to literary agents for review. He died in his daughter's home in Portland, Oregon, in 1940. Soon after, his family received word of the interest of a major New York publisher but the Captain's success had been stinted again. The manuscript required an editor, they were advised, but the publisher's staff had been drafted for World War II. The family could not afford to hire one privately so the collection and materials were boxed and stored in a closet. There they remained for nearly 40 years. His inquisitive granddaughter, Elizabeth Richardson took an interest in the collection after her mother's death. Realizing its potential significance, she contacted me.

From that day forward, it has never been far from my mind if not right in the middle of it. Captain Beavis has beguiled me with his stories of an exceptional life. Now perhaps he will do as much for you.

M. S. Kline
Redmond, WA.

ACKNOWLEDGEMENTS

I did not want to do it. But my many friends badgered me so. Continually they have been at me. Now I have my chance to get back at them. One of the first was the old CONWAY captain, Captain A. S. Balfour, O. B. E., late of the Indian Marine and now of Edinburgh who by his kindly letters gave me encouragement. Then Mr. Lubbock, the world-wide historian—who so kindly has written the Foreword. My friend Bill Adams who served his time with L. D. Douglas, commander of the R. M. S. JAPAN, years ago in the old SILBERHORN. Bill Adams now resides in San Francisco or I should say Oakland having deserted Dutch Flat, after writing that classic of the sea, *Ships and Women,* which I had the pleasure of reviewing.

Again my thanks and many of them are due to my friend Noel Robinson, that versatile journalist and free lance of Vancouver. Also my friends in the Province Building—Ronald Kenvyn "Over the Foreyard," Cecil Scott, L. V. Kelly and that charming little lady, the literary editor Kathleen Mathers.

Also the shipping community of Vancouver who have often given me their support: Commander B. L. Johnson, Lloyd's Agent; Captain Crawford of the Empire Stevedoring Company, the Wallace Brothers of the Burrard Drydock, and many others who, when I was editor of *Sea Lore,* not only gave me their support but a friendly shove. And lastly, but not least, those friends in the City Museum. Curator T. P. O. Menzies and Mrs. R. Corbett but for whose kindly aid in typing, their help and advice, this would not be finished. They must have had a terrible time making out my handwriting, often I can't myself.

To these and all, including my god-daughter May Lawson who helped so with her letters, I tender my sincere thanks.

L. R. W. Beavis
LASQUETI ISLAND
British Columbia
September 1938

ELIZA LIHN (ex-AUSTRALIA)

Some days I wish I had known Lance Beavis but through the years I have begun to realize that I could not have been closer to him if we had been the best of friends in his lifetime or mine.

I have never been afforded a greater opportunity to study world history, culture and geography from an eyewitness perspective.

A most sincere thanks is extended to George Bayless of Seattle who generously stored and insured the collection and provided work space. Captain D. A. Webb, USCG(ret) spent hundreds of painstaking volunteer hours sorting, filing and cataloging nearly 1800 photographs. His records were transformed to computer format by LT(jg) Eunice Kempt, USCG(ret). This collection formed the basis from which the publisher illustrated the book and provided an excellent manuscript reference.

The Vancouver Maritime Museum, descendent of the museum which first suggested to Beavis that his journals should be published, and the Vancouver City Archives have extended continuous enthusiasm and cooperation in publishing this work. The City of Vancouver has honored the Captain's memoir's by recognising this book as a 1986 Vancouver Centennial publication.

Members of the Conway Club, a world-wide organization of alumni of the CONWAY and Beavis's early training, and two of its members, Derek Wyndham and Cedric Hawkshaw, have afforded the editor of this book support and perspective.

The Vancouver press has continued to assist this story through Jack Ramsey, *The Vancouver Sun,* who helped us reach former acquaintances of Beavis and his daughter in West Vancouver. These people, Norman Hacking, and the late Reverend Ramsey, graciously shared their memories of the old sea captain. There were many others who reviewed the manuscript and assisted in its production. To each of them, a word of thanks.

A very special thanks is owed to Captain Beavis's granddaughter, Elizabeth Richardson and her husband Tom. The Richardson family perceived the importance of Captain Beavis's work and made efforts to preserve it. Their direct assistance in the publication of this work is an indication of their willingness to share this treasure with those who are interested.

We are grateful to the patient but tenacious and skillful Barry Provorse and his company, Documentary Book Publishers, for a special and dedicated interest in this project.

To these friends and to my loving and resourceful daughter Galena, I offer my sincere gratitude.

M. S. Kline
Editor

"Homeward Bound"

CHAPTER I

RECOLLECTIONS OF BOYHOOD DAYS

My first vague and misty recollections are of an old chateau, some five or six miles outside of Boulogne, France. I remember crossing the Channel at various times, clutching my mother's arm. Father was there, his stern face pressed against the wind.

It was before the Franco-German War of 1870. I was born in 1864. My father, Richard Beavis, was becoming a well-known British artist, a painter of military, marine and animal subjects in oil and water colour. His pictures were to be hung regularly for thirty years on the walls of the Royal Academy.

Our neighbours in France were the Wyllies with whom we were very friendly. W.L. Wyllie would one day become a noted marine artist and Royal Academician.

As the only brother among seven sisters, I appreciated their female attention and my power among the girls. Our family was of Devonshire stock. Father was from South Devon and Mother, who was a Rafarel, was from Instow and Bideford. This may possibly explain why I had sea predilections.

Those days were filled with warmth and laughter, ease and charm. But when the Prussians invaded, our world of beauty and brightness was shattered. We were forced to return to Mother England.

I began to have a better memory after this.

Whilst living in France, my father kept studios in Berners Street, London, but when the family moved back to London, he took No. G, Belzize, Park Gardens, London. This was the house that the Royal Academician and great marine artist, Clarkson Stanfield, had lived in and where he died.

My father bought most of Stanfield's studio gear and some of his furniture. He told me that in his young manhood days, some of his work had been shown to Stanfield by a mutual friend. Stanfield's comments were curt:

"Tell the young man he had better go back to Devonshire and go lobster fishing."

Fortunately my father did not heed the rude advice.

Captain L. R. W. Beavis

1

As I grew older, I was admitted into the schoolroom with my sisters' governess. Evidently I was a handfull, for soon afterwards, I was sent to a dorm school as a boarder. The lady who kept it, a Miss Elkington, had been governess for Dr. Jex Blake's children. Dr. Blake was then master of Rugby School. Miss Elkington was a spinster who had her mother and sometimes a sister living with her. I was the first boarder at the school.

Even to this day, I remember the way the spinster punished us. I do not think she was a fit person to have charge of children of tender years. She used to lamb seven bells out of the boarders for any little fault. Not the day-boarders, though; they would have told their parents when they went home.

I ran away twice. The first time I had a three week holiday. The second time I was hauled back at once, and, of course, licked.

The cook stood up for us on more than one occasion. She was a red-haired wench by the name of Sarah, and Irish at that. The time that I minded most was when, after we had all been thrashed and were going to get more, Sarah came to the rescue.

"Don't you dare hit those boys again, not over my dead body, wull ye, ye limb of Satan!"

Sarah was dismissed. Then how we missed our beloved defender!

I was brought home suddenly, when my baby brother died. The nurse, whilst giving me a tub, called my mother and father in to look at my back. It was covered with bruises and great weals, the scars of which I bear to this day.

I did not go back to Miss Elkington's school. I think my father interviewed the lady. He could be irate when the situation demanded it.

By this time my parents had moved from Belsize Park Gardens to 38 Fitzroy Square. We lived in a large house built by the famous Adams Brothers and owned by G.R. Ward, the miniature painter.

Sir Charles Eastlake, the president of the Royal Academy, lived in the square on the east side. Gow and his son, Andrew lived on our side (to the south) two doors from us. Maddox Brown lived next door. The artist Frank Dicksee, not then a Royal Academician, lived on the northeast side. With all of this artistic environment, I *ought* to have been a painter. My parents would naturally have liked me to have followed my father's profession, but I never showed any talent along those lines. As a little lad, I remember drawing horses and cows from my father's Landham studios. These were done on newspapers on the floor of the studio. Yet, most of the artwork I did was after I had been at sea. Then it was always ships, quite a few of which I lined on the inside lids of sea chests.

A peculiar thing about Fitzroy Square was that houses on the south and east sides were built many years before the other two sides and were the work of the Adams Brothers. There were stone stairs and mahogany balustrades which were a delight to my sisters and me. We used to slide down them, the latter being detrimental to my pants. The doors were also very lofty and of solid mahogany. There were deep areas in front with iron railings and oh, what vaults and collars. Our lovely old house was a maze of secret doors and passages. Iron pillars were hung in front of the house and near the front door for holding lanterns. Gas lamps lighted the streets and a man used to come along about dark to light them. He was a source of great interest to children.

The square was paved with cobblestones and it was very noisy with traffic. Later it was macadamized which was thought to be very up-to-date.

Often my father would take me for walks in the early morning in Regents Park. While he sketched, I would watch the many sheep grazing in the park. Father would tell me the names of the different trees.

On Sunday afternoons, all dolled up in my little velvet suit, Father would take me in a hansom cab to visit some of the prima donnas. We had an old friend, an Irishman by the name of O'Toole, who had taught many of these great singers the Irish melodies. It was

H. M. S. CONWAY ('Rock Ferry')
British training ship on the River Mersey
Photo taken on Coronation Day, 22 June 1911, King
George V.
*"It was the CONWAY for me since the WORCESTER,
stationed on the Thames, was thought to be too near
home. We were then living in London.*
*"... but I have never regretted my father's actions. I
made many sterling friendships and have always been
proud of being a 'CONWAY' boy."*
Beavis joined the CONWAY just as she was first
turned over by the Admiralty to the Merchant Marine
Service Association in 1876. The vessel continued in
service as a training ship until the early 1950s.

through him we came to know the ladies. I suppose I must have been a nice little boy; they used to make much of me, such great singers as Adelina Patti, Christine Nielson, Etelka Gerster, and Minnie Hank. They all kissed me but I think Christine Nielson was my special favorite.

Those were great days for me. How I enjoyed the ride in the hansom!

I was sent to a school in Regents Park as a day-boarder. "Barford's" or "All Souls Grammar School in connection with King's College" was its high-sounding name. We thought a lot of "King's College" being tacked on.

My school days at Barford's passed happily enough. I suppose I had the usual number of fights, sometimes getting the worst of them. I remember I had a fight with Goodall, the artist's son. Having gotten the better of him this time, my dear old Guv'nor was rather elated over it. "My son licked yours," he told the other artist with satisfaction.

Just before I left school, a big boy named O'Connor, a son of a friend of the family, joined my class. He, like a good Irishman, was a scrapper and invariably I had to be his second. We got to be rather notorious, in fact.

Whilst I was still at this school, my father leased from the Earl de la Warr a pretty little place called "The Cottage" at Buckhurst Park. It was right in the Park, about a mile from the manor house and the same distance from the agent's house, a Mr. Gregory.

One day I was fishing in a little stream in the Park, armed with authority from the agent, when along came the old Earl and two of his daughters on horseback. I ran in a blue funk to open the gate for them and hastened to tell them I had permission to fish. The gentleman thanked me for opening the gate and told me I could fish and shoot rabbits anytime. I thought that was very nice of him. I also thought his daughters looked very pretty on their ponies. One had red hair—she was the prettiest.

But, my hat, wasn't I scared. I had never before seen an earl, much less spoken to one.

Those were happy, irresponsible times, my boyhood days.

The holidays, mostly spent at Buckhurst Park, were never to be forgotten. The village consisted of just a few cottages, amongst which were the Dorset Arms, the village inn, and a blacksmith's shop on the green. The station was at Withyham, about a mile and three-quarters from our cottage, through the Park drive.

Generally I had a school chum staying with me; we must have been a sad worry to my sisters, especially the elder ones. We kept goats and of course, I would fraternize with the Billy and then romp into the room where my sisters were having afternoon tea, probably with the vicar or someone equally respectable.

"Oh! That horrid boy. He's been amongst the goats," and their handkerchiefs would go to their noses. I was relegated to the back kitchen. No doubt I *did* smell.

H. M. S. CONWAY
In the Menai Straits. Hundreds of young British sailors were trained aboard this ship permanently moored in the Mersey. Today there are CONWAY alumni clubs around the world.

Generally, however, I managed to break even and get my revenge. Once I got the plaster head of one of my father's lay figures and put it in one of my sister's beds, and this, when they retired for the night, nearly frightened them to death. Not a nice thing to do, but I often did things that would hardly be called nice.

I had a brother in those days who was seven years my junior. He was a nice boy who reminded me of what I was not. I had a violent temper, a source of sorrow to my parents, and all through my life it was the cause of my doing things that I would be sorry for afterwards. Yet, I don't think I ever did anything really bad.

The immediate cause of my going to sea was a fit of this uncontrolled temper. I threw a chair at my father when the old gentleman had the gout. I did not wait for the consequences. I ran for my life and Father, forgetting the gout, ran after me. He did not catch me but his condition worsened and so did mine.

A very old friend of the family, Captain Walter May, R.N., offered advice when Father told him of my wickedness. "Send the boy to the CONWAY or the WORCESTER," the old sailor said.

It was the CONWAY for me since the WORCESTER, stationed on the Thames, was thought to be too near home. We were then living in London.

STAR OF FRANCE

CHAPTER II

A SAILOR'S LIFE FOR ME

So it happened that I was sent to the CONWAY. I was only twelve years old but I have never regretted my father's actions. I made many sterling friendships and have always been proud of being a "CONWAY boy."

I joined the CONWAY in 1876 after the summer holidays. She had just been turned over by the Admiralty to the Merchant Marine Service Association, following her arrival at the Mersey River on June 23, 1876. Captain Franklin, R.N., was the commander. He was a great stickler for discipline.

The vessel was just fitting out when I joined her. This was the third CONWAY. She had been the NILE, a 92-gun ship, before fitting out for use as an impeccable training ship. As the NILE she had served in the Crimean War.[1] Everything was very strange to me. The ship was in great disorder; however, that was soon remedied. The shipwrights were still working on board for several weeks after I joined, and the ship was in considerable confusion. Her engines and boilers had only recently been removed. Being a new boy I was put into the starboard fo'castle. After a few weeks, I was made a foretopman, port watch. The way of it was this: all new boys were forecastle men, small boys were mizzentopmen, medium boys were foretopmen and the big boys were maintopmen.

I can still see in my mind's eye, Saturday evenings on the main-deck, when we gathered around the piano with Mrs. Franklin and her daughter, Dolly. If we had not been black-listed we were privileged to dance with Dolly. These were the days when we used to *dance*, not this modern sliding, walking business, like a ship caught aback and gathering stern-way. We used to do the Highland schottisch. Great Scott! but it makes my mouth water now at my age.

We did not have all of the amenities of life that we enjoy today. In those days there was no heat and no electric light and all of the water had to be brought from the shore by boat. The CONWAY grace after a meal was: "For these and all His mercies the Lord's name be praised." [John Masefield, in his book, *The Conway* (William Heinemann LTD, London, 1933) records the dietary table allowed per head per week to the CONWAY boys: "7 pints of milk, 7 pounds of bread, 14 ounces of sugar, 4 ounces of butter (or cheese), one and one-half pounds of flour, 1 pound of rice, 1 pound of oatmeal, 5 pounds fresh meat, 1 pound salt meat, both without bone; half a pint of peas, quarter of a pound of suet, quarter of a pound raisins, three and a half

---

[1] ed. note. The CONWAY had been launched as the H.M.S. NILE in 1839 but was not commissioned until 1852. In that year she was docked at Devonport and fitted with engines and propeller. She took the water January 30, 1854, and did 6.8 knots on her trials. The engines were removed in 1876 when she was outfitted as a training ship. The engine room space was later used as a gymnasium and the shaft tunnel was used as a rifle range. In 1937, at the time that Beavis was writing this manuscript, the CONWAY went into dry-dock for her first major repair job in 41 years.

pounds potatoes and vegetables, and tea and coffee as required."]

I can still remember some of the CONWAY boys, especially those of whom I was most fond. Haddock of later Olympic Games fame was on board with me, also Ned McKinstry. Ned was a great favourite of Mother Taylor of the tuck shop. He was also well-liked by her niece, Bessie, whom he later married.

"APPRENTICE DAYS"

At age sixteen in 1878, I left the CONWAY for an apprenticeship to Corry Bros. of Belfast.[2] I joined the beautiful jute clipper STAR OF FRANCE in London, Captain E. Hughes, master. After two Calcutta voyages, Captain Hugh Wilson took her over, having just come from the STAR OF GERMANY. The Old Man was known as "Barney" Wilson, a strict disciplinarian, yet absolutely fair, and he was a very hard sail carrier.

All the time I was in the STAR OF FRANCE I never saw a ship pass her, it was always the other way about. Her sister ship, the STAR OF ITALY, had the best record, yet I don't

think she was any smarter. We were never in company at sea although several times we were in port together. This often led to arguments between the crews which generally ended up in a free fight. I wonder if the youth of these times have the same love and regard for their ships. (The Lord forgive me for calling them ships.) No, I am sure they don't.

These two ships, the ITALY and the FRANCE, were the product of Harland & Wolff, and were 1,570 tons net register. They were identical in all respects, except the figureheads. These were beautiful ships, smaller than the STARS of BENGAL and RUSSIA built three years before them, and I think they were the first ships to have screw rigging in lieu of lanyards.[3]

At Belfast the STAR OF FRANCE left the stocks four months after the ITALY. Both of these ships carried double t'gallant sails on the fore and main, but single on the mizzen which was unusually large and deep. It was quite a handful for us boys. On one voyage in the FRANCE we were in company with the STAR OF PERSIA and had a good deal the better of it, finally dropping her far below the horizon astern. I think the PERSIA would have made a better showing but for a foul bottom.

On my last voyage with the FRANCE, we were in company with the SAINT MARGARET and easily beat her into Calcutta. The SAINT MARGARET was a ship of 1,368 tons, built by Roydon of Liverpool in 1877, the same year the FRANCE was built. She was considered a very smart ship. We boys of the FRANCE rubbed it in to the half-deck crew of the SAINT MARGARET. One of our taunting remarks, was, "You may be saintly, MARGARET dear, but your nun's dress gets tangled up in your legs when you start to move, and the FRANCE will always show her *starn* to you." Boys will be boys ....[4]

A day or two after being in company with the SAINT MARGARET, the FRANCE fell in with the GREAT VICTORIA, a full rigged ship belonging to Pernie of Liverpool. Originally a steamer built as far back as 1854, she

---

[2] ed. note. The average term of apprenticeship at sea was four years, after which a lad could sit for second mate papers. But if he had been in the school ships for two years, he was only required to serve three years at sea before going up for his ticket.

[3] ed. note. Screw rigging, also known as a turnbuckle, consisted of a link or sleeve with a swivel at one end and an internal screw thread at the other, or with an internal screw thread at each end. It was used as a means of uniting or coupling and of tightening two parts, as the ends of two rods.

[4] *"This ship will be remembered as being bought by John Orth, (the Arch-Duke Salvador of Austria). She sailed from Rio de Janiero and was never heard of again. All sorts of weird yarns have been told, including that the Arch-Duke has been seen in some out-of-way port. Sailors are notoriously superstitious and not always exempt from drawing the long bow."*

STAR OF ITALY *"[The STAR OF FRANCE's] sister ship, the STAR OF ITALY, had the best record, yet I don't think she was any smarter. We were never in company at sea although several times we were in port together. This often led to arguments between the crews which generally ended up in a free fight."*

STAR OF BENGAL
Built by Harland & Wolff at Belfast in 1874.
Iron ship. 1870 gross tons, 1797 net tons.
262.' x 40.2' x 23.5'
Photo taken at Port Pine, South Australia.

STAR OF FRANCE
Built by Harland & Wolff at Belfast in 1877.
*"Top masts and lower masts in one [piece]. White yards
and masts. Steel topmasts were a flesh colour. Hulls
were black and in their early days had a gold ribbon
and gold on the quarters and bow. The FRANCE and
the PERSIA had single lower masts and fidded top
masts."*

was a long, lean thing, and the first and only vessel that I ever saw with cross-jack braces leading aft. Like most converted steamers she had a good turn of speed, but we in the STAR OF FRANCE soon gave her our dust.

I had a pal on board her named Crogan who had been in the CONWAY with me and didn't I crow over him when we met in Calcutta. Crogan, as his name implies, was Irish. He was delightful company to anyone he liked but he could be a bit of a mystic sometimes. He would talk to me leaning out over the bulwarks of the upper deck of the CONWAY, his eyes shining as he yarned of the boundless ocean and piloted us from one place to another in memory. Infatuated he was with the sea. What became of him I do not know, but I have never forgotten him.

On previous voyages the STAR OF FRANCE had scalped quite a few well-known ships. We were able to give our dust to the LAKE SUPERIOR, a beautiful skysail yarder built by Steele on the Clyde in 1868; then another time we left the LAMMERMOOR behind. She was built by Reid in 1874. This ship gave us a great race, however, and although we were in company several days, there was not much to it.

The LAMMERMOOR was a very lovely ship, carrying three skysails and double t'gallant sails and royals. Beating to windward the FRANCE had a good deal the better of it, but with a fresh, fair wind the LAMMERMOOR was our equal. As the wind came fair both ships set t'gallant and topmast and lower stunsails on the fore, and t'gallant and topmast stunsails on the main. A veritable cloud of canvas—two iron jute clippers, each trying to beat the other, both their crews keyed up and stepping on their toes. The skipper and mates were irritable, yet each ship was giving her best under their superb seamanship.

Yes, I am proud, more than proud, to have served in such ships in that epic era of sail. No wonder a ship is always called "she." What is better comparable to a lovely full-rigger than a beautiful woman? Yet sometimes, I think the ship is more lovely, more reliable, harder

to know, often times as coy; but in stress, in storm, she answers to it gallantly, as do most good and beautiful women...but nuff said by an old sailor.

This ship LAMMERMOOR was sister ship to the celebrated CEDRIC THE SAXON with the difference that the CEDRIC only sported a main skysail. The LAMMERMOOR was wrecked at Point Reyes on a passage from Australia to San Francisco in very thick weather. The man who commanded her, Captain Guthrie, was exonerated. If ever wandering the shores of that neighborhood, the traveler may come across a house with a beautiful garden. There he will find the figurehead of the LAMMERMOOR.

On my second voyage in the FRANCE, outward bound in the N.E. trades, we fell in with the HOGHTON TOWER, a White Star ship of Liverpool. We were able to beat her, but it took us two days to get away from her. She was carrying stunsails on the fore and the main, even t'gallant stunsails which we were not doing at first. We sent them aloft, however, before we dropped her astern. She was a very lovely sight.

Another time we were able to get away with the unbeatable SHEILA, and fairly easily, too. I rather fancy Captain Crugel, if he was then in command, did not enjoy that. We also passed the ARISTIDES, well-known Aber-

LAKE ERIE
Built by Barclay Curle at Glasgow for Canada Shipping Co. at Montreal.

deen flyer and the commodore ship of the Thompsons.

One of the hardest tussles the FRANCE encountered was with the speedy CHARLOTTE CROOM, a ship built by Connell on the Clyde in 1874. She was rigged like the STAR OF FRANCE, a five t'gallant yarder, but had a main skysail and at this date sported stunsails on fore and main. We were in company with her in the N.E. trades and she was a cloud of sail[5]. For three days we held each other, neither ship altering the bearing of the other. Then the wind fell lighter and we in the FRANCE gradually drew ahead. In light airs the FRANCE was a wizard.[6]

In the doldrums that followed we picked up the STAR OF DENMARK but as soon as we got the S.E. trades, we romped away from her. We beat her into Calcutta by some ten days.

NILE
Built by Russell at Glasgow 1886 for Brown of Glasgow.
Iron four-masted barque. 2163 gross tons, 2079 net.
A. A. Clark master 1889—92.
Photo taken at Ayn.

[5] *"The CHARLOTTE CROOM carried t'gallant stunsails set, and lower stunsails on the fore. We in the FRANCE were carrying topmast and lower stunsails on the fore, and topmast stunsails on the main."*

[6] ed. note. Beavis noted in a 1937 newspaper clipping that the STAR OF FRANCE, like the old CONWAY, was still afloat but that she had been "degraded to a sort of dance hall at Redondo, California." From "Over the Foreyard," by Ronald Kenvyn, *The Vancouver Province*, Oct. 23, 1937.

"CALCUTTA"

My apprenticeship was out in Calcutta in November 1882 and my father had sent me one hundred pounds to come home at once by mail steamer. I was twenty years old and I was expected to pass for second mate and join a new ship then building in Glasgow. She was the MICRONESIA in which Father had taken thirteen sixty-fourths of the shares.

My dear old dad made the mistake of making the draft out to me instead of my captain. Old Captain Wilson was very dubious. Too much money. He wanted to buy my ticket but I would have none of it, making all sorts of promises which my skipper did not believe. He could not stop me getting the money and turning it into rupees. It seemed an awful lot to me. Soon it got wind among the other apprentices; they were all very willing to help me spend it. For a short time I stayed at Spence's Hotel. Of course I had a royal time, boy-like, never thinking of the morrow. Calcutta in those days was a gay place if you had money. All my CONWAY chums came around me; some of their names I remember, but not all. There was Brandy Wyndham, so named from the colour of his hair, and Leake in the COLUMBIA (one of Sandbach's large ships); Colbarn, Line and Moxon were in the WALDEN ABBEY (belonging to Poole of Liverpool). I couldn't forget Long and Chops Sinclair in the old BATTLE ABBEY (also one of Poole's ships) and Tolcher, McArthur, Beaumont and Hodges in the THALATTA. Crogan in the GREAT VICTORIA was there and so was Bairn Stevenson (as Scottish as you make 'em and true as steel) in the FRANKISTAN. Then there was Bennett in the GODIVA (another of Sandbach's). A number of others whose names I have forgotten were present, too, because the STAR OF BENGAL, the SAINT MARGARET, the OREALLA from New York—all were in port.[7]

Calcutta was a sight to see, a mass of splendid sailing ships but very few steamers, and they were mostly mail boats. All good things must come to an end and soon I was broke. I had to get a ship and that quickly if I was to eat. In desperation, I signed on as A.B. on the old CITY OF CARTHAGE, one of Smith's steamers—a compound engine. They were mostly all Scots onboard; I was a "furriner." Yet withal I fared no bad.

"Three masts and a funnel drifting," was an expression used to describe steamers since they sat very low in the water. Moreover, the City Line steamers had the reputation of being the cleanest vessels passing through the Suez Canal.[8] I remember we had a bit of a dusting in the Gulf of Lion and I was not prepossessed with the CITY OF CARTHAGE. She was my first steamer and I was not a little scornful of her.

Times have changed since then.

---

[7] "Alas, now nearly all have passed to the great majority. Some made great names in the war but were wiped out."

[8] ed. note. The Suez Canal of Egypt runs from Port Said to Port Tawfig. It has no locks and can accomodate ships of almost any draft. The modern construction of the canal was completed between 1859-69. Great Britain was the largest shareholder in 1875, purchasing the interest of the Egyptian khedive. In 1888 all major European powers declared the Canal neutral and free for passage as a result of the Convention of Constantinople.

SIERRA MIRANDA at left, GLENGARRY at right,
the first EULOMENE is ahead of GLENGARRY. At
Calcutta.
*"My apprenticeship was out in Calcutta in November
1882 and my father had sent me one hundred pounds
to come home at once by mail steamer. I was twenty
years old and I was expected to pass for second mate
and join a new ship then building in Glasgow. She was
the MICRONESIA..."*

WHITE PINE (ex-QUATHLAMBA)

THIRD MATE DAYS

oing up Channel in very thick weather and clearing a little at Dungeness, we finally docked the steamer CITY OF CARTHAGE in London in Victoria Dock on Monday, February 25, 1883.

It felt good to be home. The dear old smoke looked cheerful to me. My people made a lot of me at first but it took me over a week before I dared to tell my father that I had worked my passage. I had gotten home nearly as quickly as if I had paid a fare, and more over, this way *I* was paid. I had had the time of my life in Calcutta, too.

I was too busy, I thought, to go to school and study so I did not pass for second mate. I had to go as third mate. My father was rather disgusted with me.

I went to Glasgow to join the MICRO-NESIA in the Queen's Dock. She was fitting out and loading under the command of Captain A. Greig. He stood well over six feet and was a fine type of Scot. He had a long white beard and keen blue eyes that looked you through and through. The MICRONESIA's mate (whose name I have forgotten) was a sturdy man about fifty, a consummate seaman. The second mate was named Wilson, hailing from Aberdeen. I was third mate and again, the "furriner" among Scots. The carpenter was the Old Man's son. The sailmaker and doctor (the cook) hailed from Peterhead, as did the master and his son. The steward was named Miller but came from Glasgow. There were no apprentices, but instead, four ordinary seamen in the half-deck.

Glasgow was full of fine ships fitting out and loading. One steamer I especially remember was new. She was the Cunard liner AURANIA, barque-rigged, with royal yards across.

The MICRONESIA loaded a heavy general cargo for Sydney, New South Wales, and was towed to sea in the latter part of March, 1883 by the FLYING HUNTRESS. We stopped for a short time in the Careloch to adjust compasses, then again proceeded. Letting go the tug soon after, we had a good run down the Irish Channel. Off Tuska, the wind came ahead and blew hard from the southwest. We had to set up the rigging—what a god-send screw rigging was!

Crossing the Bay of Biscay, our spare spars went adrift and one of the sailors was rather badly hurt. The Old Man blamed the mate for the spars not being securely lashed. He was down on him for the rest of the voyage. After that we soon picked up the northeast Trades and fine weather. Being a new ship, there was plenty of work to do both aloft and on deck. The MICRONESIA was fitted with a spike bowsprit—a real plus, since we no longer had the jibboom to worry about.[1]

Near the equator we spoke the BATTLE ABBEY and the STAR OF BENGAL. The BATTLE ABBEY was carrying stunsails on the fore, but the "Belfast crack" was coming up on her fast. Captain Greig sent me away in

---

[1] ed. note. A spike bowsprit is one formed of a single spar.

the gig with letters and a couple of bags of spuds. As I left the ship, the other two ships were a long way off, in fact hull-down. There was very little wind, only the tail end of the Southeast Trades and a long southerly swell and clear sky.

The BATTLE ABBEY was the nearest so I boarded her first. The captain's name was Banks. Several CONWAY boys were on board who had been with me in Calcutta. They were much surprised to see me. Being a Saturday, the watch was busy washing decks. After a short stay we left the ABBEY since the Belfast star was close aboard and we would not have far to row at this distance.

On boarding the BENGAL Captain Smyth recognized me immediately and wanted to know what I was doing there. With a sardonic grin he asked if I had come on board to demoralize his boys again. He knew all about my escapades in Calcutta. It was quite a happy meeting in the half-deck. They, too, were washing decks. We were swapping yarns at a great lick when, on glancing out of the half-deck door, I saw my own ship close-to.

The MICKY looked a picture, all sail set and her ensign flying at the spanker-gaff; a light breeze having made up. I said goodbye to my chums and then to Captain Smyth who handed me a packet for my skipper. We tumbled into the gig with only a few yards to pull.

What a splendid sight we had in the boat, to see those three beautiful ships close to, rising and dropping on the long swell with a cloudless sky overhead and just enough wind to keep the sails full. Our gig rose and fell on the swell between the two foremost ships. The STAR OF BENGAL was passing just to leeward of the MICRONESIA and Poole's BATTLE ABBEY was just a short distance astern and to leeward of the Belfast crack. The crews of all the ships were lining the rails and the different captains were walking their poops. It was a sight I have never forgotten.

The MICRONESIA had fairly good Southeast Trades after this and sighted Martin Vas Island, where the China tea clipper FLYING

SPUR was lost. The casting was run down in forty-four degrees south latitude and one day the MICKY fell in with the PANMURE of the Dundee clipper line. In the whole sail breeze, we easily dropped her astern. All aboard the MICKY were pleased because the PANMURE was considered a fast ship and the MICKY had yet her spurs to win.

Several times running heavily in these southern latitudes, the MICKY topped the three hundred mile. One day she ran three hundred sixteen nautical miles in a twenty-three and one-half hour day; this with the fore and main t'gallant sails and the reefed mainsail. This was her biggest run so far but later in her career she did far better.

We passed Cape Otway on the seventy-fourth day out and went snoring through Bass Straits expecting to make Sydney in seventy-seven days, but this was not to be. Off Cape Howe the wind came light northerly which held her up for a couple of days. Here we were in company with Willis's HALLOWEEN, which ship carried away her main t'gallant yard whilst tacking ship in company with us. It was said that the apprentice who was stationed at the brace was so busy looking at us that he forgot to let the brace go. After that we easily went ahead.

On the eighty-first day out we picked up the tug MYSTERY off Sydney Heads, but as the wind increased she could do little with us and in the end was forced to let us go. Now we had to make sail again to a strong northerly gale. After head-reaching for three days we finally fetched-in in the forenoon of the eighty-fourth day. As we neared the Heads, the full-rigged ship NORTH AMERICAN passed us close-to outward bound. She was an old steamer converted to sail. We were soon anchored off Garden Island (Pinch Gut), and before dark we had unbent all our sails. On the following day we hove up and proceeded to Miller's Point where we discharged our cargo. I found my old ship, the STAR OF FRANCE, at a wharf close-to. She had arrived some three weeks earlier, making the trip in the same time but reporting very bad weather. The HAL-

MICRONESIA leaving Iquique.
"I went to Glasglow to join the MICRONESIA in the Queen's Dock.... I was third mate and again, the 'furriner' among Scots.
"The MICRONESIA loaded a heavy general cargo for Sydney, New South Wales, and was towed to sea in the latter part of March 1883 by the FLYING HUNTRESS."

LOWEEN arrived the day after us.

These were happy, carefree days in Sydney. The senior apprentice used to go every morning to the newspaper offices and get the day's paper and then foregather at some pub with the other ship apprentices. Usually someone was able to dig up the price of a drink, sometimes the barmaid would "stand treat". The girls at these pubs were all a little soft-hearted to the brassbound apprentice boys. We would take care to get down to our various ships as eight bells were striking; wash down the decks; hand the mate his paper and the steward the Captain's paper. Taking it by and

HALLOWEEN
Iron ship built by Mandsley, Son & Field at London in 1870 for John Willis & Son, London.
"Off Cape Howe the wind came light northerly which held her up for a couple of days. Here we were in company with Willis's HALLOWEEN, which ship carried away her main t'gallant yard whilst tacking ship in company with us. It was said that the apprentice who was stationed at the brace was so busy looking at us that he forgot to let the brace go."

large it was not bad. Life was worth living at any rate in port.

The STAR OF FRANCE went to an anchorage in Snail's Bay to load shale for San Francisco and we followed suit, loading coal for San Pedro. The Aberdeen clipper MILTIADES was also in port and the DEVERON and the ANGERONA.

I was rather lucky having an uncle living in Balmai whose house and some three acres of ground was on the waterfront of Snail's Bay. He had a nice big boathouse. I introduced my skipper, Captain Greig, and Captain Wilson of the STAR OF FRANCE to my uncle. The MICRONESIA's gig accommodated the two captains nicely, so we used my uncle's boathouse.

Our leisure days seemed short-lived. The STAR OF FRANCE got away first, some three weeks ahead of us. Then came the day for us to leave. It was like leaving home, saying good-bye to the girls we knew. What promises we made! Looking back through the long

vista of years I'm sure these lassies kept us straight, kept us off the streets and, to a large extent, away from the pubs. They were good girls, wholesome and nice, and to this day I take my hat off to the bonnie Australian girls.

We towed out through the Heads in company with the ANGERONA, she being bound to San Francisco, and we were headed for San Pedro. It was blowing a fresh northerly with a falling glass [barometer] and a lump of a sea. Just as soon as we got outside, our decks were awash and things not secured were fetching away. The little ANGERONA piled the muslin on, even to royals. She went away fast; we only set the upper topsails and foresails. Old Greig, good man that he was, knew what was coming. The glass kept falling. By 5:00 p.m. we were under three lower topsails and foresail and shortly after, the foresail was furled.

It blew hard all night from the northeast. At daybreak nothing was to be seen of the ANGERONA, but the wind was coming fair and we were soon making sail. By noon three royals were set. When the wind began to come easterly, we had a good run to the north end of New Zealand, so the Old Man let her go to the northward.

We sighted Mangai Island. Passing close-to, it looked a very lovely spot. There was a trading schooner hanging on and off with her white sails gleaming in the brilliant sunshine. Being just to leeward, the perfumed smell of tropical plants was exotic and wonderful.

We had strong trades with sometimes heavy squalls; it was a case of stand by royal and t'gallant halliards, luffing through the squalls. We were able to weather through the Sandwich Islands [Hawaii] and the first land we made was one of the islands of the Santa Barbara Channel. I was aloft when we were standing through the channel in a light wind with thick fog below the upper topsails but it was clear as a bell above. I could see all the high land. Here we picked up the only pilot who was cruising in a small sailboat on the lookout for an American ship. He was not expecting us for a week or more. We anchored

on the forty-fifth day from Sydney, a record for time I believe stands to this day.

San Pedro consisted of only a few houses on a cliff. The coal was discharged into lighters from the Southern Pacific Railway. These lighters were towed down from Wilmington, some two or three miles up the creek. There was no breakwater in those days. The ships lay at anchor about four miles off the shore and the anchorage was considered unsafe after November until the following March. Being exposed to southeasters, the moored ships kept all their sails bent. We had a donkey engine brought off from the shore. The lighters held from two hundred to three hundred tons. Some of the ships discharged one end first, others amidships but, at that, unless you kept the ship on a fairly even keel, it was a case of riding out any gale that came along.

The skippers of the various ships generally went ashore in the forenoon and stayed until about 5:00 p.m. It was nice work in the pulling boats because you escaped working the coal. One nearly always had a nice breeze in the afternoon so there was not much hard pulling. Often we bathed from the boat, although warned to watch out for sting rays. There were quite a few pelicans, too.

The stevedore company was General Benning and even today the principal stevedoring company is of the same name [1937], not that *we* had any longshoremen. It was a case of the crew shovelling coal from 6:00 a.m. to 6:00 p.m. No wonder the third mate and the boys liked to be in the boat.

It took us about three weeks to discharge our coal and, keeping seven hundred tons on board as ballast, we sailed for San Francisco. We had sent our royal yards on deck. Standing off shore with a fresh northwest wind, we soon dropped Catalina Island, in those days only tenanted by goats.[2]

2 *"Now in 1937, it is a highly prosperous summer resort in the town of Avalon. This change was chiefly wrought by chewing gum. Wrigley owns the island. Two large excursion steamers now ply there twice a day."*

ANGERONA Beavis exchanged prints and swapped stories with tugboat skipper/photographer H. H. Morrison of Port Townsend, WA.

We spoke several ships on the way up but we found we had too little ballast. The LORD DOWNSHIRE, a four-masted barque passed us easily carrying all three royals and gaff topsail. We could barely stand the main t'gallant sail and laid over so far that it was quite a job to walk. Then along came the GARFIELD a day or so after with the wind strong northwest. We had the upper topsails and foresail set. The GARFIELD was swinging its three single t'gallant sails. We loosed the main t'gallant sail, but before we had mastheaded it, we had to take it in. The MICKY nearly capsized.

The GARFIELD was a splendid sight, sweeping by just to the leeward of us, as stiff as a church with a mile or so of white water streaming by. Then finally, when in sight of the Farallons near California, the great skysail yarder A.G. ROPES was in company. But by now the wind was light, and we were able to hold our own and a little better.

On arrival we found that the ANGERONA had not yet arrived and some anxiety began to be felt for her. The STAR OF FRANCE was at Howard Street Wharf. Green's SUPERB was there, too. What names to conjure with!

We went to Long Wharf, Oakland, to discharge our coal ballast and take in wheat stiffening. The COPLEY was there discharging and the four-masted barque FINGAL. Oakland was only a village and grass was growing in the main street. The Long Wharf has disappeared but even in those days it was full of holes and dangerous to walk on at night. Yet, we used to walk on it every night because coffee and doughnuts in Oakland were very good.

After discharging her coal and taking some five hundred tons of wheat for stiffening, the MICKY towed up to Port Costa to finish loading wheat at McNear's Dock. There were a few ships there, one of Smith's CITYs, I think CITY OF LUCKNOW. A barque called the SCOTTISH WIZARD and Allan's GLENFINART were also there.

After loading was completed, the MICKY was towed down the bay by one of the Red Stack tugs, and while lying at anchor awaiting our crew, the little ANGERONA came in. She had taken the eastern passage around Pitcairn and met with very unfavourable winds, for she was no slouch. We in the MICRONESIA boasted privately that we were a much finer ship. With two good passages to our name, we were beginning to suffer from swelled head.

Two days later we sailed in company with the GLENFINART and the SCOTTISH WIZARD. Outside the Farallons the wind was ahead and all three ships had a boating match. The MICRONESIA, a very weatherly ship, soon had her opponents' hulls down to leeward. The next day, they were not to be seen.

On the way south we sighted Pitcairn Island but the weather became squally and threatening. The captain did not lose any time, although we all would have liked to have had a yarn with the islanders who had put off in their boats when they sighted our ship. Realizing that we would not stop, they quickly returned to their island home.

Off the Horn we picked up the COPLEY. She had sailed some ten days before us and was bound to Liverpool. We passed her quite easily, carrying our main royal, three t'gallant sails and courses. She was plugging along under main t'gallant and mainsail fast. A few days later we were in company with the GLENFINART again, so we had not gained anything on Allan's fine ship.

We crossed the equator far to the westward eighty-eight days out. There were strong northeast trades. After sighting Flores, Western Islands, [the Azores] we had mostly southeast winds and finally worked into a steady easterly wind. Just a few days before making the Irish coast we had fallen in with the SUPERB which had left the Bay of San Francisco over a week before us. Although she was carrying three skysails, we went by her to windward, very much to their disgust. Captain Berridge, who had his wife with him, asked Captain Greig to dine with them. Our skipper declined when he saw that we were outsailing the old SUPERB so quickly; I was much disappointed as I would have gone with him in the gig. I felt as if I had been done out of a dinner; these ships of Green's fared well because they carried quite a number of passengers.

On falling in with the Irish land, more and more ships were met all beating against a strong easterly wind. Once again we tried conclusions with our old opponent, the GLEN-FINART, and although we were able to weather on her, there was another ship coming up hand-over-hand at present, far to leeward of the whole fleet. Soon she was filling us with dismay. We were able to recognize her—it was my old ship STAR OF FRANCE. She was superbly sailed, and before dark, she was out to windward of the whole fleet. Like a wizard, she spread-eagled the lot of us. She beat every one of us into Queenstown, Ireland, and anchored hours ahead.[3] The MICKY was the next in, just ahead of Lyle's CAPE OF GOOD HOPE and Carmichael's MEDEA. From below Galley Head we had sailed through a fleet of square-riggers and anchored in Queenstown Roads, 125 days out from San Francisco.

Even though we had technically beaten the STAR OF FRANCE in time, it was only through the fact that she had been held up by the easterly winds more days. The GLEN-FINART was only a few hours astern of us. After three or four days in Queenstown, we received orders for Limerick.

In Queenstown the various ships' boats were waiting for their respective skippers one afternoon, and to while away the time, some of the apprentices were skylarking with several nursemaids. Irish girls are very attractive. Some of these nurse girls had perambulators with babies in their charge. Suddenly, before the girls could say "Jack Robinson," four or five brass-bounders were tearing down hill each with a perambulator and a baby; yelling like mad, whilst several other brass-bounders tore along with them to keep the course clear and see who won the race. Unfortunately, just at the winning post, they ran into several ladies, some of whom were the babies' mothers. These ladies were very angry. The boys all bolted for their boats, leaving the baby buggies. Next day we were all court-marshalled by our skippers. The mothers had gone to the various ships' agents swearing vengeance. I ought to have known better, being a third mate. I often wondered how the poor girls got off, I expect a lot worse than we did.

Leaving Queenstown again in company with the GLENFINART (she being bound for Galway), we were able to give her our dust. Passing near to and sailing through her lee, she presented a wonderful sight. So close were we that we could speak to those on board. She had everything set, even to a dainty main skysail. Both of us close-hauled on the port tack with a moderate southerly wind.

The GLENFINART was rising and falling to the westerly swell. Her crew was lining her rail above her wet, gleaming sides. As ever and anon she would give a slight roll to windward.

The MICRONESIA made a quick run to the mouth of the Shannon and sailed up to an

[3] ed. note. Queenstown was later renamed Cobn in County Cork, South Republic of Ireland on the south shore of Great Island in Cork Harbour. It was originally called Cove of Cork, but the town was renamed Queenstown when visited by Queen Victoria in 1849. The name Cobn was resumed in 1922. Large docks and stations of naval stores were found there. Situated on the slopes above the harbour and having a fine climate, Cobn has become a seaside resort. It is the headquarters of the Royal Cork Yacht Club, the oldest yacht club in the world, and they sponsor an annual regatta. Steel is manufactured at nearby Haubowline Island. Cobn's population in 1971: 6,049. From *The New Columbia Encyclopedia*, (Columbia University Press).

p. 25 top

GLENFINART (above)
Steel ship built by Rodger at Port Glasgow in 1895 for Sterling of Glasgow.

COPLEY (below)
"We went to the Long Wharf, Oakland, to discharge our coal ballast and take in wheat stiffening. The COPLEY was there discharging and the four-masted barque FINGAL. Oakland was only a village and grass was growing in the main street."

CITY OF AGRA

"... the MICKY towed up to Port Costa to finish loading wheat at McNear's Dock. There were a few ships there, one of Smith's CITYs, I think CITY OF LUCKNOW."

anchorage at Bay Castle, some eighteen miles below Limerick. Captain Greig went up to Limerick in a jaunting-car and it was three days before he returned, very stiff and sore.

The ship had a wait of some days before she could go up on the top of spring tides. It was toward the end of April 1884.

Limerick struck me as a very clean town with lots of gorse growing in it.[4] Due to the hostile Irish uprisings, all of our firearms were taken out of the ship by the authorities in case the Fenians should get hold of them.

I left the ship here and went home for a few weeks, having been promised the second mate's berth if I passed. In this I was successful and was rewarded with a few weeks holiday in the home of an uncle and aunt living in a small village called Cwmbran, some five or six miles from Newport, Monmouthshire. My uncle was general manager of the Patent Nut and Bolt Company, their coke ovens and their collieries. I had a most delightful time and, like most susceptible sailors, I fell desperately in love. I chose my aunt's half-sister, a very beautiful girl. She was only my aunt by marriage and I saw nothing wrong with the relationship. My uncle did but that did not deter me. We plighted our troth.

[4] ed. note. Gorse, also known as furze, is a spiny, yellow-flowered evergreen shrub common on European waste lands.

GARFIELD

"We could barely stand the main t'gallant sail and laid over so far that it was quite a job to walk. Then along came the GARFIELD a day or so after with the wind strong northwest. The GARFIELD was swinging its three single t'gallant sails.... The MICKY nearly capsized."

COUNTY OF AYR
On Fletcher's slip at Port Adelaide in 1900.

A. D. Edwardes, Knoxville, S. Australia

CHAPTER IV

CLIMBING

I rejoined the MICRONESIA in the Salthouse Dock, Liverpool. She was loading a general cargo for Melbourne. I was now second mate and engaged to a very lovely girl. It behooved me to be good and try to be worthy of her. Another mate, James Glazebrook, had joined the ship and he and I became firm friends. I feel I owe a great deal to this fine shipmate.

The MICRONESIA made a very fair, average passage of thirty-two days to Melbourne. Nothing out of the way happened except that in the northeast trades we overhauled and passed the COUNTY OF MADDINGTON, one of Craig's big four-masted ships with a reputation as one of their smartest. She was a pretty sight, square-rigged on all four masts and swinging everything she could carry. Yet, we easily went away from her. A day or so later we passed the DUNDEE, another four-poster and barque-rigged. The DUNDEE belonged to Charles Barrie of Dundee, Scotland. She, too, was renowned for her speed, so we began to think we were some ship.

We were getting down south and running our easting down. On a dull, dirty day with misty squalls and not much visability, a large four-masted barque with painted ports hove in sight before our weather beam. She was cracking on with her three upper t'gallant sails and full courses. We were able to distinquish her just as she faded out of sight, alas, ahead. It was the PORT JACKSON, a very noted ship and no disgrace to be beaten by

her. Very few ships could keep up with her. Our skipper and Captain Crombie were great friends, both hailing from the "land of cakes," [Peterhead, Scotland] and being such, they had a new hat on the outcome of the race. Although she left us, we arrived at Port Philip Heads, Australia, a few hours before she passed the Otway bound for Sydney, so Greig got the hat.[1]

Melbourne was a different place. Much different than it is today. They had tremendous gutterways to the streets, like miniature rivers when it rained. People had fallen into those gutters and drowned. Of course it has been said they were drunken sailors but I doubt it. Most sailors never got much further than Williamstown or Sandridge.

We discharged our cargo at Williamstown close to the Aberdeen flyers MILTIADES and SALAMIS. The DEVERON was there, too, a beautiful full-rigger built by Steele and belonging to J. Russell, Greenock. They also owned the GRYSE, another full-rigger built by Steele. It is remarkable the way some Scottish shipowners know where to go for a well-built and speedy ship. Whilst at Williamstown, Green's MELBOURNE hauled off to an

---

[1] "It was a white one and very tall at that. The Old Man used to sport it in 'Frisco, calling it a democratic hat. I remember one time when Crombie was in Sydney with his splendid ship, he was keeping open house so to say for his friend, Playfair, the butcher who was running for mayor. Crombie drove a team of piebald ponies up and down George Street with a big sign that read, "Vote for Playfair." Playfair was elected. Evidently the advertisement was good business."

anchorage from Sandridge. I think she looked better as the MELBOURNE than she did later as the MACQUARRIE. Sentiment, pure sentiment.

Williamstown was quite a thriving seaport. Many years later I visited it—and wondered. The grass was then growing in the streets and everything looked changed, desolate and forlorn. Perhaps it was only youth that in those early days made it seem so delightful.

We were a month or five weeks discharging our cargo and had a happy time. On Saturdays the decks were washed down and the main yard, which had been topped for discharging, would be let run and squared on lifts and braces. All other yards were squared and ropes and braces neatly coiled down.

The various pubs were very homey and pleasant; I can remember one or two. There was the Woolpack with a girl named Julia Rolfe, very much in demand by the various mates. The old Courthouse Inn was owned and kept by Mrs. Thwaite who had several daughters, all of whom were pretty and charming. They were good musicians; the second eldest daughter had a wonderful voice and sang beautifully. I was privileged to meet several of them in future years and they all married well.

Mrs. Thwaite was like a mother to the apprentice boys and she would send them into the kitchen where the younger members of the family were congregated. This kept the boys away from the bar, and many a young boy has Mrs. Thwaite to thank for keeping him from drink. We mates used to have the entry to a little parlour off the saloon bar where there was a piano. Jimmie Glazebrook had a fine baritone voice and how we used to sing! Sentimental songs were in vogue so we sang them with the girls. Jenny was the eldest girl, Maud, the next oldest and the best singer; then Ada, and the youngest girl whose name I have forgotten. It was the youngest however, who eventually became a noted singer.

2 ed. note. Australasian slang.

Captain Meston of the SIR WALTER RALEIGH was one of the ship masters who had entry to the house. He was a great friend of the family. But chief of all was old Captain Perrot of the Aberdeen clipper MILTIADES. Phillips of the famed SALAMIS was there, too. All these men were of the "Courthouse" clique and were reckoned more as friends than as customers. Mrs. Thwaite was especially solicitous for the welfare of Captain Perrot. She generally sent him on board his ship in the charge of a water policeman who had strict instructions to see him safely on board. He was not to let him fall into the she-oak net.2 At that, in spite of all these precautions, one night he managed to fall into it. The she-oak net was spread under the ship's gangway; there to catch any unwary person who had imbibed not wisely but too well.

Whilst at Williamstown, the VICTORIA REGINA, a 2,000-tonner built by Oswald Mordaunt in 1881 for Coupland, was at Sandridge. One of Duncan's ships, the well-known PERSIAN EMPIRE was also there. They sailed together for Newcastle, N.S.W. in ballast. Off Wilson's Promontory the wind came ahead and both ships collided on opposite tacks. The PERSIAN EMPIRE was struck just abaft the fore-rigging on the port side and was holed almost to the water's edge. By plugging up with the spare sails, she managed to limp back to Melbourne, a very narrow squeak. The VICTORIA REGINA was hardly damaged and continued to Newcastle. I was on board the PERSIAN EMPIRE to view the damage. Duncan's ships were painted pea-soup colour; you could hardly call it beautiful but they were fine ships and well kept.

Leaving Melbourne the MICKY made a quick run of fifty-two hours to Newcastle. We laid to an anchor to discharge our ballast and I was delegated night watchman. Incidentally, I nearly lost my job as second mate. Captain Greig was determined to keep his crew to work the ballast out, and they were equally determined to skip if they could. That was the chief reason I was made night watchman. The very first night soon after dark, I had just

PORT JACKSON

"We were able to distinquish her just as she faded out of sight alas, ahead. It was the PORT JACKSON, a very noted ship and no disgrace to be beaten by her. . . . Our skipper and Captain Crombie were great friends, both hailing from the 'Land of Cakes,' and being such, they had a new hat on the outcome of the race."

passed the fo'castle door and was close to the fo'castle head. Whilst taking a turn forward, a man suddenly came to the rail and, looking down from the fo'castle head, hailed me softly. At first I thought it was one of our crew but he sang out, "Now's your chance, boys, I have the boat under the bow."

That was enough for me. I dashed to the ladder and closed with him saying, "You damned son of a bitch, get to hell out of here or I'll holler for the mate and skipper."

"All right, ole son," he said, "but don't make such a bloody noise," and he slid down one of the jib down-hauls that conveniently had been left trailing in the water by some of our crew. As soon as he was in the water I drew my knife and cut it. He fell some thirty feet or more, the ship being in ballast. He just missed falling into his boat, splash! into the water. I let a yell out of me and started ringing the ship's bell like mad. The skipper and the mate came on the run, both of them armed with revolvers. We watched the man climbing into his boat and the skipper fired a shot over him as his runner pulled away.

The crew was cussing and intimated that the heart and liver of the young second mate [me!] ought to be carved up and fed to the gulls. The Old Man was very pleased and called me into the cabin. He gave the mate and me a snort of Scotch whisky and also a loaded revolver. He told me I had better not go ashore whilst in port as it was Sullivan's boat and he would be laying for me. He and the mate thought it would be wise to have one of the apprentices with me to keep watch, so Hagan, an Irish boy, was given to me. All went well that night.

The next night when everything was quiet, I called Hagan and discussed the routine with him, saying it was no good for two of us to be on watch. Hagan heartily agreed. So it was arranged for him to have a sleep and I would call him about 2:00 a.m. and have one myself. After calling Hagan and cautioning him, I layed down on the hen coop and was soon dead to the world. He was to call me at 5:00 a.m. and the cook as well. I was awakened by the

cock crowing, broad daylight, nearly 7 a.m. The ship's boat was gone from the davits, no cook was called, and Hagan was fast asleep with his lamp alongside him. Looking in the fo'castle I found all hands home except two.

This was a nice kettle of fish. I called the mate, Jimmie Glazebrook, and told him my sad tale, hoping he would break the news to the skipper. All he had to say was, "Go and tell the Old Man, I'm not going to." So in I went and what he said to me will not bear repeating. I came out a very sorrowful young man. I was relieved of my job as night watchman; instead I had to run the ballast baskets on the stage.

A few hours later we recovered the boat. The Old Man was sore at me for a long time, though eventually he forgave me.

One of the ships at the Dyke [Newcastle] was the full-rigger MAGICIAN, a large 1600-tonner built by Richardson Duckworth in 1881 and commanded by Captain Hastings who sailed with his wife. She was a fine, powerful looking ship that was afterwards sunk in collision with the BEN DOURAN in the vicinity of Pernambuco, Brazil, in November, 1885. Fernie's ARISTOMENE was also at the Dyke.

On leaving Newcastle Captain Greig took the middle route through the Islands and made 'Frisco in fifty-six days. Whilst discharging our coal cargo at the Rolling Mills we saw the four-masted barque EARL OF DALHOUSIE capsize. The date was May 12, 1885, and it was just after dinner, at 12:30 p.m. Jimmie Glazebrook and I were smoking our pipes, walking the main deck outside the cabin, when Glazebrook made some remark about the DALHOUSIE listing. Over she went.

We had one dinghy on the davits and both of us jumped into it with some of the boys, heading for the rescue. Most of the crew had been taken off by a shore sailboat, but old Jarvis, the skipper, was still on her bilge, together with the carpenter. "Chips" was very irate at losing his tools, cussing hard in a beautiful Scot's tongue.

34

We had lent Captain Jarvis some heavy purchase blocks to send his yards down but we did not see them again for many a day. There was a consular inquiry and the captain had his certificate suspended for six months. The vessel was later raised and the same captain took her home. She arrived in 'Frisco on November 7, 1885, after a very good maiden passage of 118 days from Dundee. Jarvis was not popular with his crew; he tried to work his cargo of coal out with them—needless to say a failed attempt—and of course, he was not much in the favour of the stevedores.

At the time of the accident he had been moving the ship over to the Alameda flats to scrub the bottom of her hull with apprentices to do the work. It was blowing half a gale at the time and one of Spreckel's tugs was plucking clear of the American ship BELL O'BRIEN. When she was finally raised she was an even sorrier mess than when the captain and crew set out to clean her. So much for economy.

When the MICRONESIA had finished discharging and had taken in some three hundred tons of ballast, she went to anchorage in Sausalito Bay to await a charter; freights then being away down. A number of well-known ships were in San Francisco at this time, amongst them were Carmichael's THESSALUS, Captain Bennett; Ismay's GARFIELD, Captain Thompson, and the HOGHTON TOWER, Captain Trimble; also the BENMORE, BRITISH AMBASSADOR, BRITISH DUKE, CROWN OF DENMARK, then new and a large six t'gallant yarder; and the ex-P & O steamer ELEANOR MARGARET.

We lay in Sausalito for several months with a full crew on board, despite all the efforts of the boarding house crimps and that of the ship by working them from 6:00 a.m. to 6:00 p.m. These men all had wages, being shipped in Australia, and they made the voyage in spite of all. They were as fine a crowd of Britishers as you could wish for.

Sausalito was a very pretty little spot, the home of two yacht clubs and a nice hotel, the El Monte. There were also a number of country cottages. The ships were all spic and span and we gave two dances on board the MICRONESIA since the ship was covered as far as the mainmast. The crew was all on board and I had a good deal to do, but after 6:00 p.m., I was mostly free. We had many friendships and the American girls were just lovely. I especially remember Captain Thomas who had two very pretty daughters. They were staying at the El Monte and were in great demand at all the dances. Captain Thomas was later governor of San Quentin.

Captain Banks was also laid up in Sausalito Bay. He was very popular at the yacht clubs. We seldom went to San Francisco. We were all so interested in Sausalito whilst we stayed there. There were lots of boats to sail and rowing races.

THESSALUS
"Other ships making good passages that year [1888] were the THESSALUS from Portland, Oregon, 97 days and the WENDUR from Tacoma was only 99 days to the Fastnet and was several times in company with the THESSALUS, arriving within an hour of each other."

ALCIDES
*"In those far-off days I had youth on my side, and
although poorly paid and not much to boast of in the
way of food, we had health, life lay ahead, and all the
world."*

36

The DURHAM, which had been bought by Herron of Liverpool from Money Wigram, came over to Sausalito to lay up. Captain Campbell commanded her, a great dandy who wore a tall hat. After leaving the DURHAM he was given command of the LORD RAGLAN, a new ship of Herron's, and was lost in her with all hands a few years afterwards. A hard-case Nova Scotian man by the name of Butler took over the DURHAM and made a name for himself.

At last we got orders, chartered to load wheat destined for Cork. We left Sausalito on a Sunday, not without many regrets. Sunday was a favorite day for Old Man Greig; he used to get his son and family over from 'Frisco for a trip up the bay and river. We loaded at the Nevada dock, then new. Some of us felt pretty badly leaving Sausalito, so one Saturday I took the ship's dinghy and a couple of the apprentices and sailed down to Sausalito. We nearly met with disaster when the boat started to leak badly, thumping into a head sea most of the way. Fortunately we were able to fetch up alongside a flat bottomed sailing scow at anchor, repaired our damages, and had hot coffee and doughnuts. The crew of the scow thought we were mad-brained Britishers, and no doubt, they were right.

We finally arrived alongside the DURHAM about five in the morning. Needless to say there was a girl at the bottom of it. After spending all of Sunday ashore and having a happy time, we put off to the DURHAM, had our supper, and left again. With a fair tide and a favorable wind, we arrived back at our ship before *turn to time*[3] on Monday evening. What risks youth will take for the sake of a petticoat, a risk that I would not have taken in later years in a small fifteen-foot boat.

We had all our crew on board and all sails bent. After completing loading and towing down the river and bay to an anchorage, there was no delay. One of the ships at anchor was the CALISTOGA; she was waiting to go alongside to discharge.

We sailed on July 9, 1885, and being very foul, made a long passage of 146 days. This was the MICKY's worst passage but most of the ships leaving at that time made long passages.

This was my first introduction to using a patent scrubber, a vile contraption consisting of a tank about six feet long covered with a bristly mat that had to be hauled fore and aft along the ship's bottom. It could only be used in a flat calm, so generally it was boiling hot. The watch was yoked to it, walking fore and aft the decks in a tropical sun. It was not much fun. The wheel used to be lashed so that the helmsman got his part of it, too.

From Queenstown the MICKY went to Belfast to discharge and I left for home, having had a letter from my betrothed that I did not quite understand. She said she had met her fate, I wondered what it was. The letter was written from a little village called Strines, not far from Manchester. I made up my mind to stop off.

After all these years I can remember with what a beating heart I went to the little house called Ivy Cottage. An old lady answered my knock at the door. She looked rather askance at me when I asked for my girl by her maiden name, thinking she was staying there with her aunt. Then the old dame really looked me up and down.

She told me the only people living there was a married couple. I was non-plussed for a moment when a clever thought struck me, although I was far from happy at the moment. I had a small photograph in the back of my watch and I showed it to her. The old woman nodded her head, but said the lady of the photo was out. So I went for a walk and came back later.

This time I saw my "faithless one." She had jilted me for a German music-master. I gave her all the letters she had written to me and went home sadder and perhaps a wiser young

---

[3] ed. note. When heaving the hand log (an instrument for measuring the distance run through the water) the order is given to "turn the sandglass and start timing" in order to calculate the ship's speed.

man. She cried bitterly on parting. What could I do? There was nothing that could be done that would not make matters worse. Evidently I still loved her for I told her if she ever wanted me to let me know. Years afterward I heard from her but for the moment I went home very sad.

I passed for mate in London before Captain Rankin. He gave me a pretty thorough overhauling and nearly failed me in seamanship, telling me to come back the next day. What could you expect from a young fellow who had just been jilted by his best girl?

I didn't tell the examiner that when he said, "You kept those jibs down until the anchor was off the ground and her head had started to cant. You have been in fine ships both as second and third mate, you ought to have known better." I agreed.

When I got my blue ticket I made for the nearest pub. It was a little place called "The Grapes," just off the Minories in George Street. I felt I needed bucking up and the daughters of the house soothed me.

The next and third voyage of the MICRONESIA was from Liverpool to Sydney and I cannot recall much out of the way about it. The passage took eighty-seven days, not as good as on her maiden voyage, being held up by calms for a week or more on the equator. However, in the northeast trades we overhauled and passed the LUCIPARA, a four-masted barque belonging to Denniston of Glasgow. She was then on her second voyage, and later had quite a reputation for speed. These ships of Denniston's were mostly commanded and officered by Germans and a goodly proportion of the crews likewise. It always left a bad taste in our mouths. Why were these foreigners—Dutchmen we called them, allowed to command British ships? We were not allowed that privilege in German ships even if we had wished to serve under an alien flag.

Running our easting down in 45 degrees 8th latitude with strong westerly gales, the MICKY did several good runs of over three

hundred miles and on one day made three hundred thirty-six miles in the twenty-three and one-half hour day. Old Man Greig was up all night and in the early hours of morn, as daylight crept in, we passed a ship running under topsails and foresails—very comfortably. We were carrying the main royal. The old Scotsman turned to me with a cynical smile, saying, "That's a sensible, cautious man, Beavis. He's had a nice sleep all night." That was more than we had had. The Old Man went below then, telling me not to take anything off her; watch the steering and not to carry anything away. Very comforting orders, or at least I thought so.

One day with a howling northwest gale blowing and the glass falling rapidly with every prospect of a dirty night, we fell in with the WATERLOO. She was a lovely four-masted ship, belonging then to W.A. Brown of Glasgow. She was a little abaft our beam and coming through the water like a railway train, swinging her three big t'gallant sails.

WATERLOO
"I thank God that I have been allowed to see these glorious ships, visions of beauty, now gone forever."

The WATERLOO crossed the skysail yards over royals and single t'gallant sails. She was one of Connell's creations and at the time Connell was building only beautiful ships; later on building ones that were well-made to carry. We were driving the MICKY but the WATERLOO proved a bit too much for us. She gradually faded away ahead, losing sight of her altogether in a blinding squall of wind and rain. The picture she made was one that will always remain in my memory. I thank God that I have been allowed to see these glorious ships, visions of beauty, now gone forever. The sea—our sea—is now desecrated by monstrosities enough to make old Neptune vomit when he has to consign one of them to Davy Jones's locker.

Both the MICKY and the WATERLOO were being driven to the limit, and the WATERLOO ever and anon would appear to

SIR ROBERT FERNIE
Built for W. J. Fernie, of Liverpool, in 1889, the SIR ROBERT FERNIE was sold to the Germans in 1912. Renamed ELIZABETH, she was a hulk at Callao by 1917. She was finally wrecked at Lobos Island in August 1924.
"We were a month or five weeks discharging our cargo and had a happy time. On Saturdays the decks were washed down and the main yard, which had been topped for discharging, would be let run and squared on lifts and braces. All other yards were squared and ropes and braces neatly coiled down."

those of us in the MICRONESIA to be taking pretty heavy water aboard, sometimes a mass of spray and spume. We were flooding our decks, and with life lines stretched fore and aft, 'twas no mean job the steward had to get the cabin grub along safely from the galley. The only dry places were on the poop and forecastle head.

Leaving Sydney for San Pedro we had continuous easterly winds which forced old Captain Greig to take the passage to the westward of the Fijis. We sighted several of the islands and passed to leeward of Midway without sighting it. We made Port Fermin on the forty-seventh day, picking the pilot up (now in a motor launch) in the early morning. We anchored the same day off San Pedro.

We were asked if we had seen anything of the DUNOTTAR CASTLE. This ship had left Sydney a month before us. We in the MICRONESIA had been quite chummy with the mates of the DUNOTTAR CASTLE in Sydney and also with those on board the full-rigger SUDBOURNE and the four-masted ship WATERLOO. These three ships, expecting to sail together had arranged a race amongst themselves, the WATERLOO being the favourite although the DUNOTTAR CASTLE ran her a close second as she had made the passage from London to Sydney in seventy-two days, one of the best that year. The SUDBOURNE was not considered to be in the same class as these two, although a fine looking ship.

The DUNOTTAR CASTLE never arrived, and before we sailed from San Pedro we had word of her fate: totally wrecked on Cure Island but without loss of life. The mate had safely made the long journey to Honolulu in the ship's lifeboat, taking fifty-six days. A steamer with the mate on board was despatched to Cure Island only to find that the rest of the crew had been taken off by the Nova Scotian ship BIRNAM WOOD a few days previously. The men were eventually landed at Valparaiso.

San Pedro had grown but little since the MICRONESIA's first visit. There were proba-

bly a few new houses on the bluff but nothing recognizable. The ships discharging coal included the American ship BELVIDERE, Captain Gibson; the beautiful little barque COOLEEN, Captain Barclay, and the CAERMARTHEN CASTLE, a main skysail-yarder, commanded by Captain Richards.

The COOLEEN and the MICRONESIA were chartered to load wheat and flour in San Pedro for Liverpool. The others had to go seeking. Both BELVIDERE and CAERMARTHEN CASTLE were totally wrecked after leaving San Pedro, although we did not know of this until long afterwards. The BELVIDERE was wrecked at Bonille Point, Vancouver Island, on the twenty-ninth of November in a dense fog. She had been bound for Departure Bay. Having struck a reef there, she was pulled off by the tug TYEE, but she foundered before the tug could beach her. The CAERMARTHEN CASTLE stranded near Nestucca Bay at three in the morning of December 2, 1886. She was in ballast, bound for Portland, Oregon. As far as I can recollect no lives were lost on either ship.

Discharging and loading in San Pedro was a slow job and occupied some two months. One afternoon we were rather late in sailing off to the ship in the MICRONESIA's gig. We had Captain Gibson of the BELVIDERE with us and, as we rounded the stern of his ship long

CAERMARTHEN CASTLE was an iron ship built in 1874 in 11 months by R. & J. Evans of Liverpool.

after sunset we noticed—and so did he—that his ship's ensign was still flying. He passed some remark to Captain Greig about his mate. The rest we heard as we left his gangway. It was lurid.

The MICKY's gig was a beautiful six-oared boat built of elm, thirty feet long and yawl-rigged and fitted with a rocker keel with lead in it. Captain Greig was very proud of his gig and so was I. All teakwood thwarts and turned teak stanchions and gratings. Could she sail? Why, there was nothing could look at her on a wind. The CAERMARTHEN CASTLE was rather proud of their lifeboat, schooner-rigged, fairly fast off the wind. It was nearly always a dead beat tie windward, coming off from the shore but the MICKY's boat generally had it all her own way.

One night we left our rival ashore, her second mate having departed from virtue and imbibed too heavily of San Pedro fire water. We took Captains Richards and Hall of the MACDUFF, another full-rigger. Staying to supper, Captain Greig sent me back to my ship with instructions to return later. After my supper, I returned to the MACDUFF and hauled the boat out to the yardarm clear of the gangway. There was a nice fresh breeze blowing and a little later along came the CAERMARTHEN CASTLE's boat. The drunken mate was steering and two apprentices were in the boat. It was a bright moonlit night and he was yawing all over the place and the boys were yelling like mad. We heard it all—and so did the skippers who were on the poop.

A gruff drunken voice cried out, "To hell with you," and CRASH! the boat sailed right into the ship, smashing her bowsprit and stem. What was said to the second mate by his skipper, which I overheard, will hardly bear repeating.

This poor old chap was disrated, but I think Captain Greig pleaded for him because a little while after he was reinstated. Our Old Man loaned our carpenter to help repair the boat as Richards of the CAERMARTHEN CASTLE was going to soak the second mate for the damages. Incidentally, the second mate in dispute was a Scotsman and Richards was Welsh. Old Greig did not care for the Welsh. How the good old Scots hang together.

The skippers sought recreation and one of their favourites was to go shooting up the coast. One day Old Man Greig and Hall of the MACDUFF, with Barclay of the COOLEEN all went away in the MICRONESIA's gig, and I, the second mate, was taken along to act as dog. And did I like it? In a hot sun, retrieving the game?

Well, we went up the coast past Point Fermin to a little bay called Portugee Bend, a deserted whaling camp. It was all right but for the fleas. How the old skippers stood it, I don't know. I suppose that being younger, my hide was more tender. Anyway, after being nearly eaten alive, I could stand it no longer. I went down to the beach and got on board the boat. There I slept peacefully enough.

The next day was spent shooting chiefly jack rabbits, a hare which, if hit but not killed, cried like a child. It was mournful to hear. I was getting well fed up being "dog" when the party was broken up much to my delight. Captain Hall of the MACDUFF was starting to shoot a jack rabbit when a rattle snake jumped up in front of him. Hall's gun went off in the air and he fell backwards into a cactus bush. Cactus is a painful plant and decidedly poisonous. Poor old Captain Hall swore horribly and also started to swell, that is, his afterend did. We all took turns picking cactus out of his rudder. There was nothing for it but to return to the ship.

All the way back Captain Hall could not sit down; he had to kneel in the boat and he never stopped cussing. Barclay of the COOLEEN (and Irish at that) drew his wrath when with a grin he said, "Hall, you shouldn't cuss so when you are praying."

43

The climax came when we arrived at Hall's gangway. Getting him out of the boat and onto the gangway, one of the skippers gave him a shove on his rudder. He let a roar out of him and murder was in his eyes. Old Greig was the culprit saying, "Hall, behave yourself, there's your good wife waiting for you." Poor Mrs. Hall was making the voyage and had an awful time with him. His language was something to remember.

The other two skippers had a good laugh over it in the quiet of their cabins, no doubt accompanied with a drop of whisky. I enjoyed the whole incident as I did not like being the "dog."

The COOLEEN finished loading some time before we did, and the day she sailed the captains and apprentices of all the ships in port helped to make sail on her. She had been at single anchor a long time and her cable came up in a terrible mass of kinks. All of the ships' boats were congregated at her gangway and the boys were all on board. When the COOLEEN gathered sternway, most of the boats got foul under her headgear. There was a wild stampede to get them clear. The afternoon breeze was northwest so the little COOLEEN soon began to step out and one by one the different ships' boats left after keeping her company for a mile or two.

The MICRONESIA was the next to go and was escorted in like manner. She sailed about the middle of November.

Whilst in San Pedro, the DURHAM, the same ship that had been with us in Sausalito a previous voyage, had arrived. She was under command of a different skipper than before. The man who now commanded her was a Captain Butler, a notorious hard case and bucko. When she sailed most of her crew were in irons, chained to the 'tween deck stanchions. The apprentices from other ships had to make sail on her as none of the sailors from the ships in port would do so. Butler had his wife and children on board, and for some reason or other, his wife's maid was locked up in the spare room.

The DURHAM had lots of cabins, having been a passenger ship belonging to Money Wigram before the Herrons bought her. She was undoubtedly a very fast ship. On this passage she was bound to San Francisco and on his arrival, Butler narrowly escaped serious trouble. This was caused not only over his crew but also on account of the maid. Herrons seemed to have a liking for hard-case skippers.

On the way to the Horn we fell in with Bates's NEW YORK and with a fair wind easily dropped her astern, although it might have been a different tale on a close-haul reach. Bates's BREMEN and NEW YORK were old North German Lloyd steamers; each was over 328 feet long. They would have been better rigged as four-masted ships. They were hurricane-decked fore and aft and carried three skysails over, royals, and single t'gallant sails. Captain Hughes had command of the NEW YORK. She had been carrying coals between Departure Bay and San Francisco for several voyages. Hughes had a black bear as a pet, a cub at first but growing bigger, it caused some consternation on board. One time in San Francisco the bear got loose and disported itself on deck. It finally located in one of the spare cabins next to the second mate's room, much to the mate's dismay.

Funny incidents happen on board ships. The Old Man's son who had been carpenter had settled in San Francisco and we had another carpenter in the MICRONESIA. This one also hailed from Peterhead, Scotland. The sailmaker, another Peterhead man, roomed with him. At Port Costa they had caught a snake and, after killing it, had preserved it in a pickle bottle full of whisky. They intended to take it home to Peterhead. As we neared the Horn, New Year's Day loomed up. Chips and Sails kept looking at the snake in the bottle and the temptation was too great. They were both good Scots; it seemed a pity to them to waste good whisky. After much deliberation, out came the snake and down went the whisky. They did not know if the snake was poisonous, and for the next few days they were very sorry for themselves. If they felt a pain, no doubt it was the poison working. Of course, the rest of the crew was all certain the snake was poisonous. This did not help matters any. Being hardy Scots, they survived. The snake was dried and hung up in their berth. It, too, may have reached Peterhead.

Off the coast of Ireland, we fell in with several Scottish fishing boats, some of them hailing from Peterhead. One came alongside and how they gammed. I could not understand half of it but they all seemed to know one another. Their boats were beautiful and powerful, lugger-rigged and double-ended. They looked as if they could stand any weather that came along. They were then maybe a hundred miles from their home port.

The MICRONESIA arrived in Liverpool March 8, 1887, after a smart passage of 113 days, having beaten the COOLEEN by ten days. Going up the Irish Channel with a strong westerly blowing and all sail set, we passed a four-masted steamer, the BRITISH KING, inward bound for Philadelphia. As we tore along quite close aboard, various rope-ends were dangled out by our crew to show their scorn for the steam kettle.

Squire Lecky was in command of the BRITISH KING and he came on board in Liverpool to congratulate our skipper, saying it was the finest sight he had ever seen, a delight to the sailor's eye, as we went slashing by. Then he turned to me and spoke as one "Conway" to another. He told me to stay in sail until I got command. This advice I eagerly heeded.

EURASIA at Wellington wool wharf

SHIP EURASIA.
© J. DICKIE.

CHAPTER V

SECOND MATE DAYS

I stayed by the MICRONESIA to see the cargo out and, incidentally, to let the mate, Jimmie Glazebrook, go on leave. When he returned to the ship, it was in dry dock. I bade him and my old skipper good-bye and went home to have a holiday and pass for master. I had little difficulty in passing before my old friend Captain Rankin.

After a month's holiday I joined the EURASIA as second mate in the East India Docks. Captain Parkes was the Commander, a little man with iron-gray whiskers. One of the best. When I joined, the mate was leaving and a Welshman named David Hughes joined as mate. The EURASIA appeared to me, after just leaving the MICRONESIA, a very heavily sparred ship. Her fore and main yards were 103 feet square and her corses very deep. She had a great sheer and, unlike the MICRONESIA, had 10 to 12 foot poles above her royals. Her half-round was very like the STAR OF FRANCE, although her poop was not so long. She also had a chart-house, which I thought a very splendid innovation.

We were loading a general cargo for Melbourne, as was also the MICRONESIA in Liverpool. I think this was the time Queen Victoria opened the People's Palace in London. I happened to have lodgings in Burdett Road. I could have gone home from the docks to Campden Hill Square where my father lived but that was my excuse, as the procession was to pass along the Burdett Road and right past my diggings. I arranged a party of several bar-maids from the Three

Nuns in Aldgate. This was fine but somehow or other my sisters got to know that my rooms commanded a good view. Three of them came barging in. Of course I had to introduce them to the other ladies. They were very nice about it, but didn't they pull my leg afterward.

The EURASIA was chartered by Houlder Bros., so all the time we were in dock their house flag was flying both night and day from our main royal truck. The after 'tween decks were fitted up for steerage passengers; 49 adults were carried without a doctor. They were emigrants to Australia, and this type of crossing was all they could afford. Altogether with infants and children, there were close on 70. Father came down to the docks to see me off. It was raining and the poor devils in steerage were huddled amongst their baggage whilst the carpenters were putting the finishing touches to their quarters. "Wet when we came aboard and wet, damned wet, when we got ashore," was the refrain of some of them on arrival in Port Melbourne. There is a tale connected with this which you will hear.

Passing through the lock gates on the afternoon of August 25, 1887, our crew came tumbling aboard, a very drunk and pretty tough looking lot. They did not belie their looks when later, trouble developed. We did not anchor at Gravesend but proceeded straight to sea. Our royal yards were on deck and, as the wind came fair early next morning, up aloft those yards had to go.

It was my watch on deck from 4:00 a.m. to 8:00 p.m.; I had all three yards crossed and was mastheading the mizzen royal when the mate came on deck. I had bent the sails before sending the yards aloft. They were some yards, too—the fore and main were each 48 feet square—not bad work with a crew only just recovering from a heavy bout with booze.

All day long we romped down the channel with "a bone in our teeth", passing steamer after steamer and looking upon them with scorn and derision. Our passengers were mostly sick now. In the saloon[1] we had two ladies and one gentleman and a couple of children. The other 60 passengers remained in steerage. The only light they had down below was from the deck light seeping through the crevices in the deck. The EURASIA had a big teakwood booby hatch and a ladder down. The fittings were just rough deal boards and bunks with benches and tables.

We carried our fair wind across the Bay of Biscay and ran right into the northeast trades without any calms. The trades were well easterly and a day or so after, we sighted the MICRONESIA. She had left Liverpool the same day that we had left London. There was a lot of dry-pulling and sweating-up; my old ship was heartily damned. She came up from dead to leeward, just abaft our beam when we first saw her. Passing close under our stern she looked the thoroughbred that she was. We finally lost her on our weather beam. Old Parkes congratulated himself that the MICRONESIA had not passed us although she had undoubtedly weathered on us.

We crossed the equator on September 12, eighteen days from London and seventeen days from Start Point; passed Cape Otway November 6, seventy-three days from London and seventy-two days from Start Point. We anchored in Hobsons Bay off Port Melbourne, just seventy-three days from Start Point and

seventy-four days from London Docks. It was a passage that compared favorably with any of the wool clippers.

One day in the northeast trades I had the forenoon watch and was aloft in the main t'gallant rigging on some repair work when I suddenly noticed a commotion on deck and observed several frantic women passengers, screaming and running. I slid down the backstays on the run and found the whole watch below knocking seven bells out of the third mate, a man named Chambers. Snatching a heavy teakwood capstan bar from the rack around the after capstan, I laid several of the fellows out. The mate and the captain came into the fray with revolvers. We put a couple of the ring leaders in irons and dumped them in the sail locker which was in the fore part of the poop. After we had them, all hands came charging aft but, as we had revolvers and meant to use them, they gave in quickly.

It appeared that our passengers had been getting liquor from the steward and passing it along to the crew. After this, all liquor was stopped. When the two ringleaders sobered up and promised to behave, they were released. But from then on we kept a vigilant look out. Altogether they were a turbulent lot, although good sailormen. Strange to say, they did not appear to bear any malice toward me, although I had laid three of them out. It was the third mate they had it in for.

This was a good job and we made a smart passage. Otherwise I feel sure we should have had more trouble. We were getting down to the longitude of the Cape of Good Hope when one of our passengers died. He had been ill most of the time from consumption and only a few days before his death, we had put him in the chartroom. He was married and his wife had accompanied him on the voyage. She was a canny person and after he was dead, she removed all his clothes except his undershirt. The stairway and passage to the chartroom was very narrow and the corpse had to be carried out that way to be sewed up on deck.[2] Due to the consumption, the steward refused to touch him, as did all hands. The corpse was

---

[1]ed. note. The saloon was the main accommodation for passengers in a passenger carrier, but it was also the officers' mess in a merchant ship. These were probably the same or shared quarters on the EURASIA.
[2]ed. note. The deceased on ships were usually sewn into a canvas "mummy bag" by the sailmaker before burial at sea.

BARON ABERDARE
Iron ship built by Watson Sunderland in 1874 for
Greenock owners
"The Old Man had commanded the GUINEVERE
NO. 2, a noted China tea-clipper, and the BARON
ABERDARE.... Often he would spin yarns to me of the
old China tea days. I loved the old man and he was
always a good friend to me. The mate was very jealous;
the Old Man did not particularly like him, mainly
because he was a teetotaller, which Parkes was far from
being. I had no objections along that line and would
take a drink when it was offered."

now stiff and cold and unwilling though I was, I humped him on my back and carried him down the stairs. His bones cracked and his long lanky arms were hanging around my neck. Ugh. I can feel him to this day. Backing the mainyard and tolling the forward bell, we buried him at sea.

We ran our easting down in about 45 degrees south latitude with strong, fair winds, capping 300 miles several times. Old Captain Parkes was a great man for having his tacks boused[3] well to windward. He used to have a spare rigged out for the main tack and another one on the cathead for the foretack. This was in the trades, and he also carried what we called a watersail on the lee bowsprit guy. The tack was boused down to a spar up to what would have been the martingale or dolphin striker.[4] It pulled like the very mischief when the wind was a little free, but often filled with water. On the fore-royal stay we would carry a jib-topsail with a very long tack. The EURASIA carried a tremendous spanker in fine weather; they *all* helped.

The Old Man had commanded the GUINE-VERE NO.2, a noted China tea-clipper, and the BARON ABERDARE, one of McCann's famous BARONS. Often he would spin yarns to me of the old China tea days. I loved the old man and he was always a good friend to me. The mate was very jealous; the Old Man did not particularly like him, mainly because he was a teetotaller, which Parkes was far from being. I had no objections along that line and would take a drink when it was offered.

It was late in the day when we anchored off Port Melbourne or Sandridge as it was then called. The MICRONESIA was at anchor, having arrived the previous day. She had beaten us by one day from where we had spoken to her.

[3]ed. note. To "bouse" means to pull down on the rope or the fall of the tackle.
[4]ed. note. The "martingale" or "dolphin striker" was the short wood or metal spar suspended downwards from the end of the bowsprit.

We landed our passengers the next morning in Holland's sail boat. Holland used to do a roaring trade landing passengers from ships at anchor. We had a heavy teakwood gangway and this was used for them. The mate had sent me into his room with the newspaper reporters to give details of the passage from the ship's logbook. It was really his job to do this, but he was not fond of talking or spinning yarns, although a good seaman. Whilst I was doing my best with the reporters, there was a tremendous crash and cries of "Man overboard!!" Jumping out along with the newspapermen, we found the teakwood gangplank had carried away and that five or six of the passengers were in the water. The mate had foolishly allowed a whole crowd to get on it and away they went. Soon all were fished out and hauled on board. That is how the phrase I referred to earlier originated, "Wet when we came aboard and wet, damned wet, when we got ashore." These poor people were in their best togs and no doubt were very sore at us. Fortunately, the women were all safely in the sail boat when the gangplank collapsed. We sent the men along to the steward for a good tot of rum.

The next day we hauled alongside the Sandridge Railway Pier and had the outermost berth on the starboard side—or to explain more aptly—port side to quay. On the outer berth the ship had both anchors down. Our berth was usually allotted to the SOBRAON, but as she was not expected for several weeks, we had it. Captain Vine was the Harbour Master and a great friend of Captain Emslie of the SOBRAON. We had been alongside over two weeks when news came that the SOBRAON had passed the Otway and was inward bound. Orders came for us to shift, but Captain Parkes refused. There was quite a hullabaloo, and I believe it was taken up in the Parliament House. We would not shift and they could not force us to do so. However, the matter was settled by the agents of the SOBRAON offering to pay for our moving and also a day's demurrage. So we shifted to another berth and the queenly SOBRAON

GARTHPOOL

had the berth at the end of the pier. Captain Vine never forgave Captain Parkes. I don't think we were over popular with the Sabraonites and Captain Elmslie. What did we care?

After staying five weeks at Sandridge and taking in some 800 tons of ballast, we sailed on December 16, 1887, for Newcastle, N.S.W. We arrived there December 21, five days out. We had light head winds for the first three days and then struck a southerly buster off Wilson's Promontory and fairly flew the rest of the way. We discharged our ballast at the Dyke. We had discharged the entire crew at Melbourne and took runners around.

After loading about 2,800 tons coal, we sailed on January 15, 1888. We had had both Christmas and New Years in port. We made a fast passage of 47 days, arriving at San Francisco on March 2, 1888, only to find the MICRONESIA had again beaten us by two days. We had nearly twelve hours off Christmas Island when Captain Parkes, imagining that there was a shipwrecked crew, sent me ashore in the ship's lifeboat. We were ashore several hours but we discovered nothing but land crabs and some deserted huts. All water we found was brackish and not in the least palatable.[5] We were glad to get back to our ship.

We discharged at Beal Street Wharf and whilst in 'Frisco I saw the DOVENBY HALL dock with the notorious Captain Bailey. She had had a quick turn around and was with us at Port Costa and had sailed a little before us. We bent most of her sails since she had no crew—and no wonder. Bailey was murdered on the way home by his coloured steward two weeks after leaving 'Frisco.

Whilst in San Francisco the little MERIONETH came in, making the passage in 96 days from Cardiff.[6] The MICRONESIA was with us at Port Costa, both ships being at the Nevada dock, as also was the ELEANOR MARGARET, an ex-P & O steamer. At that time the Nevada dock was considered to be most up-to-date, having two decks and conveyors or endless belts for loading grain. The grain came in 100-pound sacks and one man turned these sacks in the hatchway as they came down the sheets, twisting them continually from port to starboard or vice versa.

Captain Parkes and Greig were great cronies and always together. Greig was a fine looking man and stood six feet, three inches in his stocking feet, with a great white beard. Parkes was a small man. One night, coming down to the ship at the Nevada dock after spending the evening with Greig (who was seeing him aboard), Parkes slipped and fell between the ship and the wharf. It was a wonder he was not killed. Hearing the commotion—I was in bed at the time—I jumped out when I heard the mate say, "Let the little b———r drown." We did not let him drown and he was always my friend after that; I don't think he ever forgave the mate.

There was in San Francisco harbour a wonderful sight of fair ships in that spring of 1888. I have a photograph showing the BROWNRIGG, EURASIA, ELEANOR MARGARET and HERAT all ready for sea. There were also, (although not in the photograph) the MERIONETH, LINLITHGOWSHIRE, MICRONESIA and others. All these beautiful ships were keyed-up and keen on making a race. Most had great reputations.

The EURASIA sailed on April 1st in company with the LINLITHGOWSHIRE, the BROWNRIGG following later in the day. The MICRONESIA had left the day before in company with Bate's HERAT and the four-master ELEANOR MARGARET. Outside the Farallons we found the weather hazy and a light northwest wind. The next two days we kept company with the LINLITHGOWSHIRE and then we lost her in the haze. We had favorable weather and good trades, crossing the Line on April 16, fifteen days out.

[5] *"Since those days, I believe Lever Bros. has owned the island, which is quite a size, and established a copra trade. Christmas Island has since become a depot for air ships."*
[6] *"I was on board her and saw the silk flag that Spreckel had presented to her; it covered the whole of the poop."*

Captains Greig, Kirkbride and Parkes
Photo taken in August 1889

The only island we sighted was Ducie Island, a coral island with a lagoon not far from Pitcairn. We rounded the Horn May 16, forty-five days out, with fine fair winds. We spoke the LINLITHGOWSHIRE, also 45 days out and were in company for a day or two. We overhauled a day or so later and spoke the four-masted ship ULRICA. She was from Portland. We were out of sight of her the same day. Crossing the Line—Atlantic side, 68 days out, we spoke the MERIONETH the same day, only 65 days out, having left April 4. This took the wind out of our sails but we were consoled when we left her astern and beat her into Queenstown by three days, thus making the same passage.

On June 27 out of the haze suddenly appeared our old friend MICRONESIA. She reported speaking the BROWNRIGG off the Horn. From then on we kept company with the MICRONESIA, not being able to shake her off. Together, we arrived at Queenstown on July 4 and one hour later the LINLITH-GOWSHIRE arrived. The times were: LINLITHGOWSHIRE, 95 days, MICRO-NESIA, 96 days, EURASIA, 95 days. The MERIONETH arrived on July 7, also making the passage in 95 days, although all three ships had beaten her from the equator. The EURASIA was 27 days from the Line, as also was the LINLITHGOWSHIRE. The MICRO-NESIA was only 26 days. Bates' HERAT of the straight stem, a main skysail yarder which had left with the MICRONESIA, was 156 days to Falmouth. She had a cautious

master and no reputation for speed. The BROWNRIGG, a skysail four-masted ship of Houston's, had also left the same day as the EURASIA and was spoken by the MICRO-NESIA off the Horn. She passed the Lizard on June 29, only ninety days out, and arrived and docked in Hull on the 97th day. The ELEANOR MARGARET was 98 days to Queenstown.[7]

The EURASIA left Queenstown July 5 and arrived at Harre July 7, ninety-eight days out from 'Frisco after calling at Queenstown. I left the EURASIA with regret but I was unable to get on with the mate. And so I went home.

[7] "Other ships making good passages that year were the THESSALUS from Portland, Oregon, 97 days. The WENDUR from Tacoma was only 99 days to the Fastnet and was several times in company with the THESSALUS, arriving within an hour of each other. They sailed together again and docked on the same tide at Fleetwood, England. One other ship, Heap's PARTHENOPE was 99 days from 'Frisco to Queenstown. These were not at quite the same time as the others, but, taking it altogether, it was a very favourable year for North Pacific passages homeward. At the same time ships from the East Indies were making unusually long passages. Such magnificent passages, such close passages of these iron ships and such a number, had never before been equalled."

BRYNHILDA off Flattery

55

CHAPTER VI

ADVENTURE

After having been home for a few days and being at a loose end, nothing in view, I went to Liverpool and was able to sign on the R.M.S. UMBRIA as A.B.[1] The UMBRIA and the ETRUIA were crack ships and the fastest on the Atlantic. They were single screw ships, barque-rigged. We averaged close on 19½ knots, the fastest I had ever been through the water. But I did not like steam so I managed to be discharged in New York.

After looking around New York City, which had not yet been developed into skyscrapers looking toward heaven, I took the train to San Francisco and from there went to Nanaimo, British Columbia, as A.B. in a collier called the WELLINGTON, master Captain Jordan. It was Captain Jordan who told me that a second mate was wanted in the TITANIA then belonging to the Hudson's Bay Company. He gave me a letter to Captain Dunn. He also advised me to call on the manager at the Hudson's Bay Company in Victoria. It was entirely through his kindness that I was paid off and started afresh.[2]

Not only did I land the berth as second mate of a wonderful ship but I made a good friend in Captain Dunn. We arrived at Port Moody, near Vancouver, some time in September 1888. It was just two years after the fire that destroyed the city of Vancouver, then newly incorporated, when I presented myself to Captain Dunn.

Captain Dunn was standing on the wharf and, after looking me over, he told me to follow him on board. He looked over my papers, asking various questions, but it was Jordan's letter that made him engage me. Thus I became second mate of the famous tea-clipper of which Captain Shewan of the NORMAN COURT in his reminiscences observes, "After the ARIEL, which I consider the fastest ship afloat, I place the TITANIA. Then the THERMOPYLAE, CUTTY SARK, SPINDRIFT and LEANDER, and very little to choose between any of them."

The TITANIA had been twice cut down afloat and was now rigged as a barque. Captain Dunn cautioned me that I would find her very different from the iron ships I had been in. We were loading at Port Moody a mixed cargo for London and sailed from there in tow on September 28, 1888. We called at Victoria and sailed from there on October 3. I remember that the little bit of a towboat only plucked us a short distance clear of Brotchie Ledge, and we made all sail to a fresh easterly wind which by the time we got to Flattery on October 4 had developed into a hard southeast gale.

This was my first introduction to a China tea-clipper and the little beauty was a wonder and an awe-inspiring sight to me. Under reefed upper topsails, reefed foresail and mizzen staysail, the mainsail being fast, she tore out to sea, determined to get an offing,

---

[1] ed. note. "A.B." is an able-bodied seaman classification.
[2] *"Years after, I met Captain Jordan again, by then a Bar Pilot at San Francisco, and I was able to thank him."*

MERMERUS was a celebrated wool clipper
generally in London with the TITANIA.

Gould's, Gravesend

standing off to the southwest and slashing through the rapidly making sea. She was very wet but not with heavy water.

Captain Dunn was not the man to let the grass grow under his feet and he kept her going all that night. Towards six in the morning the wind had shifted to the westward and we were a ship in a blinding rain squall to the southward. Gradually the wind hauled to the northwest and then the TITANIA began to show her paces like the little thoroughbred she was, kicking her heels up and dashing off. In a short time it was out reefs with the fore and main t'gallant sails on her. By noon all plain sail was set. Now she tore through it, lifting her head and throwing a shower of spray as she shouldered the old southeast sea, yet making no fuss about it like the lady she was. I had been in fast ships before, but never had I seen her equal. Dainty as her namesake, she was a thing to conjure with. Captain Dunn eyed me and smiled saying, "Could your old iron ships keep up with her, eh?"

This slant held right in to the northeast trades. Soon we were picking up the grain fleet from 'Frisco and always we left them astern. We rounded the Horn on the 55th day out from Flattery with a strong westerly gale. The TITANIA had a habit of dishing the water up on her lee counter when running heavily and had to be watched carefully. We passed a number of outward-bounders, head reaching under lower topsails; whilst we fled before the ever-freshening wind under t'gallant sails and foresail, sometimes flaunting our main royal.

On the equator we tried conclusions[3] with several homeward-bounders from Australia and New Zealand. In the light winds nothing could touch the TITANIA. How she could ghost along with the flap of her sails. It was always a case of ship ahead, say at daybreak,

alongside her by noon, and dropping her below the horizon before dark. I remember one day we overhauled the THYATIRA, an Aberdeen White Star ship with quite a reputation. She was not in it, however, with our little ship. (They must have been relieved when they discovered we were the renowned TITANIA. It was not so bad to be beaten by a tea-clipper, although cut down.)

We arrived on soundings[4] January 16, 1889, and passed the Lizard the same day, being 104 days from Flattery or land to land. We arrived off Gravesend January 19, 1889, and docked the same day in the West India Docks. My people were not expecting me home for several weeks. Captain Dunn asked me to stay on and I promptly decided to make another voyage with him. I was in the ship all the time in London.

Victoria, B. C. is shown here before the construction of the Parliament Buildings and the Empress Hotel. The city looked like this in the days of the TITANIA in 1890.

[3]ed. note. "Conclusions" were judgments of comparative valuations of ships, a race.
[4]ed. note. "Soundings" were a way of determining the depth of the water with a lead and a line.

I remember the MERMERUS was in the berth close to us and the mate and I were very chummy. My father and sisters came on board to see an out-and-out clipper and were entertained by Captain Dunn. They thought my stateroom was terribly small and stuffy.[5]

This was the fourth outward passage of the TITANIA for the Hudson's Bay Company and the ship left the docks on March 8, 1889, bound for the first time for Vancouver, B.C. Vancouver was by then incorporated as a city, although as yet, if you signalled another ship and were asked what port, it was still "Burrard Inlet." "Vancouver" was not yet in the code book.

We anchored off Gravesend and took in powder. We were held up by bad weather and did not get away until March 12. Head winds were encountered in the Channel and we did not pass the Start[6] until the 16th of March. After getting across the Bay of Biscay we made good progress. We went through the Strait of Lemaire and slipped around the Horn to the westward without much delay. We were off Cape Flattery on July 9, just 105 days from land to land. Arriving at Victoria on July 11 we discharged some cargo for Hudson's Bay Company. From there we went to Vancouver in tow and arrived there July 25, 1889.

This was the first through-cargo from London to be discharged. All the available space not required by the Hudson's Bay Company had been taken up by Bell, Irving & Patterson. We docked at their wharf.[7] The cargo amounted to 800 tons and consisted chiefly of pipes, cement, firebrick, hardware, liquor and general merchandise.

Captain J.L. Dunn was well known in every port we visited and had gained the sobriquet of "Dandy Dunn" from the natty and stylish manner in which he always dressed. Indeed, he would have made many of the modern steamship captains appear like hoboes. He was an entertaining conversationalist and a capital host aboard his ship.[8]

After discharging in Vancouver, a city that I would live to see celebrate its 50th birthday

China tea clipper TITANIA
The TITANIA was built by R. Steele & Co. at Greenock in 1866. She measured 200′ x 36′ x 21′ and was a composite build—an iron frame, planked, with steel masts. She was owned by the Hudson's Bay Company in the 1880s, sold to the Italians in the nineties and broken up at Marseilles in March 1910.
"This photo is a copy of a picture in the possession of Captain Dunn, painted in China. [She was] a most wonderful little ship."

[5] *"Writing this in Vancouver in the year 1936, I often wonder how we stood it, and I go back and look at my ship in Hudson's Bay Store on Granville Street, a beautiful model they have in her original rig with a dainty main skysail yard crossed, but quite a few errors in her deck plan not to be noticed by a landsman. In those far-off days I had youth on my side, and although poorly paid and not much to boast of in the way of food, we had health, life lay ahead, and all the world."*

[6] ed. note. The "Start" is a bay near Dartmouth, England.

[7] *"This later formed a part of the Canadian Pacific Railway's dock, just west of the Union Steamship dock."*

[8] *"Dandy Dunn had many friends and his tragic death, the result of an accident in British Columbian waters, caused profound sorrow. It happened on the voyage after I left him in October 1890, while the TITANIA was at Bell, Irving & Patterson's wharf at New Westminster. Captain Dunn accidentally slipped off the wharf whilst boarding his ship at night and was killed when his head struck a log or pile. He is buried at the cemetary at New Westminster. On several occasions I have visited his grave, and my thoughts have gone back over the years to my old skipper and friend. Dunn taught me most of what I know of sailoring; also, in the dog-watches of those far off days, he would tell me of the China trade and those peerless clippers."*

by a jubilee, we towed around to Steveston at the mouth of the Fraser River to load a mixed cargo. Steveston was not to be compared with Vancouver, although in those days it was a rough and ready town. New Westminster was the place we liked to spend our money. When we completed loading, all but a few tons were left to be picked up at Victoria. We left Steveston in tow on September 28, 1889, and arrived at Victoria the same day. Upon completing loading and bending our sails, we left Victoria October 3 and towed most of the way down the Strait of Juan de Fuca, passing out by Tatoosh (or Flattery) October 4. We had fine weather all the way until getting down to the Horn when we had strong, fair gales. Off the Horn we spoke the LADY HEAD, a barque belonging to the Hudson's Bay Co. She was under two lower topsails and nosing into a westerly gale. She was renowned for her slowness—the direct opposite of the TITANIA.

We arrived on sounding in very mild weather on January 12, 1890, and picked up the Bishop Rock lighthouse in a howling southwest gale, exactly 100 days from land to land. We arrived in London River and docked the same day on West India Docks, 104 days from Victoria, B.C. The TITANIA's times were never beaten and I do not think equalled. They stand for all time.

The following day I said goodbye, not without regret, to my skipper and friend. I went home in bitter weather to enjoy the Christmas fare they had saved up for me and had a most enjoyable time at my father's house. He was now living at Campden Hill Square, London. My younger sisters were growing up and kept things merry. And so, the sailor was home from the sea.

SIERRA MIRANDA

SCOTTISH GLENS

EURASIA

CHAPTER VII

FLYING SCUD AND SPUME

I was home a week or two before I was offered the berth as chief mate of the EURASIA by my old skipper, Captain Parkes. I joined her in the Victoria Docks, London, where she was then loading a general cargo for San Francisco. It was our misfortune to finish loading at a berth with insufficient water for us, and on getting into the locks we found the ship was some four inches by the head. However, this did not seem to affect her sailing qualities.

We left on the 26th of February 1890, and the EURASIA soon started to show her paces. Before we arrived at Margate Roads the wind had freshened to a moderate easterly gale. It was there that the pilot left us. As we went down channel we passed steamer after steamer and we were much elated when we overhauled and passed a large P & O [Pacific-Orient] steamer. The water was smooth. Just out of drydock we were clean and had as much wind, sometimes more than our three royals could stand, but never a sheet would the captain start. The Old Man was all out to make a record.

With fair trade winds and few doldrums between trades we made a rattling run down inside the Falkland Islands. The weather showed all signs of becoming dirty and soon the wind freshened to a hard gale from the west northwest and a fast-falling glass was evident. Captain Parkes reduced sail to a main lower topsail and mizzen staysail. These sails were brand new. I thought he was over cautious at the time but the dear old chap knew. Everything was made snug and extra gaskets were put on all sails.

By 8:00 p.m. it was blowing a living gale and the EURASIA was dousing her decks freely. The weather worsened rapidly and the ship laid down with her lee rails in the water. Before midnight the mizzen staysail blew away, followed shortly thereafter by the main lower topsail. In a few moments there was nothing left of them. It was a job now to get a tarpaulin in the weather mizzen rigging to keep the ship's head up. Once we got it into the rigging and let the roll go it blew itself up.

AUSTRASIA

Such an awe inspiring sight that night was. The moon was peeping through the clouds, and the storm clouds flying by, and the sea was one mass of scud. The big ship was now down almost on her beam ends while lee rails plunged underwater and the water was high on the lee side of the poop. All hands were now aft, the fo'castle gutted, galley washed out and both doors of the carpenter's shop gone. Soon, sail after sail, well-furled though they had been, blew away and flogged themselves to pieces. Heavy water was coming aboard forward and sweeping along the decks. It was impossible to get aloft, the force of the wind pinning you to the rigging. All through that night all hands were aft.

From the chart room door on the after side we had a rope stretched to the weather poop rail and by that we hauled ourselves to windward and under the lee of the weather cloth. At times the carpenter and a sailor would venture along the decks, watching their chance to get forward and see how the watches were standing. Once on their return, they reported the lifeboats stove in and all of the doors of the midship house were gone.

The EURASIA had a great sheer, yet, she was burying herself forward and tons of water were sweeping her decks. The only way one could get forward was by crawling along under the lee of her weather bulwarks from stanchion to stanchion and being half drowned at that. So when daylight broke Captain Parkes decided we had better jettison cargo forward to lighten her bows.

We were able to get down below the hatch to the sail locker, located under the fo'castle head. With great difficulty, some hundred tons of tin in cases were got out and passed up through the sail locker hatch. We slid them down to leeward and threw them overboard. All hands were kept at this, fighting for the life of the ship and their own lives. Dangerous work it was for those on deck who, working up to their waist in icy water were often submerged completely.

Drums of linseed oil were found and used with great effect on the breaking seas. Making a hole in the drum, we let the oil run out on deck and overboard. The ship, drifting to leeward, made an oil smooth to windward. As a result, no seas broke on board from to-windward.

What a sight our fine ship looked. Aloft she was as if she had been in a snowstorm, she was covered with white wadding from the flogged out sails. The builder's good work was pronounced in that the masts and yards stood the storm miraculously. All of the lee braces and most of the running gear had worked out through the deck ports and was frayed to pieces. The main topmast staysail was the only sail left and, but for the fact that it was furled and lashed in a netting on top of the house it would have gone, too. All of the teak doors of the forward house were gone. The lifeboats on the top of the house were stove in. The dinghy had disappeared. The lee teakwood ladder to the poop was also missing. The mast coat around the mainmast had also burst and a lot of water had gotten below.

It took us two days without any let up in this weather to get that tin out of the hold. The only hot food that we had was what we managed to heat on the cabin stove. The Old Man was liberal with his rum and that helped a lot. After jettisoning the cargo forward we found the ship acted much better. In a way she was more lively and lifted her head to the seas. Running the oil had made a smooth to-windward and by now no seas broke aboard, only lee water.

We were much concerned about the leeway the ship was making but nothing could be done in that respect. Old Captain Parkes came to me on the second night of the storm. The barometer was down to 28″.20 and still falling. Saying he thought we would be ashore on the Falklands before morning, he offered me a good drink of Scotch whisky. I did not refuse, I only wondered if I would ever have another.

After three days the weather began to moderate and the glass to rise and we were able to distinquish the horizon. All through the storm the sea and sky were mingled, one mass of flying scud and spume. As it began to calm, our lee rails came up and the EURASIA began to roll and lurch heavily. It was imperative to bend fresh canvas, repair damages and get our ship under command. Although pretty well played out, we bent three lower topsails and rove off new braces on the lee side, then wore ship before having a welcome sleep. The next day the sun peeped out and we were able to get our position—none too soon. We bent a new suit of canvas, our second best.[1]

After the gale moderated the wind went to the northeast and east and we rounded Staten Island and the Horn with the royals set. It was a lucky break for us since we had only our second-best canvas to depend upon. From now on we made great headway and anchored in San Francisco Bay, only 104 days out from Victoria Docks, London. On the way north we spoke the EUDORA from New York. She reported a terrible time off the Horn and the loss of most of her canvas. We were very evenly matched, yet we contrived to beat her into 'Frisco by about three days.

In San Francisco it was a case of general average[2] and yet to look at the ship which was now spic and span, one could hardly believe she had been through such bad weather until one saw the make-shift doors and the wicked scars on her decks caused by the tin cases when we had jettisoned them. It is an ill wind that blows no one any good and we had our share of paints and oils, etcetera which, of course, should have been thrown overboard. How could you expect sailormen in such times of stress to pick and choose? Under the circumstances, the underwriters were lucky. They did not have to pay for a total loss. We were lucky, too, to escape with our lives.[3]

Whilst in San Francisco I became friendly with Captain Morse's family, especially with his eldest daughter, Bessie. She was a charming girl and we used to go out together often. One day my old skipper called me aside and told me that Captain Morse had been inquiring about me. He had wanted to know what my prospects were and if I was steady. Old Parkes said he had given me a good boost.

ZEUS (upper)
Peril was a familiar occurence at sea. The ZEUS was struck by lightening.

BORROWDALE
"It was our last tack—we were able to fetch Havre Roads. But the poor little BORROWDALE had all the Channel before her to beat against the hard north-easter."

[1] *"This and one other occasion many years after when I was in steam were the only times that I can truthfully say that the wind scared me. The EURASIA would surely have foundered but for the fact that she was exceptionally well-built and that her aloft work had been well cared for."*
[2] ed. note. "General average" is a marine insurance term employed in the case of a total loss. The owners of the vessel average out the loss of the ship and the cargo respectively to the number of shares each owner controls.
[3] *"Several fine ships foundered in that self-same storm, including the LORD RAGLAN, one of Herron's and almost a new ship."*

This made me thoughtful, since I had never entertained the idea of matrimony with Bessie, not in the near future anyway. She was a sweet girl and a little later she married Captain Gibson whom I met in San Pedro when he commanded the BELVIDERE. I met Mrs. Gibson many years later, then an elderly lady and still very charming. We laughed and joked about those early days and how her father had scared me.

Newton's BORROWDALE, a little skysail yarder, was in port with us amidst a number of other fine ships. The STAR OF RUSSIA, that lovely Belfast ship of Corry's[4], had arrived the day before we sailed. That night we had two of her crew aboard, shanghaied, drunk and doped, and their own ship not yet alongside the wharf. Such was a sailor's life. The EUDORA had sailed a week before us. The little BORROWDALE hove up and went to sea on August 16th. Two days later, on the eighteenth, wc followed in her wake.

We had fair weather most of this passage. We deserved it. We sighted Pitcairn Island and invited a number of the islanders aboard for several hours. They had come off the island in two whale boats and we traded with them for fresh fruits, yams, chickens and fresh produce.

After Pitcairn we had mostly favourable winds, freshening to gale force until off the

Horn. Here we spoke the EUDORA and the BORROWDALE, having gained a week on the EUDORA and two days on the BOR-ROWDALE. From the Horn we beat the EUDORA by one day into Queenstown, but the BORROWDALE turned the tables on us, arriving twenty-four hours ahead. Our ship arrived on December 12, the EUDORA arrived on the thirteenth and the smart little BORROWDALE was there December 11, 1890.[5]

The weather in Queenstown was bitter; a black nor'easter had been blowing for weeks. We sent down our royal yards in Queenstown while waiting for orders. The BORROWDALE received orders from Newcastle-on-Tyne and left before us. We received orders for Havre.

This was the year the Thames was frozen over as far as Gravesend. We had to beat every bit of the way, a heart-breaking job. Every time we tacked ship we poured boiling water on the lee brace blocks to free them of ice. This was the only time in my life I ever saw floe-ice in the English Channel, but all along the shores of the Isle of Wight there was a sort of field ice.

Off St. Catherines Point [England] we were in company once more with our friend the BORROWDALE and we wished each other Merry Christmas. It was our last tack—we were able to fetch Havre Roads. But the poor little BORROWDALE had all the Channel before her to beat against the hard north-easter. Never again did I see that dainty main skysail-yarder. Often I had talked with Captain Sennet, our stevedore in San Francisco, about her. Sennet had commanded her for a number of years and had made many fine passages in her.

Arriving in Havre Roads we docked the next day but could not berth alongside the quay by all of ten feet on account of the heavy ice. I had a hot bath in my cabin that night. A hot bath for anybody but the skipper was quite a luxury, and one had only a diminutive tub. It was difficult to get both feet into it.[6] I awoke in the morning to find my tub frozen solid. I was leaving for good after this voyage

[4] "She later had a sinister reputation due to the loss overboard of the mate William Finney and his whole watch one dark and stormy night."

[5] "Passages that year were as follows: the EURASIA, 116 days; the BORROWDALE, 117 days and the EUDORA, 124 days. Basil Lubbock has the EURASIA's passage incorrectly in his usually accurate The Last of the Windjammers, having us leave San Francisco on August 15. I was on board the BORROWDALE the morning she sailed, which was the sixteenth, and we had two sailors from the STAR OF RUSSIA with us who verified that their ship had not arrived in San Francisco until the seventeenth. We arrived in Queenstown the day before the EUDORA whose arrival was December 12. This should be sufficient proof of my figures."

[6] "In these days of luxury our present day officers would be insulted if they had to use such primitive methods for bathing. Not so with us of the old breed. Cleanliness was next to Godliness, at least when bound for home."

because the former chief mate Hughes was returning. [This was the mate with whom I did not get along.] I persuaded Captain Parkes to let me go under the circumstances. That frozen tub closed the deal.

The ship was not paying-off until after Christmas. The British Consulate could only manage to pay off two ships a day and there were quite a few before us. It would be a long wait.

I said good-bye to my old skipper on Christmas Eve and it was several years before I saw him again. It was not until he had put back to Liverpool from Rio de Janeiro under jury-rig with the new four-poster AUSTRASIA.

I left early in the day for Dieppe and spent hours there waiting for the Channel steamer. The time was spent chiefly in Cafe Chantants. Did I do that to improve my French?

I crossed the Channel that night, arriving in Folkestone in the early hours and then arriving at Victoria Station about eight in the morning, Christmas Day, 1890. The streets of London were covered with frozen snow and s-l-i-p-p-e-r-y! I chartered a hansom cab, but before long I abandoned ship and proceeded on foot at a jog-trot. It was damnably cold and the streets were covered with ice. I had told the cabby to follow on with my portmanteau (called a grip by the moderns). I got to my father's house in Campden Hill Square about nine in the morning, pretty nearly frozen. My sister Edith rushed to the front door; then along came the rest of the family.

What a breakfast I stowed away. Did ever ham and eggs and coffee taste so good? The family had been frozen up for weeks. There was no water in the house. A water cart came around every day and you had to buy your water by the bucket. It reminded me so much of sail that I chuckled all over to think, "Now you know what it is to have your water rationed, too."[7]

The shortage of water didn't trouble me to the extent that it did the female portion of the household. There was plenty of beer to drink and my father had a good wine cellar, and always, whenever I came home, he would

EUDORA, steel, four-masted, built in 1888 by A. Stephens & Son, Dundee.

indulge in some rare Madeira. That was followed by a touch of the gout. This vintage came from an estaminet[8] of an old friend of ours, Russel Gordon of Cossart, Gordon & Co., Funchal, Madeira. At other times my father had to content himself with whisky and Vichy water...not so bad at that.[9]

We celebrated Christmas royally. Only a few days before it had been sailing ship fare for me, salt horse and coffee. The cold weather lasted quite a time but when the thaw came, and with it the water supply, no male could have a bath until all the women of the house were fully satisfied. I was told, "You are used to being without water unless it's salt; sailors don't need a bath."

[7] *"This was Christmas Day, 1890, forty-seven years ago, and I was a very young man in my early, yes, very early twenties."* ed. note. Beavis was actually 26 years old in 1890 and to his recollections he seemed a very young man.

[8] ed. note. A cafe in which smoking is allowed.

[9] *"Many's the time I would have liked to have had it myself on a dark and dirty night."*

ARISTIDES

CHAPTER VIII

TWO YEARS IN THE MYLOMENE

Whilst home I went to Captain Baxter's nautical school in Leadenhall Street. He was in partnership with Captain LeCouteau, a Jersey man who had commanded the barque SCOTTISH LASSIE. Captain Baxter had been mate and master in the New Zealand Shipping Company and he had commanded the WAIHA in the early eighties. I had great regard for Captain Baxter and in later years we became firm friends.

It was about this time that the suffragettes were coming to the fore. One day a bus full of them passed down Leadenhall Street just as a mob of us young mates came out of Baxter's school. These were darned good-looking lassies, waving flags and jeering at us poor males. It was rather a foolish thing for them to do, especially to a lot of hefty young sailing ship mates. They must have appealed to our sailor hearts for with one accord some half dozen of us went swarming up the steps of the bus and, grabbing hold of the girls, gave them resounding kisses amid lots of screams and yells. Then we swiftly beat it to the pavement. I don't think the girls minded much, but it was a wonder we weren't run in.

I sat again before Captain Rankin and passed this time for extra-master. With this I had acquired all my certificates under sail. After getting my ticket I started to look for a ship and wrote to several shipowners, being now the proud possessor of an extra-master's square-rigged ticket. I was offered the berth of mate in no less than five ships inside of a week. One was from Carmichael of Greenook,

and as I write I have the letter from Nourse offering me mate of the BANF. Another was from Brocklebank's to go chief mate of the MAJESTIC and then, Fernie's. I do not know why I decided on Fernie's except that I wanted to go to Melbourne. The pay was the same in all the ships offered, £8. per month.

MAJESTIC
Iron ship built by Harland & Wolff, Belfast in 1875 for T. & J. Brocklebank, Liverpool.
"Bowsprit, yards and masts painted white, a beautiful figurehead of a woman and much scroll work round the bows.... A very fast ship and a wonder in light winds."

A. D. Edwardes, South Australia

71

I joined the MYLOMENE, 1900 tons—full-rigged ship, then in Dunkerque, France. She was taking ballast bound for Fredrikstad, Norway, to load deals for Melbourne. The captain's name was Cross. I believe he hailed from Manchester. The mate had left to pass for master and was to take charge later at Fredrikstad when Captain Cross would leave.[1]

Captain Cross used to fire a lot of atheist literature at me. I think Ingersoll was the author of this stuff and Cross greatly admired him. Just as the MYLOMENE was getting into the Baltic, she was nearly ashore on a reef and Cross completely lost his head and kept saying, "My God, my God," at which I turned to him and said, "I thought you had no God." He shut up like a clam.

---

[1] *"Of all the different skippers I have sailed with he was the only one I could not get along with. For one reason, he was a man I could not respect. In appearance he was tall but slovenly, then about forty-six years old. His wife sailed with him and also his little daughter. They were all "cro-jack-eyed" (squinted). When you were at table with them and thought they were not looking at you, by the Lord Harry they were. When you were certain they were looking at you—they weren't. The captain and his wife were atheists and what the child was I do not know but, she was a little beast. Just after I joined ship she got into my room and inked all the logbook and put sand in my bunk. Her parents only laughed.*

"On the way north from Dunkerque this child began playing with the mizzen topsail halliards and took nearly all the turns off the belaying pin when her father happened to notice her. He had been playing with her a few minutes before and was sitting on the cabin skylight. It was "Good girl, Ida, hold it for Daddy" and he jumped up and caught the rope from her, making it fast again. Then over his knee she went and didn't she yell! After that he got foul of me for not having the halliards hitched, I pointed out that it was he himself who had not hitched them after the tussle with his daughter. We previously had had words over the anchor when leaving Dunkerque, when he was going to knock my b—b—head off. He didn't—I took a capstan bar to him when he ignominiously fled to the arms of his wife. He was leaving the ship, however, at Fredrikstad to take command of the four-masted barque EULOMENE then fitting out, so I did not worry much about him."

[2] *"Cross gave me a very bad name to the new master, Captain Wilkin, who had once been mate on her. I sailed over two years with Wilkin and he told me of Captain Cross's initial introduction only as I was leaving. We never had any friction and remained firm friends. I was at Wilkin's wedding years later and their first-born was named after me."*

When in Fredrikstad, Captain Cross and his wife had a habit of going ashore each evening after dinner, then a few minutes later, he would pop back to see what the mate was doing. He tried to catch me at forty winks. He had performed this escapade several times, before one day I grew so hot under the collar that I told him of it and a little bit more. I referred to something about his ancestry which was not a nice way to talk about one's captain, but he was not nice. When he left, he told me he would report me to old Fernie and that if he had been going in this ship, he wouldn't carry me. I replied, "If you, sir, had been going as master, I would not have sailed one foot with you."[2]

Fredrikstad was a clean little town with several sawmills and at one we were loading. I, as mate, was responsible for the cargo and tallying all of it. It was some job. There were 950 standards of dressed lumber. While loading a lumber cargo in most iron ships, the ballast, consisting of small shingle, would be stowed in the ship's bilges, packed tight. From the main hatch aft about a foot more would be packed, otherwise the ship would load by the head. Just before completing loading, the new master, Captain Wilken, joined and old Cross departed.

One Saturday the second mate and I went by train to Kristiansand [Norway]. We took all precautions, as we thought, and put in our pockets on one side the return fare. We gaily laid ourselves out to spend the rest of our substance. Well, we had a good time. We spent all of our Norwegian money except the fare back. But to our horror when we got to the station, we found the last train was double fare. We were in a nice pickle. After much debating the second mate thought it would be better for me to get back to the ship as I was mate. He would stay in Kristiansand. We were making arrangements for it when, on feeling through my waistcoat pockets, I came across two ten-franc pieces of gold—what a god-send! We arrived back at the ship all right, but ever after that we had a dislike for Norwegian railways.

GRENADA and tugboat TYEE

"The tug TYEE towed us to sea and we passed out from Flattery on the afternoon of November 22. I did not see Mount Baker for many years after this."

The MYLOMENE was built of iron by Potter of Liverpool and was 1900 tons register. This was the largest ship I had been in so far, yet she was lightly sparred and had no hoist to her sails to speak of. All of my previous ships had been heavily sparred and very taunt-o.[3] The MYLOMENE had one abomination that was a source of worry and sorrow to me. This was her sliding gunter jibboom;[4] you could never keep the thing straight. It would cant to leeward in the least bit of a breeze. I had been with a terrific-sized jibboom in the STAR OF FRANCE and also in the smaller TITANIA, but once they were set up they would stay put. These sliding gunters of Fernie's never would hold their position. All of their ships with the short spike bowsprit were fitted with them.

MAQUARRIE (pp. 74-5)
"One weekend I took the night boat to Sydney and visited my uncle and cousins. I called on the MAQUARRIE and took one of the boys, George Newman, for an outing to my uncle's place."

[3]ed. note. Means very high or tall, i.e. "taunt-masted" or "taunt-rigged".
[4]ed. note. A "gunter" is a fitting consisting of two double eyes united by side bars, one eye in each sliding freely over the lower mast, the other serving as a step for the topmast. In the case of the MYLOMENE this fitting was placed on the jibboom.

MAQUARRIE

MACQUARIE

74

The MYLOMENE also had lanyard rigging and it had been the habit of Captain Cross to set up the fore and aft stays when any of the shrouds showed a tendency to become slack. It was because of this that in the course of time the MYLOMENE's topmasts, t'gallant and royal mast and others were all raking slightly forward. Whilst I was in her I fitted her with an entire new set of lanyards and that took some of the forward rake out of her masts. Previously I had been with lanyards in the TITANIA, but the other ships had screw rigging.

The MYLOMENE had not dry-docked for nearly two years and she was to dry-dock in Melbourne. Being very foul, (she did not sail well at the best of times) one could not get much out of her.[5] We sailed about the middle of June, going north and passing Fair Island, Scotland. We discovered just how sluggish this vessel was. Rarely, only rarely would she stay. And slow, oh how slow. There was one thing about her, though, you could carry the main t'gallant sail when other ships would have been snugged down to reefed upper topsails—that is if you were sure of your spars, and that we were not. In her earlier days the MYLOMENE had carried stunsails and the boom irons were there and one or two of the stunsail booms, but the sails had all been cut up for some other purpose.[6]

We had a long voyage out to Melbourne. Everything passed us. Old ballyhoos with windmills going would go gaily sailing past. The only thing we passed was the Crozet Islands and if it had been thick weather we

would have doubted it, but as they were anchored to the bottom of the sea we were able to do it.

We discharged up the Yarra at a lumber wharf. I had to tally all of the lumber out and it was hauled away by horse lorries. I am afraid I must have cheated quite a bit as I turned many thousand pieces over and one roll of paper. This was the first time I had been shipmates with paper made from wood pulp. We also had a number of buckets or pails made from pulp. The year was 1891 and I believe the pulp-paper industry was in its infancy.

One day, whilst we were discharging and I was busy tallying on the wharf, there was a sudden commotion on board. Turning to look, I saw stevedores on deck, all running to the offshore side. Dashing on board I found the second mate in the water; the ship's dinghy, which had been used for scrubbing the ship's side, was capsized and the third mate was holding on to her keel. The apprentice who had been with the third mate was not to be seen. There were various cries of "He's under the boat." Throwing off my coat, I dived in. He was not under the boat. The second mate and I dived again into the filthy, muddy water. The dinghy was righted and baled out. The third

RIVERSIDE
"Outside the Heads, a full-rigged ship, the RIVER-SIDE, deep loaded and bound for Sydney, went by us as if we were at anchor."

[5]ed. note. Beavis refers to the "foul" bottom and the need for its cleaning. Sailing vessels were encumbered in speed when growth and sea life were allowed to build on the ship's outer hull or bottom. Two years was an extraordinary length of time to pass without drydocking or a fresh water berth.

[6] *"We had a patent scrubber, said to be Captain Cross' invention. It required a four-knot breeze to work it in. I never had much faith in it. It took some of the growth off, but not all, and very little run. It also caused the ship to steer badly. This old ship had a donkey engine but no donkey man. We were always expecting the boiler to blow up. Some Divine Providence evidently looked after us."*

mate and the sailmaker dragged with grapnels and about half an hour later recovered the apprentice's body. Of course the lad was dead.

The boy was nearly out of his apprenticeship and was a good six-footer and quite a nice youngster. He and the third mate had been scrubbing the ship's side and were skylarking when a steamer passed, causing the wash that capsized them. Both could swim but they lost their heads even though there were several ropes for them to grab.

A few days later we drydocked in Duke's drydock and then, having taken ballast, sailed for Newcastle, New South Wales. Outside the Heads, a full-rigged ship, the RIVERSIDE, deep loaded and bound for Sydney, went by us as if we were at anchor. We were light and clean just out of dry dock, and all sail was set. The wind was on the quarter, yet that ship went by us like nothing at all. The RIVERSIDE was nearly a sister ship to the MICRONESIA, Russell-built. We were about a week getting to Newcastle. After discharging our ballast, we loaded coal for Valparaiso, Chile.

One weekend I took the night boat to Sydney and visited my uncle and cousins. I called on the MAQUARRIE and took one of the boys, George Newman,[7] for an outing to my uncle's place. I only had a few hours so it was a hurried visit. I had to return by Monday morning. Before leaving Newcastle, several of the crew had complained of feeling ill, including the second mate. I was not feeling too well, either. However, we sailed with 3000 tons of coal aboard. The first night out after making sail, I collapsed and I remember nothing of the rest of the passage. The following day the second mate was down and before many days all hands; some might be up for awhile and then cave in.

The captain had sailed south of New Zealand and the weather was stormy. The mainsail was furled, somehow, and also the t'gallant sails. But for the rest of the passage, the old MYLOMENE stormed along under six topsails and foresail. What she could not carry

she had to drag. She made the best passage of her life—36 days from Newcastle to Valparaiso with all hands down with typhoid fever except the captain, two apprentices and the steward.

Once, with a howling gale blowing, there was only the captain, third mate, steward and two apprentices on deck. The apprentices steered the ship. There was no lookout except the third mate or the captain and the boy who was steering. Tired, tired almost to breaking strain, were these men. The ship stormed through the gale like some mad creature.

I was a mere bag of bones. All this time I knew nothing. It was only through the care of Captain Wilken that I survived. The typhoid we had contracted was of the worst, most virulent variety. The sailmaker and seven crew members had died but I had been unaware of their passing. The sailmaker and one other man had had putrid typhoid, the most dangerous type.

When we arrived in port, I was just able to sit up. It was a long time before I was properly recovered. It was the captain who had saved me. The ship was quarantined for ten days at Valparaiso. We moored in the tiers, [a row of moored or anchored ships], two anchors ahead with 120 fathoms cable in each and one anchor astern. We discharged slowly into lighters. There was plenty of surf and days when no discharging could be done; then a saint's day, also no work. [Those discharging the ship refused to work on religious holidays referred to as "saint's days".] The crew was working the cargo and naturally grew thirsty. We had quite a time trying to prevent the men from getting Pisco or anisou [sic] from the launcheros. One Maori man was a splendid specimen but as soon as he got any liquor, he was absolutely crazy. Several of the crew deserted, but finally we were rid of the coal cargo and took in sand ballast. Here we lay for some time with no signs of a charter.

7 "George Newman is now master of one of the Furness Motor ships [1936]."

BRODICK CASTLE
"It took us about three days to get our anchors and cables, the water being very deep. They were lifted by a steam lighter from shore; we only had to heave in the slack cable. Leaving Valparaiso with light, southerly winds, we drifted up the coast to Coquimbo, about 250 miles north of Valparaiso."

Two ships in Valparaiso with us were the LATIMER, a heavy looking ship, and the BRODICK CASTLE, a beautiful ship with a great reputation for speed but a very mean captain of the name of Ferguson. He had a number of pigeons on board his ship. We also had a few birds and a large and airy pigeon and fowl house. Ferguson's birds soon found that ours was a better ship. There was more to eat, so they stayed with us.

One day Captain Ferguson called on us and was overly abusive about his pigeons. He was going to do all sorts of things to me, he threatened. My captain was grinning. I went to the pigeon-house and let all the birds out and told the master of the BRODICK CASTLE to take his damned birds. He was disgusted, he couldn't catch them and, needless to say, they returned and stayed with us when we sailed.

I remember going ashore on Palm Sunday and I visited several churches. They were filled with women but only a few men. The priests were going around with incense, of which they took care to give a very good dose to us heretics. I visited Vina Del Mar, a quiet, handsome spot on the northern side of the bay where there was a race course. There were a goodly number of French and German ships in the harbour.

Now as the norther season which occurs in June, July and August drew near, we were ordered to send down tophamper.[8] However, before we did this, the captain decided to shift up the coast to Coquimbo, Chile, a much safer port. It was also the South Pacific station for the British Navy.

It took us about three days to get our anchors and cables, the water being very deep. They were lifted by a steam lighter from shore; we only had to heave in the slack cable. Leaving Valparaiso with light, southerly winds, we drifted up the coast to Coquimbo, about 250 miles north of Valparaiso. On making the land in the vicinity of Coquimbo, we were close in to Guayacan.

In those days the lighthouse served the two ports of Coquimbo and Guayacan. The wind fell away to a flat calm, and by 8:00 a.m. we were so close to the rocks that for a time we could not lower our starboard lifeboat. It was only the backwash from the rocks that saved us. Both lifeboats were put into the water to help tow the ship. They leaked badly and had a number of rats in them which swam up around us. I was in charge of one, the second mate the other. Each boat had 120 fathoms of three inch manila line for a towrope. We were both glad to be in the boats, leaky and ratty though they were. The captain, third mate, idlers,[9] and the rest of the crew were on board to trim sail. They seemed to envy us in the boats.

Before we left the ship we had cast adrift hatches and all that would float, expecting the ship to strike every moment. There was 90 fathoms of water right up to the rocks. The ship was braced sharp on the port tack heading to the north and the west. Desperately we pulled for over an hour in the two boats with rocks and cliffs almost touching the ship's starboard side. Then a wispy draft of air came away from the southward and the ship's head came out. Slowly, oh so slowly, she began to pull out. Shortly after a fleet of rowboats came out from Coquimbo, headed by M.M.S. GARNET's boats. All of them took hold of us and yanked us into Coquimbo.

What a relief—to return on board again and see my captain. Even though his nerves must have been badly shaken, he was quite cool. We went in to the cabin and had a drink with the officers of the GARNET; they didn't need it but we did.

I went into my room which was just at the break of the poop and found it all in disorder, just as I had left it. For a time I had never expected to sit in it again. All my treasures, my lares et penates [sic] such as a sailor loves to collect were there. Wasn't I glad to see them.

We anchored close to the LIFFEY, an old wooden British man-of-war, then used as a store ship and also a prison for the South Pacific station. We found Coquimbo a nice town, very quiet. There was another small town called La Serena on the northern side of the bay. Here we found several small craters full of pumice stone, of which I commandeered quite a lot to clean the ship's bright work. The officers of the GARNET were hospitable and we visited often, went to church on board her on a Sunday and stayed to lunch. These were very happy days for us all.

One day the captain said to me, "I'm going to give the hands liberty and so many dollars."

I remonstrated with him, saying, "They'll only get drunk."

[8]ed. note. The upper masts, sails, rigging of a ship.
[9]ed. note. An idler was one who had constant day duties on board ship, and hence kept no night watch.

"Yes," he replied, "I know that, and they'll be locked up in the Caboose and have to clean the streets. Then the captain of the port will fine them $50 each, $25 for himself and $25 for me." Well, he did it and they did it. I did not like it. No wonder, a few days later most of our men had deserted.

We lay at anchor several weeks before receiving a cable to proceed to Royal Roads, B.C. for orders. As we were short of most of our crew we had some difficulty getting men; what we did get was a pretty poor lot. These were beachcombers, the scum of the Chilean beaches. We finally got away with fine weather and fair winds all of the passage, so, to make the most of it, I rigged out stunsail booms at the fore and with two main topmast staysails had jib-headed stunsails on both sides. Being light we made a fair, average passage and anchored in Royal Roads, only to find everyone ashore down with small pox. The year was 1892. No one was allowed to go ashore. After a few days Captain Wilkin decided to go across the Strait of Juan de Fuca some seventeen miles to Port Angeles and thus be clear of the contagion.

One morning early, with the wind off the land, we hove up anchor and set our topsails. Within three hours we anchored behind Ediz Hook at Port Angeles. This was a much better and safer anchorage than Royal Roads. It was here, though, that trouble developed amongst our crew of beachcombers. One man especially would not work and feigned sick; the captain ordered him aft to be taken care of and attended by the steward. This meant durance vile—a slop diet and no tobacco. He refused to go. The second mate and I went to get him. He had armed himself with an ax and a murderous knife. We made a dash at him—I was badly cut in the groin, but we would have caught him anyway if not for the rest of the crew piling on top of us. The second mate and I were badly knocked about.

The Old Man had been standing outside the fo'castle door with a small pin fire revolver which would not go off, so we beat a hasty retreat. On getting aft, the second and I

cleaned ourselves up and repaired our bruises. The skipper and the apprentices hurried ashore for assistance. I let the hands stand easy for the rest of the morning.

Having matured a plan in the meantime, I waited until after dinner before I went forward to call all hands out of the fo'castle, with the exception of the so-called "sick" man. I sent them into the sail locker to move some sails. They were quite unsuspicious. The sail locker was under the fo'castle head and had a heavy hatch. As soon as they were all below I clapped the hatch shut and put the iron bar across it. I stationed the carpenter there with an axe in case any of them managed to break out. Then the second mate and I dived for the fo'castle door. Our sick man was sitting there smoking, not expecting anyone. Did we beat him. His own mother would have had a job recognizing him.

Just then the skipper returned with the sheriff and a couple of hard looking officers, all armed with 45 calibre revolvers. The captain also had guns for us. They had a look at our man and casually remarked that we seemed to be able to take care of ourselves. Then we let the crowd out of the sail-locker. They were sheepish and crestfallen. The skipper and the sheriff gave them a severe tongue-lashing. They saw how heavily armed we were.

Going aft to the cabin we discussed the problem with the sheriff. He advised us to let them desert if they wanted. That night one of them swam ashore, stole a boat, brought it off under the bow of the ship and before turn to time next morning, all hands were gone, with the exception of one. We were not sorry; they were a tough lot. I had had a narrow escape when the malingerer knifed me, requiring several stitches. This life had its unpleasantries.

Now with only two apprentices and one man who happened to be a decent sort, we were a happy ship. Very soon we had the MYLOMENE painted and spic and span. The captain had friends in Vancouver, B.C. and visited them, leaving me in full charge. Port

A. D. Edwardes, South Australia

Angeles in those days was a small community, just one street. At times, bears, cougars and deer still roamed through town. It looked quite imposing from the Straits at night though, because it was well lit with electric lights. (I think the electric lights were put in before the town.)

Once I chartered a horse and buggy and taking the second mate along with me drove to New Dungeness, a distance of some 25 miles. The road was through the virgin forest of huge Douglas fir, some of them well over three hundred feet tall. In many places we had to make detours around fallen trees.

We enjoyed this outing immensely, it was a great treat to be on our own and away from the ship. We had a nice dinner at the village inn and started back just as night was falling. We were warned to keep a sharp lookout for bears.

MILLWALL
Iron barque, 1222 tons, built in 1863 for D. Duncan, Liverpool. Sold several times before out of register in 1900.

It was after dark when we got back and stabled the horse without the liveryman seeing it. Next day when settling the bill, the livery man said we had nearly killed the horse. It was a good thing he had not seen it the previous night!

Whilst in Port Angeles I made a trip to Lake Crescent some miles inland. There was a small launch running on it. I visited a cabin owned by a Mrs. Michelle who was the postmistress whom I had met on several occasions when she had come into Port Angeles for supplies. Her ne'er-do-well husband was then living in San Francisco. She was trying to eke out a living there in the woods. She was a charming lady who had travelled extensively both to London and Paris.[1]

Whilst in Port Angeles the whale-back steamer C.W. WETMORE put in on her last voyage. She was totally lost at Coos Bay after leaving Port Angeles September 8, 1892. In October we received word that we were chartered to load wheat at Tacoma. So we started to discharge our ballast overboard. We were at anchor in ten fathoms of water and someone ashore who did not like our captain made a kick about it.[2] Whilst the skipper was ashore, the sheriff and another man, both with heavy revolvers, (they must have remembered how the second mate and I had beaten that malingerer) came off and ordered me to take soundings. I refused to do so, informing them that I knew what water I had. I was not very polite in spite of their revolvers. They left the ship in search of a lead-line and returned to take their own soundings whilst we looked on. On leaving the ship they met Captain Wilkin ashore and arrested him. There was quite an uproar in the community;

WILLSCOTT (later STAR OF ICELAND)

Capt. P. A. Gruelund

the townspeople had made money out of the ship whilst she had been lying in their port. They were quite irate with the law. The trouble was quickly adjusted and as there happened to be a 20 fathom patch a short distance further out, we lifted our anchor the next day and kedged out to it. Neither the sheriff nor his satellites came out to verify our soundings—they had had enough.

Late in October we towed to Port Townsend and from there to Tacoma. We went straight to the buoys and secured ballast logs; then we discharged the rest of our ballast. With a clean-swept hold already lined to receive wheat, we waited our turn to go alongside and load.

Whilst waiting, the STAR OF ITALY came off to the same buoy fully loaded. She brought back memories of my old ship, the STAR OF FRANCE that I had been in as a young boy fresh from the CONWAY. She made the MYLOMENE look like a barge. Her tauntness was apparent for her royal yards on the lifts were away above our trucks.[3] With the great rake of her masts and her beautiful sheer, she was like a yacht compared to us.

When she came off to the buoys they just ran a line and her crew, hauling on that line by hand, chantied her off. For the most part she had a coloured crew and could they sing! You could hear them all over the harbor. The

[1] "I remember, too, that the butcher and principal ship chandler in Port Angeles was a man of the name of Metcalfe, related to the Cumberland family who originally came from there."

[2] "According to U.S. maritime law we were not allowed to throw ballast overboard in less than twenty fathoms."

[3] ed. note. A truck was a small wooden cap at the summit of the masthead, usually having holes in it for running signal halliards.

mate's name was Edwards, and he had skippered the ship to San Diego after the STAR OF ITALY's master, Captain Cotter, died during the passage. Believing that his command would continue, Edwards brought the STAR OF ITALY to Port Angeles. But here to his dismay he had been relieved by Captain Reed. The mate's disappointment was displayed through his actions.

We followed the STAR OF ITALY on the grain berth and loaded 3,000 tons of wheat. We sailed November 21, 1892. The STAR OF ITALY had left November 17. We were forced to recruit an entirely new crew, but for a wonder, we managed to get a pretty decent lot. The tug TYEE towed us to sea and we passed out from Flattery on the afternoon of November 22. I did not see Mount Baker for many years after this. As we towed out past Tatoosh, a hard southeaster was making up fast and we had to carry all the sail she would stand to gain an offing. By midnight we were snugged down to three lower topsails and foresail, plunging heavily into a rising southwest swell which foretold that before long we would have the wind from there. At 4 a.m. the shift came in the form of a blinding squall of wind and rain and we wore ship round on the starboard tack.

It blew hard all day shifting to westward as night fell. We had, however, managed to get searoom and when the wind again backed to the southeast, we were able to carry full topsails, foresail and mainsail. The MYLOMENE was not a fast ship, being like all of Fernie's she was undersparred. As we drew further south and into the southeast trades, we fell in with quite a few of the 'Frisco grain fleet and they all left us astern. One night in the southeast trades, to our astonishment we overhauled and passed a full-rigged ship. Captain Wilkin was thinking of heaving-to, but since we were doing well, he refrained. By morning, she was out of sight astern. We never knew what ship it was but it was the only ship we ever passed whilst I was on the MYLOMENE. We sighted the "Diego Ramirez" and rounded the Horn on

February 10 in fine weather and strong winds. It was summertime in those latitudes during January and there were long hours of daylight. Two days later we fell in with four of the Australian wool fleet on four consecutive mornings.

On the first of these mornings we sighted the Aberdeen flyer SALAMIS. With a fine sail breeze, the SALAMIS passed us in the early afternoon. The next morning the ARISTIDES of the same line repeated the performance. We reported the SALAMIS ahead. The following day along came the MOUNT STEWART, swinging her main skysail. Then, on the fourth morning the famous MER-MERUS passed close to us, also carrying her main skysail. We reported the position of the others.

Captain Cole was in command of the MER-MERUS and he evidently did not like the other ships being ahead because he signalled, "I did not drydock this time." [He was excusing his tardiness, having the disadvantage of a foul bottom.] Evidently the other ships had. We saw them no more.

Captain Edwards
"The mate's name was Edwards, and he had skippered the ship to San Diego after the STAR OF ITALY's master, Captain Cotter, died during the passage.... Edwards brought the STAR OF ITALY to Port Angeles [Washington]."

Oliver Godfrey, Newcastle

Fortunately we escaped the ice that so many other ships were caught in. In the tail end of the southeast trades, we fell in with the RODERICK DHU, outward bound to 'Frisco. She was a very lovely sight with her six t'gallant sails and her main skysail fluttering above her royal. Like all of Williamson-Milligan's ships she was beautifully kept and painted white on the topsides. She looked the thoroughbred that she was.

Crossing the equator with very light winds, we gave the crew a taste of Cross's patent scrubber. I was heartily glad when the winds came too strong for its use. As far as I could see it only made the ship steer badly and the MYLOMENE was none too good before it. The northeast trades were poor and soon petered out in 23 degrees north. Calms and light airs followed, and to make matters worse, we were short of provisions. Apparently the steward misinformed the captain about his stores before leaving Tacoma. Long before reaching the equator we had that steward grinding wheat in the coffee mill. He was grinding meal for mush and burnt ground wheat for coffee. We had no butter, no sugar, no milk. The salt beef had given out. The salt pork had been gone long before it.

Just north of the equator we fell in with a small French barque, outward bound, and we got a barrel of salt pork and a little flour. The pork was very good, and unlike our pork, the head of the pig had been salted down in the barrel, too.

As time wore on things got worse and the worst catastrophe occurred when the tobacco ran out. Sailormen will stand a lot, but no tobacco, that was the last straw. Old beds were broken up and the straw smoked. Old pipes were ground up. The continuous head winds and calms and a surly, mutinous feeling amongst the crew was not at all pleasant for the mates.

TALISMAN (p. 84)
"It blew hard all day shifting to westward as night fell. We had, however, managed to get searoom and when the wind again backed to the southeast, we were able to carry full topsails, foresail and mainsail."

One morning, after sighting several homeward-bound ships, we were fairly close to one of Andrew Weir's barques, the CASTLEBANK. The captain's name was Boyd and he was not a very pleasant fellow. All we could barter was a very small sack of sugar. At that I had to sign for it.

Whilst I was on board the CASTLEBANK, along came one of the North German Lloyd steamers, the SAALE. I was in charge of the MYLOMENE's lifeboat so I immediately cast off and pulled towards the steamer. My ship had hoisted "N.Y. short of provisions, starving" and the steamer stopped. She was bound to the westward and was full of passengers. As I came alongside, the captain hailed me and asked if any sickness was on board. "None at all," I replied, and I was allowed on board the steamer. The ship's master spoke excellent English. He inquired which provisions we were short. "Everything," I replied. "Disgraceful," he said. The chief steward was called and given orders to provision the boat. I offered to sign for everything we received. But the German commander said, "No, you are short of provisions, aren't you? The North German Lloyd doesn't do anything like that." He sent for a great plate of ham sandwiches. Oh, how good they were, washed down with cold, foaming beer. The captain added a large case of beer and several bottles of whisky to the boat for my captain.

The steamer captain was in a hurry, things moved quickly and, bidding him good-bye, I went along the deck to our boat. What a sight!—my four sailors were all helplessly drunk. The passengers had been lowering bottle after bottle of strong German beer to these men. Their empty stomachs and lengthy absence of the taste of liquor crippled them into total helplessness. They were completely knocked out from the suds.

The boat was loaded to the gunwale with provisions—new potatoes, vegetables, fresh meat and case goods and, best of all, tobacco. The boat's crew was so drunk, uselessly lying on top of the provisions and the boat so overloaded, that I had to scull her back to the ship.

Fortunately, it was not far away. The passengers lined the rails and laughed. We must have looked a comical sight, as well as a rather disreputable lot of mariners. We were sunscorched, bare-footed wearing only pants and shirt, lean, healthy and *drunk*. (What the ladies thought, I do not know, but I will admit to caring less just then).

Once clear of the steamer my one thought was a smoke, and so, smoking and sculling, I passed close to the CASTLEBANK. Captain Boyd wanted me to give him a sack of potatoes. "Nothing doing, old chap," I told him. "You couldn't spare anything but a measly 50 pounds of sugar and that you got out of your cargo."

Getting alongside the MYLOMENE at last, (fortunately it was a dead calm) we had to get the drunken sailors out first, hoisting them aboard. Soon the provisions were out and the boat hoisted. One could not blame the men. Five months at sea and nearly starving. What a glorious feed we had that night with new potatoes, fresh meat, vegetables and good coffee. No more of that vile burnt wheat! Our meal was followed with a glorious smoke. Everybody was happy.

A day or two after this with a fine fair wind, we spoke the QUEEN MARGARET on April 14. This beautiful four-masted barque, although in ballast trim, presented to us sailormen an awe-inspiring sight. The wind was strong from the west and she passed close to us, swinging her six topsails, foresail and reefed mainsail, just as much as she could carry. She had not long left port and was wonderfully clean, laying well over on the port tack, showing most of her boot topping. Her skysail yards were on deck. Sometimes when she lifted to the swell you would see almost to her keel; down she would go to bury her hawse pipes into the foaming sea. She was bound to Philadelphia. She is said to have made the voyage in 45 days from Greenock.

[4] *"Years after, in Vancouver, I met Captain T.F. Morrison who commanded the QUEEN MARGARET from 1902 to 1905, and we used to yarn about the old ship."*

That was the last time I saw this magnificent vessel, but I never forgot the sight of her.[4]

Our luck had turned now with plenty of provisions and tobacco. The winds came fair and the old MYLOMENE plodded along towards the Irish coast. Off the coast we had strong southerly winds and by carrying a heavy press of sail, we managed to hold our own with one or two homeward bound vessels. We finally anchored in Queenstown Harbour, Ireland, on April 24—156 days out. The STAR OF ITALY had arrived over three weeks before us, 131 days out.

Whilst at anchor in the outer harbour I saw my old ship, the MICRONESIA, come sailing in. I easily recognized her when she was yet far out to the south. She was from Australia with wheat and had been dismasted that voyage on the passage out to Australia. She, too, was a lovely sight as she sailed into port at a great lick and made a running moor not far from us. I believe her captain's name was Bridges. However, he was leaving when she got to her discharging port.

We received orders for Limerick and the SARAH JOLIFFE was sent to tow us around. Most of the crew were paid off in Queenstown as we did not require them. Using the ship's bow cable and the tug's steel hawsers with a heavy manila spring line, we proceeded in tow to Limerick. After rounding the Fastnet we had a hard gale from westward with a regular western ocean sea. The MYLOMENE rode it out easily, paying out 60 fathoms of chain cable. It was a wonderful sight to see the little tug away up on a sea and then to lose her altogether as she went churning down the other side.

We were just able to catch the spring tides at Limerick, docking on April 29, 1893. Once again I was in this city after an absence of nine years. The previous time was in April 1884. There was not much change in the town. Just as many jaunting cars as there were before. These were the days before motor cars became the fashion.

One thing about Fernie's ships, they were well found in gear, although nothing to boast of in provisions. I remember Captain King, the ship's husband (now in modern times called the marine superintendent), meeting us at the dock gates with a brand new coil of 5½ inch manila and 90 fathoms of 2¼ inch pliable steel wire—quite a godsend. Captain King had his own ideas about mooring ships in dock; all the forward lines had to lead forward and all the after ones aft, no springs.

Captain Wilkin and all the apprentices went home on leave; I was left to the tender mercies of old King and had to see the cargo out. I slept on board, but as there was no cooking, I used to go ashore for my meals. These I greatly enjoyed.

Every morning about 9:00 a.m. King used to come on board and I had generally not gotten back from breakfast. He said to me one morning, "Young man, you take a long time over your breakfast."

"Well sir," I replied, "I've quite a walk before I get to it, and quite a walk after getting it, and I'm pretty well ready for another." He just smiled.

King always sat in the after-cabin on the transom where he could look along the passage-way and out on deck. There he would smoke strong Burmah cheroots and knock ashes out on the carpet. Day by day the pile grew. There was no steward, only a night watchman. Generally King left for lunch and would come back in the afternoon for a short while. As a rule, by three in the afternoon I would tidy up. Sometimes the girls in the little restaurant I frequented would come down to the ship and we would walk back to supper. Once I happened to meet Captain King. Next day he said to me, "Now I know why you take so long at your meals."

"Do you blame me, sir?"

"No," he answered, "you are only young once and by gorra, they were pretty girls."

After a month of discharging, the cargo was out. The captain returned and also the apprentices. I was now free and said good-bye to the old ship and Captain Wilkin. They were going to Cardiff. I had been on board two years and three months and I wanted to get home. Summer time was coming and everything was gloriously green. I left Limerick and, travelling to Dublin, crossed to Holyhead and so, home.

LINDSTOL

CHAPTER IX

THE MICRONESIA AGAIN

Arriving home one fine day in June my father and sisters were glad to see me. My sisters always had a gayer time when I was home. However, I was not to be with them for long.

One day I had a wire from Jimmie Glazebrook saying he had been appointed to the command of the MICRONESIA. "Would you like to come mate with me?" Sure I would—in my old ship and one that could sail! My old chief officer as captain would be dandy. We had always been great friends and had had many adventures together. I had known his wife before they were married, when she was Miss Geddes. Indeed, I had memories of a fearful and horrible accident that happened to me at her mother's house in Liverpool. I had been invited to dinner, along with Jimmie Glazebrook. We had dolled up and made ourselves very nice. At any rate I thought we had. I was much the younger of the two; Jimmie was a good ten years older than me. It was only a short walk to the Geddes's house, a lovely old home with polished floors and rugs. We were in evening togs and I was growing out of mine.

As we entered the big hall, my foot caught in one of the rugs and down I went on my rudder—just as several pretty girls came into the hall. Jimmie came to my rescue to help me up, also the girls. "Not on your life," I said, "not until someone fetches me a petticoat." I had felt the cold polished floor and knew the seat of my pants had gone west. There were roars of laughter, a petticoat forthcoming, and

I had to go back to Glazebrook's diggings and change into my uniform. That was my first introduction to the charming ladies of the Geddes family. They never forgot it and neither did I.

The MICRONESIA was loading in Barry for Rio de Janeiro. Barry was quite new then and was full of tall ships. I think the dock had opened in 1889. When I joined, the ship was out at the buoys in the middle of the dock with 800 tons of coal aboard. A few days after this we went under the tips [sic] and completed loading.

We towed out to sea on July 1, 1893. We had beautiful weather from the start and, after getting rid of the coal dust, we soon got the old ship looking trim. The paint on the hull had been changed to French gray, no black topsides now. She had a pretty good crew, mostly Britishers, a new second mate and the third mate was one of the apprentices, just out of his time.

The "MICKY" had been dismasted the previous voyage, losing her fore and main topmasts, only her mizzen remained standing. At the time it happened there was an apprentice named Carley on the mizzen-royal yard when all that top hamper at the fore and main came crashing down. He finished furling the royal and descended to the mizzen t'gallant sail and helped furl that. Some lad.

The MICKY made a smart passage to Rio, arriving early on the thirty-seventh day out. She went up to Gamboye, close to the small pox hospital to discharge. The coal was con-

NORMA (ex-ELIZABETH) built in 1884

signed to the Brazilian government. All went well and we were getting on with the discharging which was done with our own crew and a donkey engine from the shore. All of a sudden during the night of September 5, a full-blown revolution on the mainland broke out.

The Brazilian army and navy were at loggerheads. President Piscato, head of the army, wished to stay president for all times. Admiral de Mello, head of the navy said, "No, let me have a shot." This was our observation of the situation at least, and I don't think we were far off. The AQUIDABAN and the TRAJANA, both warships, and several torpedo vessels were now very active. Firing commenced between these two Brazilian vessels and the forts at the entrance to the harbour. Often the bullets were flying over the MICRONESIA so the forward house was abandoned (being of teakwood) and the crew slept under the fo'castle head. I plugged up my porthole with a thick Lloyd's Register. At first when the firing started, I often went aloft to watch. It suddenly occured to me that when the bullets would swish by me, those that I had heard had *passed,* but the one that might hit me I would not hear. After that enlightened discovery—NO MORE watching from aloft.

All work amongst the ships ceased. Our captain went ashore in the ship's gig but returned at once without being able to land. The crew was rather elated at not having to work coal. One Sunday [September 10, 1893] a rebel gunboat came alongside and took charge of us. A score or so of marines with fixed bayonets in the charge of a naval officer made us

unmoor and heave up our anchors. It was very hot and sultry; you can imagine the language of our crew heaving in cable on a fearfully hot Sunday and that, too, at the point of a bayonet. What they called those Dagoes does not bear repeating—no doubt it was a good thing they did not understand. They gathered from our manner, though, that they were not popular.

From the Gamboye side they towed us over to the Nitheroy side of the harbour amongst their own ships, no doubt with the intention of using our coal which was consigned to the government. However, Captain Glazebrook immediately went away in our beautiful five-oared gig with the brass-bound apprentices of the ship and the old red-duster flying at the stern. He was off to the H.M.S. SIRIUS and Captain Lang. The French admiral was the senior officer, but Captain Lang was the controlling spirit.

By this time quite a few warships had arrived, one French, three British, two Italians, two German, two Americans and one Portuguese.[1] As usual, the Germans played a lone hand and kept aloof from the others, anchoring on the other side of the fairway. After a short talk with our captain, Captain Lang took action at once and sent the BASILISK and BEAGLE with guns trained on the rebel warships and orders to extend an apology to us. They were to immediately return our ship to her previous anchorage. How I loved that dear old white ensign!

Those Dagoes had the tables turned on them that Sunday afternoon. They had to heave up our anchor, and I even made them stow the cable in the chain locker. Needless to say we had a lieutenant and a score of blue-jackets from the BEAGLE keeping the peace. Our crew was looking on and making faces at the Dagoes and using derisive terms and then some. We were protected by the British flag.

Back we went to Gamboye escorted by the two British warships and a roar of cheering went up from the other British ships. A very crestfallen lot of Dagoes they were as they went on board their war tug.

[1] ed. note. Brazil had gained independence from Portugal in 1822 but did not become a republic until 1889. It was largely under military rule after that date and revolutionary turmoil was evident for many years. During the early 1890s foreign countries were wary of these internal developments in Brazil and the European and American warships were likely to have been present to protect the interests of foreign investors and shippers.

All the time we lay at anchor, I never allowed any bathing overside and never used the water from the bay to wet the decks. We wet the decks with our fresh water. I think that is why we escaped smallpox and yellow fever.

Since we couldn't get rid of our coal, Captain Glazebrook decided we would try and get ballast. We towed over to the ballast grounds in Nitheroy. This was against orders, we had been ordered to anchor behind the British fleet. Well, it was a case of taking a risk. If we stayed, we were sure to get yellow jack and die, so we might as well take a chance of being shot. At our old anchorage in the Gamboye there were the British four-masted barque KINROOSHIRE and the three-masted barque NORMA and several other vessels. We started loading stone ballast. It came in lighters and there were a few launcheros to help pass it in, the method being to rig stages over the side and pass it up by hand baskets. Several times we were under musket fire, but we were getting on with the ballast and getting used to the fire.

One day Captain Glazebrook had a narrow escape. I had often asked him to be more cautious, but he had always laughed at me. This time he had some ladies in the ship's gig and they were fired at from the shore. The boat's mast was shot away and some bullets went through the side of the boat even though the ensign was flying from the flagstaff at the stern of the boat. Fortunately, nobody was hurt.

Another time, whilst taking in ballast, a rebel gunboat took refuge under the lee of our ship and brought a hail of bullets from the shore. I called all hands on board off the stages and ordered everybody to get behind our iron bulwarks, then ran to pull our ensign up. The firing was too hot for me and before I had pulled the ensign half up, I dived down the companion way below. One launchero was shot through the back of his head, the shot tearing a great hole in his forehead. He died before I could get him ashore.[2]

At last we got all our ballast aboard and towed back to our old anchorage. The weather was infernally hot and muggy. Yellow fever was increasing and most ominous was the continual passing to and from of the death boat—a boat with a lateen sail and black crosses on it. It was used to pick up the dead bodies from the ships and hospitals.

We had to try by every means in our power to get rid of our coal. Finally it was arranged with the Government ashore that they would give us lighters, but we would have to tow them with the ship's boats. To this we agreed and so, after bringing off an empty lighter we would load it up with coal and sticking a boat hook in the pile of coal with the red ensign attached, we would tow the lighter to the shore. It was a dangerous proceeding as more often than not the very people who were to receive the coal would fire on the lighter. The insurgents sometimes took a hand in the game and once, we lost a whole lighter and some 200 tons of coal.

At last we were rid of all the coal. Now came the job of getting fresh water. All the water boats had been seized by the insurgents so we had to get the water from ashore with the ship's lifeboats. Finally, after bending sail

[2] "Whilst in Rio our warships sent boats to gather white sand for cleaning the ship and they took the opportunity to make a picnic of it. The place where the white sand was to be had was in a small cove some seven or eight miles down the bay. The Government's arsenal was located there. It was then in the hands of the rebels. They had just finished having a lunch when there was a terrific explosion, some two or three hundred tons of explosives went up in smoke. An entire boat's crew, including a first lieutenant of the H.M.S. SIRIUS, I think, was blown to pieces.

"The MICRONESIA was at anchor at that time in the Gamboye some ten miles from where the explosion occurred. She rolled and rocked and several tons of ballast fell down in the main hatch. I had men chipping overside on stages and they just climbed aboard and rolled into the scuppers. I was walking along the deck and fell flat. The steward ran out of the cabin scared stiff, a lot of crockery being broken. It was my first thought that we had been shelled. It took some minutes before we regained our equilibrium and realized that we were not hurt. Half an hour afterwards, it rained black, sooty rain."

93

and getting all ready, we received permission to sail and we were allowed a tug. On November 9 we weighed anchor and proceeded in tow only to get fired on by the forts. The shooting became a bit too accurate for our taste, a shell falling between the ship and the tug. Back we went and anchored astern of our warships. This time it was the Government that had to apologise. It would not occur again, they assured us. We could go to sea on the "manana". The following day, November 10, we again proceeded. I remember well it was a beautiful day. On each side of us were warships, the BEAGLE on one side, the BASILISK on the other. We went to sea under escort and passed the forts, not a shot being fired from either side. When we were well outside, our two warships returned to port. We made sail never more gaily or briskly. The tug was let go and soon we were making the white water fly.

Once more we were out at sea with fresh salt air filling our lungs after that long spell of clammy heat. A short time after leaving Rio horrible boils broke out on nearly all of the crew, but after that everybody became well—no smallpox, no yellow fever. I congratulated myself that by ordering no swimming and not wetting the decks with harbour water, we had evaded the two worst scourges.

We sighted Tristan d'a Cunha and were tearing along with a fine, fair wind when a boat's sail was seen approaching the ship. Although loath to lose the fair wind, we hove the ship to in case it was a shipwreck crew. Bye and bye they came alongside, in a fine, double-ended boat but with a very old and dilapidated sail—part of the scheme to cadge canvas. They were natives who had brought off some half-dozen sheep with immense horns, also a few vegetables. The islanders appeared to be almost half-castes and looked very much like Dagoes. There were eight of

them in the boat, including the shipwrecked third mate of the ALLANSHAW.[3] He wanted to get away but they evidently did not wish it. He reported that the second mate of the ALLANSHAW, an elderly man, had married and was quite contented not to be rescued.

We did a little trading, giving them flour, tea and sugar, also light canvas for a boat's sail. I cannot say much for their honesty because, after they had gone, I missed a good pair of serge pants, some shirts and a pair of boots out of my room. As soon as they had left us, we squared away and it was all we could do to carry the main royal. Before they were out of sight, with the aid of our glasses we saw a perfectly good sail go up in the boat. That confirmed our opinion of them. The sheep were about as tough as you could raise them. They went charging around the decks and God help you if you got in the way.

We made a very good run to Melbourne and averaged 222 nautical miles for 27 consecutive days and on one occasion logged 300

SYDNAES (ex-MOZAMBIQUE) at Havre, 1915-16

[3] *"I believe it had just recently been shipwrecked there on March 23, 1893."*

miles in 20 hours. Passing the Otway on the fortieth day out, the MICRONESIA anchored in Hoboons Bay 41 days out on December 21, 1893. Just at this time the four-masted ship TRAFALGAR had arrived with the boy Shotton in command. The captain, officers and a number of the crew had died of Java fever. Young Shotton was quite the hero and created a sensation both in Williamstown and Melbourne, Australia. Both the MICRONESIA and the TRAFALGAR laid at Williamstown.

An amusing incident occurred in Williamstown Police Court. The sailmaker, a rough diamond but a good sailor, had been made an officer by Shotton during the passage. "Sails" was much given to imbibing strong waters. After a usual Saturday night's spree he was locked up and brought before the magistrate on the following Monday morning. He was charged with drunkenness and disorderly conduct. When asked what he had to say for himself, he replied, "I'm the 'ero of TRAFALGAR." The magistrate discharged him, cautioning him that if he came before him again he would be no hero.

Both the MICRONESIA and the TRAFALGAR loaded wheat for the United Kingdom. Captain Bowden arrived from England to take over the TRAFALGAR. He had lately commanded that lovely and fast ship the CHARLOTTE CROOM. The ships got away within a day of each other, the TRAFALGAR being the first to leave. It was at the end of February. Both ships were notable as fast and a number of bets were made by the shipping people. The MICRONESIA left on the first of March and went south of New Zealand with all the wind she wanted. Glazebrook was a great sail carrier, but withal prudent. Bowden was evidently more cautious.

Down by the Diego Ramirez, blowing a whole gale with hard squalls, the MICRONESIA went storming along under a main t'gallant sail and reefed mainsail, logging all of 14 knots and more in the squalls. The wind was west southwest and howling, and the visibility was not too good. It was the forenoon watch when between squalls, I sighted a four-masted ship head-reaching under three lower topsails, the jigger topsail being furled. At first I thought it was an outward bounder and so reported it to the master. Very soon I recognized it to be the TRAFALGAR.

I gave the Old Man another call and he was on deck in a moment. Excitedly I said, "Let me set the fore t'gallant sail and main royal."

"No, no, you'll burst something."

"No, I won't, and if I do I'll pay for it."

The Captain replied, "All right, go ahead."

Jumping forward I roared out, "Loose the fore t'gallant sail and main royal."

Two of the apprentices were racing aloft on the main, a couple of sailors were skinning up the fore. The watch below all tumbled out to give a hand. It was near seven bells, so with all hands, the fore t'gallant sail was sheeted home and mastheaded and then the main royal. Just then a hail squall came sweeping along. The MICKY was going like a driven deer with two hands at her wheel.

As the squall passed the TRAFALGAR showed up, now quite close, under three topsails and nothing else but a weather cloth in the jigger rigging. We could make out the oilskin-clad figures of Captain Bowden and the mate and the helmsman just clutching the spokes of the wheel and a few heads of the watch on deck. She was dipping her nose into the great Cape Horn rollers and lurching and rolling heavily. What a sight we must have been as we went foaming by, swinging our main royal, all of our canvas straining to the very limit in that terrific squall. If ever the MICKY topped seventeen she was doing it then. Both ships had little storm ensigns flaring out in that wild wind from the gaffs. We waved to the figures on the poop and they waved back sorrowfully we thought.

Soon she was out of sight astern as another blinding squall came along. When it had passed, the TRAFALGAR was only a dim speck. It was slow with the main royal up and then the fore t'gallant sail. All hands willingly helped and those sails came in without a seam being started. "Well, I'll be damned," the Old Man said, smiles all over his bronzed and bearded face. The steward was at the cabin door with a welcome cry of "Grog oh" and all those oilskin-clad sailors had grins on their mugs, old and young alike, for had we not given the TRAFALGAR the go-by in grand style? The sailormen had a regard for the sailing qualities of their ships and in their hearts they appreciated it when those ships were handled well. I went below and had a whisky with my skipper. All he said was, "Good man, Beavis, but the MICKY had all she could carry."

We kept the wind with us and for three days in succession topped well over three hundred miles. As a matter of fact we ran 1,236 nautical miles in four days.[4]

Later on when we met the TRAFALGAR and Captain Bowden in the Barry docks, he explained that he had hove-to as he had feared his jigger stays. From what we saw as we passed her, they were being put to a much severer test head-reaching. He said that the following day they sighted the Diego Ramirez Islands and had fine weather and light winds. We beat him from there to Queenstown by 23 days. He thought we were mad the way we had been carrying sail. We thought he was very, very cautious.

The proof of the pudding is in the eating, and by carrying sail we kept the wind with us. The picture of the MICRONESIA must have been most inspiring—the dull grey sky with furious snow squalls blotting out the horizon, the storm-swept ocean mingling with the sky and two ships. One four-poster was head-reaching and diving into it; the other a full-rigger flying for her life before it, driven to the limit. Such a sight will never be seen again.

The MICKY made a very good passage of 89 days to Queenstown. From there she was ordered to Plymouth where she arrived on June 8, 1894.

Captain Glazebrook kindly consented to my going on a few days leave, and I got married.

My father did not approve of my marriage and would have none of me for many a long day. But I knew I had won a treasure, and so it proved through a long and happy married life.

After this I returned with my wife to Plymouth rejoining my ship. We spent many delightful days exploring the neighbourhood. Captain Glazebrook had his wife with him and she and my wife became great friends.

It was summer time and the weather was glorious. Ah! what a lovely spot Devon is, especially when you are young and honeymooning.

Whilst in Plymouth there was a small barque, the ALLEGIANCE in the dock. The skipper was part-owner and was living on board with his wife. Everybody else had been paid off. He had a stage slung over the side and was doing some chipping and painting. He did not like being watched by us. Sometimes, perhaps often out of pure devilment, I would pop my head over the rail and, with a main topsail voice let out a roar— "Get on with that chipping, damn you! Don't let me catch you loafing again and put that pipe out."

Poor man, at last he quit. He couldn't stand it. It wasn't nice of me, I'll admit. Both my wife and Mrs. Glazebrook called me down. But my skipper would only laugh and then he was called down, too, by the women. Oh, we were young in those days.

The time soon passed and we had finished discharging and taken ballast. We were to tow round to Barry. The owner would not allow our wives to go with us so they went by train.

---

[4] ed. note. The United Kingdom nautical mile equals 1,151.51 statute miles.

Wreck of the BACCHUS

*"... She was dipping her nose into the great Cape Horn
rollers and lurching and rolling heavily. What a sight
we must have been as we went foaming by, swinging
our main top royal, all of our canvas straining to the
very limit in that terrific squall. If ever the MICKY
topped seventeen she was doing it then. Both ships had
little storm ensigns flaring out in that wild wind with
the gaffs. We waved to the figures on the poop and they
waved back sorrowfully we thought."*

S. P. HITCHCOCK of New York

CHAPTER X

TRAGEDIES

Barry in the summer time was not bad at all. A nice hotel and some pretty walks made life interesting. The docks were full of fine ships. The beautiful THYATIRA was here belonging to Woodside of Belfast and loading a cargo of coal—what a desecration for a wool clipper. Poor freights had driven colonial and jute clippers to smudge their fairness with cargoes of coal. We were doing the same. We were loading for Rio de Janeiro.

In Barry we renewed our friendship with Captain Bowden and the TRAFALGAR. Young Schotten, "The Boy Captain" as he was called, had left. I was offered the command of the little vessel FIRST LANCASHIRE. She was bound to Santos, then a hotbed of yellow fever. Captain Glazebrook was very much against me taking this command and began talking with my wife about it; well, what with my wife, Mrs. Glazebrook and the captain, too, they persuaded me to turn it down.

We left Barry early in August, 1894, and made a fair passage to Rio, passing our friend the THYATIRA in the northeast trades. She was barque-rigged. One day in the doldrums, whilst the watch was busy cleaning ship, one of the apprentices, a young lad, was cautioned by me not to draw water over the side. I shifted him to another place. At the time we had a fishing line towing from the poop rail, it was for albacore and had a ratchet that would notify you if anything bit. A matter of an hour passed with the breeze freshening when, happening to walk aft to look at the compass, the man at the wheel suddenly said to me, "Somebody's overboard, sir."

"Where?" I exclaimed and looking astern, I saw what looked like a body some hundred yards astern. Throwing a lifebuoy overboard and letting a shout "Man overboard!!", I told the man at the wheel to put his helm down. By this time the captain was on deck but I was the only one in shirt and pants so I took a header overboard from the poop rail and swam to the lifebuoy where I had seen the body. The water was warm and I soon reached the lifebuoy but not a sign of the boy was to be seen. How quickly the ship seemed to go away while I searched the waves. Rising on a swell I could see the main yard aback and a boat being cleared away—what a time they seemed. I was getting tired and not a little scared of sharks.

Soon the ship's boat came along and pulling me in, I took charge and cruised about for over an hour. Still no sign of the youngster. We sorrowfully returned to the ship with the lifebuoy. On mustering the crew, the only one missing was the young apprentice. It appeared he had disregarded my warning and had gone to the rail to draw a bucket of water. He was jerked overboard. Some of the watch had seen him doing this, but no one actually saw him go. But for the man at the wheel we would not have known how he was lost.

This cast a gloom over the ship for several days. I was none the worse for my impromptu swim but I felt badly over the loss of the boy. I found fault with myself for not keeping a more stringent eye on him and I also blamed the sailors who working close around, heard me give my warning and yet allowed him to draw water overside the moment my back was turned. I felt that if I had seen him fall overboard I could have saved him before he got so far astern. He could not swim, poor little lad. Captain Glazebrook in his kindly way would have no moaning. Grasping my hand, he said, "You did all that was possible, risked your own life in shark infested waters. You as chief officer had the whole ship to look after as well as the boy."

This time in Rio there was no delay. My old ship the MYLOMENE was here. Captain Wilkin was married and had named his firstborn after me. I never knew why he gave him my surname. Captain Wilkin and his wife were stalwart friends of mine. One day he said to me, "My wife makes me wear a collar all the time, does yours?"

"You bet," I replied, "when she has the chance, but you see, she's not always with me like yours." Mrs. Wilkin happened by just then and looking at me commented, "Just as disreputable as ever." I had no collar.

Leaving Rio we made a good passage in ballast to Wallaroo, South Australia. On the way across one of the young A.B.s fell from the lower topsail yard to the deck. I was below at the time but his screams woke me when he was brought aft and laid on the grating outside the cabin door. One leg and his wrist were broken, but so far as we knew, this was all. We turned the mess-room into a hospital and set his broken limbs. He seemed to be doing all right, then we became doubtful. He had no pain. It dawned upon us that his back was broken. Plucky he was, living several days. Then the day came when he began to fail rapidly. Going forward I told his shipmates to come at once. They gathered in the mess-room, rough sailormen all but sterling at heart. Dying, he looked at them saying, "What do you buggers want, what are you doing here?" He asked for his pipe and drawing a whiff, so he passed. Passed to his God.

The merciful God of all poor sailormen, who would weigh the pros and cons, and I think the sailorman would have a lenient Judge. The next day was Sunday and we buried our poor broken sailor. It was a strong whole sail breeze when hauling up on the mainsail; letting fly the main royal we backed the main yard. Slowly and mournfully the ship's bell tolled, rung by the ship's youngest apprentice. All hands were gathered aft and the skipper read the burial service. Then the grating was tipped and the body slipped from under the ship's ensign to that boundless deep. The bell ceased to toll, the yards were trimmed down main tack aft sheet, main royal halliards. Once again the ship was flying on her way.

On arrival at Wallaroo we had orders to proceed to Port Broughton, a little further up the gulf, and there load wheat and channel for orders. Port Broughton was not much of a place, just a few houses and a shed or two. The MICKY was the only ship there and lay some six or seven miles from the shore. Everything had to be done by the crew, discharging ballast and taking in wheat. There was no donkey engine to be had so it was a case of hand winches.

The wheat in Australia was always in 200 pound sacks, a back breaking job. It was not like California where they used 100 pound sacks. The weather, too, was abnormally hot, so hot that to save our decks we covered them with gunny bags that we kept wet. Our fresh meat, chiefly mutton recently killed and brought from shore, was fly-blown and rotten before it arrived at the ship. At last to obviate that, we got live sheep and killed them on board.

At the time the MICRONESIA was at Port Broughton, the community was suffering from a plague of field mice. We got hundreds of them off in the grain sacks, mostly dead, but not all. It seems they generally had a plague of something or other; one year it would be snakes, another year frogs, the mice were the least objectionable.

At last the day arrived when we were loaded; we had bent our sails and readied for sea during intervals of waiting for grain lighters. Then we waited for a favorable breeze before getting underway. No tugs were available here and there were several banks with shoal waters. Two more days passed before we were underway, setting all sail to a very light breeze, but after getting down the gulf a few miles the wind petered out and we anchored, leaving our topsails mastheaded. Later in the afternoon the following day, a light breeze sprang up and we managed to get out of the gulf. Here we found the wind strong south easterly and, after a day of beating, the captain decided to square away for the Australian cape of Leeuwin and so went about around the Cape of Good Hope. We were to regret this decision many times in the following weeks of the voyage, although at first we did fairly well to Leeuwin. Then, keeping way to the north to pick up the southeast trades, these proved very light. Never a ship did we sight. It was a case of a lonely ship upon a lonely ocean.

In the vicinity of the Mauritius the glass fell ominously and gave all indications of a hurricane. This, combined with the rising sea and the alarming appearance of the sky, gave us plenty of warning. Sail was reduced to two lower topsails although there was little wind, but the sea was running in all directions and the barometer fell to 28″.50 with the wind constantly shifting and taking the ship aback. All hands were kept on deck continually hauling the yards around for several hours. Fortunately it was daylight. Finally the wind came from the southwest and blew terrifically, and the barometer started to rise.

We had heavy westerly gales off the Cape of Good Hope with a tremendous sea running and the decks full of water. We sighted Cape Agulhas one morning and three weeks later sighted it again. We spoke Brocklebank's MAJESTIC with her two reefs in her t'gallant sails. She was homeward bound from Calcutta and had a hard tussel in which she had little the best of it. At last we got a slant from the southeast which took us into the trades and we went rolling along to St. Helena. Pass-

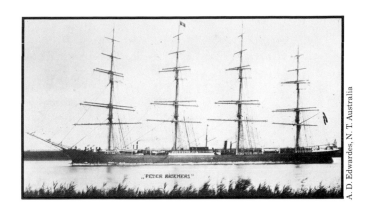

PETER RICKMERS at Antwerp

ing the island at night, we had no chance to freshen our supplies. St. Helena is noted for its watercress besides harbouring the tomb of Napoleon.[1] The following day we were in company with a German wooden barque, the ELISABETH RICKMERS. She certainly gave us the go-bye. Later on in the doldrums we picked her up again but when the trades came away, she just romped from us.

On a fine morning we sighted Ascension Island, its tall mountain peak visable from a great distance.[2] As we passed the anchorage we could see a warship there.

The northeast trades proved very disappointing and drove us far to the westward. Then another spell of calms occurred in the horse latitudes with nothing but gulf weed around. After that, easterly and southeasterly winds all helped to make a long and tedious passage.

At last the MICKY anchored in Queenstown and after two days was ordered to Dublin. From Queenstown we had a fair wind and made a quick run along the coast. Picking up a tug, we unbent all our canvas and jogged up the gear. The MICKY was a picture when she docked.

[1] ed. note. Napoleon died at Saint Helena in exile in 1821. His remains were not entombed in Paris until 1840.
[2] ed. note. Ascension Island was a British depot northwest of St. Helena off of the African Coast.

My wife was there to greet me on arrival; she had come over with Mrs. Glazebrook. We had a most enjoyable time. Captain Lowe in the barque CARLETON lay close to us and he asked me to go mate with him. Nothing doing. I was to have command of the MICRONESIA when we arrived in Liverpool. Captain Glazebrook was leaving to go into steam. I stayed by the ship all the time in Dublin, seeing the cargo out.

CARLETON
Steel barque, built in 1881 in an 11 month period by J. Reid & Co. at Glasgow. Built for J. Kerr & Co. of Greenock, the barque measured 234' x 37'5" x 23'4". She had a gross tonnage of 1358, net measured 1299 tons. Her code flags were WFDK; official number was 81828. Captain Lowe joined her as master in 1883.

"Captain Lowe in the barque CARLETON lay close to us and he asked me to go mate with him."

Opie, Ltd., Falmouth Cornwall

BAY OF PANAMA
Built by Harland & Wolff at Belfast in 1883 for Bullock
Bros.
294′ x 42′ x 24′3″, 2282 tons net, a 7 t'gallant yarder.
A jute-carrier, the BAY OF PANAMA was caught in a
snow storm March 10, 1891, and driven into the cliffs.
The ship was swept by huge waves from bow to stern,
and nine people were lost overboard, including the captain, his wife and four apprentices. The mate forced
the crew members into the rigging where six froze to
death overnight. Seventeen of the original crew of
forty survived until morning. They were carried
ashore in a breeches-buoy, numb with frost bite. This

was one of the most famous and grimmest ship wrecks
in history. [Story told in *Shipwreck,* Photography of
the Gibsons of Scilly by John Fowles (Little, Brown
and Company, 1975)]

E. R. STERLING (ex-LORD WOLSELY)

CHAPTER XI

IN COMMAND

Leaving Dublin in tow, the MICKY arrived in the Mersey early in September, 1895. We towed across to Liverpool with a crowd of runners.[1] Colonel Goffey sent along a gang of Tom Gray's riggers who knew the ship well. I had an easy time. These were my last days as mate. Captain Glazebrook was leaving to go in the Moss Line of steamers. Although I was very sorry to sever our connection, it was a promotion for me. In all the years I had sailed with him, I had always found him to be one of the staunchest and finest shipmates.

Anchoring in the Mersey with a very hot flood tide making, the pilot in rounding-to brought the ship up too short a scope. We lost our anchor and 45 fathoms of cable. We had to let go the other anchor in a hurry.

The MICRONESIA loaded a heavy general cargo for Melbourne in the Waterloo dock. As I assumed command the owners informed me that they were sending me Charles Sharrock as chief mate. He had recently been mate of the ORANASIA with Captain Grieg and had been with the Company a number of years. Although a smart seaman, he had failed to pass for master several times. I pointed out to the owners that I would prefer a man with a master's ticket in case anything happened to me. They overruled my objections and those of Captain Glazebrook.

[1] ed. note. Rope used to increase the mechanical power of a tackle. The rope runs through a hook-block with one or both ends fixed. The hook-block is attached to the object being moved.

With the ship in the berth, loading was a slow job. After the mate joined, I managed to get a week's leave. My wife and I travelled up to London. We stayed with my wife's people but spent a good deal of time with Father, too. It was a great wrench, saying good-bye to him. I was never to see him again and I can picture him now as he turned and leaned against the mantlepiece in his studio. He was broken down. We had made up all our differences and

Captain L. R. W. Beavis

HOLT HILL

were jolly good friends, and he was very fond of my wife now, as well. A sailor's life is made up of partings and as recompense, joyous home comings.

It had been very warm when we left Liverpool for London, but on our return the weather had turned cold. On our arrival in Liverpool, my wife went straight to our lodgings in Birkenhead and I went down on board the ship to see the mate and get my ulster overcoat, then went off to the office to interview my owner. After that I went home by train through the Mersey Tunnel. It was hot and stuffy in the train, and soon a horrible smell developed. Passengers avoided me, moved away. The smell seemed to be coming from inside my collar. It was terrible. Ladies were looking scornfully at me, my brow was wet with perspiration and embarrassment. I plunged my hand inside my coat pocket for a handkerchief—My God! I felt fur and O' the smell. Off came the overcoat; everybody moved back. Coming to my station, I gingerly carried my overcoat to my lodgings. My wife ran to meet me but poof: stepping back, she said, "How awful you smell."

"Don't rub it in," I said. "There is a dead rat in my overcoat pocket," and I threw it on the floor. My dear wife jumped on a chair and yelled; our landlady came to the rescue with a pair of tongs and pulled out a great rat, all decomposed. Trying to get out of the pocket, it had gnawed a hole before dying. I could not wear the coat for days. At first I admit to thinking the mate had stuck the rat in my coat, but my steward told me no one had been in my cabin. I had to let it go at that.

The MICRONESIA completed loading early in November. Wild weather was ravaging the coast at that time and delayed us quite a bit. I said goodbye to my wife on a Saturday morning and packed her off to London on Lord Mayor's Day, 1895 [November 9]. The great four-poster HOLT HILL, belonging to Price of

Liverpool, Captain Jenkins commanding, had completed loading and was ready for sea. The weather was none too good and the barometer was erratic. The owners of both of our ships were anxious to get their vessels away and to this avail used this unconvincing but challenging argument, "Oh, the HOLT HILL is going to sea." That was said to me. I knew I was mad and positively rude to my owner saying, "Oh hell, if the HOLT HILL can stand it, the MICKY can and will, 'blow high' or 'blow low'." And to Jenkins they said, "Well, the MICRONESIA's going." So against our better judgment both of us put to sea.

It was as dusk was falling that we pulled out into the Mersey in tow of the old HOTSPUR, a paddle wheel tug. The HOLT HILL followed a little later in tow of the STORM COCK but soon passed us. The pilot was not at all enthusiastic and wanted me to anchor. But by now my fighting blood was up and I would show them, those shipowners of ours, and at any rate there was Holyhead to put into if utterly distressed.

The pilot left at the Bar, and we continued towing. The crew was all drunk, only the officers and apprentices were available to do anything. As night fell the weather rapidly became worse. A hard gale with driving rain and a falling barometer lessoned the visability and at times we could hardly see the tug. Now the sea began to make and the MICKY was taking water over the bow. Black was the night, black as the hobbs of Hell.[2] Toward the dawn in a furious squall of wind and rain the hawser parted and we were adrift. It was a case of making sail. On the darkness with a drunken crew, before it could be sheeted home, the main topsail blew to ribbons. I decided to wait for daylight. There was no sign of the tug by then.

As daylight slowly broke, the HOTSPUR suddenly emerged from the murk to leeward of us. Chalked on his boilers was, "MAKE SAIL. I'M OFF."

The first thing to do was to get the tow rope in. It belonged to the tug, but he was never going to get it again. Ninety fathoms of steel

2 ed. note. A "hobb" is a mischievious sprite, an imp or elf, such as Puck, or Robin Goodfellow, in Shakespeare's A Midsummer Night's Dream.

wire and some twenty fathoms of heavy manila were left. At last we got it aboard and set the fore and mizzen lower topsails. By now it was blowing a hurricane but the crew at least was sobering up. No use yet to attempt to bend another main lower topsail. The sails were badly bent and the apprentices had to put in a lot of new ropands.[3] I spoke to the mate about the slovenly way the sails were bent and we had some words. He found that he had a young shipmaster with which to deal, not an old man.

There was no chance of getting into Holyhead, Wales. That night we were off the Isle of Man, a British possession. It was a case of wearing ship every few hours.[4] Next day with all hands at it, a new main lower topsail was bent and set.

The weather continued vile and it was many days before we got a slant, then one night the wind favoured us a little, coming off the Irish land. How I drove the MICKY that night. With reefed upper topsails and reefed foresail, we plunged into the heavy southwest sea, diving into it as far as the foremast, washing her decks fore and aft.

The next morning we were off Tuskar. Although it was piping up and drawing ahead, now I had sea room. I passed and spoke the THEODOR, a large, four-masted barque that had been a steamer. She had left Liverpool a week before me and was bound to Vancouver, B.C. This helped some, we were not the only one lagging. Still the weather remained bad, gale after gale. It was not until the night of December 1st, just 22 days after leaving Liverpool, that we sighted the Bishop Rock Light on the Scilly Isles and had it abeam before morning.

All this time the HOLT HILL had been safely in Holyhead, behind the breakwater. Captain Jenkins had been relieved of his command, so much for the judgment of Liverpool shipowners.[5] The MICRONESIA might have been there, too, had I been able to get in. I could not without a tug, however.

A few days later the MICKY overhauled and spoke the PAMONA. She had once belonged to the Allans of Glasgow but was now owned by Andrew Weir. She had left Barry a few days before us and had reported the same fearful weather. I think she was bound for Rio. We were later in port together at Newcastle, N.S.W., and compared notes. The weather remained stormy until passing Madeira, Spain, but from there the MICKY began to move. Once again I sighted the lonely island of Tristan de Cunha [Atlantic Ocean] but it was in a howling gale, and none of the islanders came off to greet us.

Down south in the Roaring Forties with a strong increasing wind late one afternoon, I sighted the RODNEY. She had left London on November 1, eight days before we left Liverpool. She was reducing sail but I held on until I had dropped her below the horizon. That evening we had a hard gale from the southward and I carried sail to the limit. During the night a man was washed overboard from the bowsprit while furling the inner jib. Nothing could be done to save him, as under the press of sail he was miles astern before the alarm was given. Calling all hands aft, they gave me their assurance, "No, nothing could be done, sir."

We anchored in Hobson's Bay, Melbourne on the 96th day out from Liverpool or 74 days from Scilly. I had done well after the long delay. The RODNEY arrived the next day, 105 days out. Captain Corner of the RODNEY and I became friendly.[6]

---

[3] ed. note. These were small lengths of line passed through the eyelet holes at the head of a sail to attach it to the yard or jackstay.

[4] ed. note. Putting the vessel on the other tack by putting the stern into the wind or in other words, running off before the wind and sailing round to the other tack while trimming sail.

[5] *"We did not learn this until I spoke the HOLT HILL in the trades."*

[6] *"I had known him before and we both used the same club, The Athaneum. One night when staying ashore something went wrong with the lights and both Corner and I shared a small candle stuck in a beer bottle to go to bed by. Needless to say we did not sit up late."*

There were a number of fine ships in Melbourne. Captain Loutitt who had once commanded the RODNEY was surveyor for Corner's ship and mine. It was most interesting to yarn with him when at lunch. He shared repast one day on the MICRONESIA and the next day on the RODNEY.

My ship was fixed to load Duckenfield coal at Newcastle, N.S.W., for the west coast of South America and a strike of the miners had been called. The RODNEY was to load for London. Knowing the strike was coming, I cabled my owners and urged them strongly to break the charter. This they refused to do. They later regretted that decision greatly since I had been offered the same rate as the RODNEY to load for London. After finishing the discharge of cargo and taking in ballast, we sailed for Newcastle and made a quick run around the coast.

A few days after arrival the strike commenced and all the collieries ceased working. A large number of deep water sailing ships were in port and I found there were eight to load ahead of the MICRONESIA for the Duckenfield collieries. I managed to get an inside berth at the Dyke. The four-poster DUMFRIESHIRE was just ahead of me and the bald-header KING DAVID tied up outside of me with two other ships. The barque CLONCAIRD lay astern of me.

Soon the port was full, 108 deep water sailing ships were held up. They lay four deep for the whole length at the Dyke and were anchored two and two, bow and stern in the stream. Over at Stockton they were also four deep. No men were allowed to be discharged unless transferred to another ship. Such were the desperate conditions in the 1896 coal strike. Chipping hammers were going from early morn till 6:00 p.m., an infernal and incessant racket. Some ships were able to break their charters and get away but were soon replaced by others arriving.

One night, Captain Caddell of the CLONCAIRD and I had been over in town. We returned late and came aboard my ship to have a whisky and soda. Captain Caddell left

for his own ship but a few minutes later he was on the wharf calling to me. He was yelling that Hill of the SOUTH-ESK was there and in trouble. Going ashore I found Hill remorsing that his lady passenger, a Mrs. Welldon, was dead on board. I went with Caddell, Hill and the water police on board the SOUTH-ESK, then at anchor in the stream. Mrs. Welldon was lying on the cushions on the transom in the after cabin. She was fully dressed with her hat on her head and looked happier than she had looked for some months.

At the inquest it transpired that she had taken an overdose of chloral after a quarrel with Captain Hill. Her husband, a master mariner who was murdered soon afterwards by Butler, was silently condemned by most of us—for leaving her so much alone with Hill. She left behind two young children in England.

Most of the shipmasters in port attended Mrs. Welldon's funeral but few if any of the women did. Women are hard on their own sex if they stray slightly from the path of virtue. Only the week before, this lady had been a guest at a picnic on the Hunter River. She had been cruelly cut and ignored by the other women present, not one of whom could hold a candle to her for looks or breeding. No doubt this had preyed upon her.

One ship that I remember well during the strike was the MACCULLAM MORE. She was commanded by Captain Gaze who had previously had the MORIALTA. The MACCULLAM MORE was a lovely ship, a six t'gallant yarder with a main skysail yard topping her royals. The previous master, a Captain Smith, had been in her for some years and had taken a great interest and pride in his ship. Some of the inlaid work in the cabins was the most beautiful seen, all accomplished by Smith's own hand. She had also a famous gig that rivalled ours in the MICRONESIA.

Time laid heavy on our hands so a strike committee was organized and meetings were held on the various ships—chiefly to protest the intolerable delay.

The strike at last was settled and the miners went back to work. It had caused a great disturbance amongst the shippers after being idle for over six months. Finally the MICRONESIA was loaded and out to the Farewell buoys.

The MICRONESIA was a colonial clipper carrying mail and passengers. Leaving Newcastle I was thought to be a little high toned by the regular West Coast traders partly

Stockton Newcastle N. S. W.
1896 Coal Strike—when 108 deep-water ships were tied up
"A few days after arrival, the strike commenced and all the collieries ceased working. A large number of deep water sailing ships were in port and I found there were eight to load ahead of the MICRONESIA."

because I had a flash gig which was beautifully kept. Taking our big cutter on one occasion, I made an expedition to Chimba Cove [Australia] a few miles away. It was a desolate spot; the only inhabitants were condors, a species of the vulture. There we found a number of graves, mostly open with skeletons. Some of this find we brought back to the boat, intending to give Captain Thomas Motley of the WALLACETOWN a pleasant surprise; he had earlier expressed a desire for a petrified skeleton. But Mrs. Motley who sailed with him would have none of them. I had to take them on board my ship, but what I intended to do with them is hard to say. I feel sure my wife would not have had them, either.

We were ordered to the port of Antofagasta, Chile. I had five passengers, including two ladies, one with a small baby. We towed to sea in September 1896, but the long delay in port had made the MICKY foul and she did not sail as well as she could. However after we got a breeze, some of the growth dropped off. I went south of New Zealand and for a time, I had all the wind I wanted.

During bad weather the baby on board became ill and had convulsions. The mother was a rather helpless sort of person. I did not know much about babies but I remember my mother saying she had saved one of us (I don't know which one) by giving hot baths. I recommended this and the baby was better for a time, but the mother refused to give him more hot baths and the poor little infant died. I had quite a time with the mother before she would allow the sailmaker to sew the little thing up. Gently the sailmaker laid the baby in a soap box and he was sewing canvas around the tiny body when I found horny old Sails wiping his eye. We buried the wee corpse in the morning, a hard gale blowing and shipping heavy

water. I dared not heave to but all hands turned out in oilskins and seaboots as I officiated.

A few days later in finer weather the young father and mother appeared to have gotten over their grief. The lady remarked to me that they would probably have another and it was lots of fun making them. I thought I better go away before I heard any more. In those days I was a bit bashful.

I had had it instilled in me by various west coast skippers to make my landfall well to the southward of my port as the current was likely to carry you past your port if you did not. I made the land some sixty miles south and coasted up. It was night when I made the lights of Antofagasta and stood in, not a little nervously, to be up with the anchorage by daylight. As daylight broke the pilot came off and I sailed right into the tiers, 45 days out.

Antofagasta was a dreary, God-forsaken place. The town consisted of a street or two and a plaza, nothing else but a hospital. The streets, such as they were, consisted of dirt and nitrate refuse and were wetted down with salt water. One's boots soon showed white salt after going ashore. The only recreation was boat sailing and fishing with dynamite cartridges. We got lots of fish but the pelicans got more.

Our original charter to load nitrate had expired before we arrived in Antofagasta, owing to our long delay in Newcastle, N.S.W. We were forced to accept 16/- per ton for nitrates or else go seeking ballast. After discharging most of our coal, keeping some 700 tons as stiffening, the MICKY left for Iquique, Chile, arriving there in November 1896. Here, after discharging most of our remaining coal, we loaded nitrate channelled for orders. Iquique was a bit better than Antofogasta. There was an English Club and a restaurant, plaza, etcetera; also the mole[7] was a little better.

About a mile or so out of the town was a little place called Cavancha. It was a surf bathing and dinner resort. A German ship, the ALIDA,[8] had wrecked here. Several times I had seen her on the rocks at Cavancha; then

[7] ed. note. A "mole" is an anchorage protected by a massive stone structure set up in the water as for a breakwater or pier.
[8] *"Originally known as the ARDMILLAN, one of Allen's fine fleet."*

112

came a day when there was little left of her but a battered, broken hull.

There was a tremendous fire in Iquique that had started near the English Club. That night of the blaze I happened to be ashore with Captain Andrews of the GLENALVON. We were aroused by the fire coming into the hotel we were staying at. A frowsy Chilean maid called me, "Capitan, Capitan, mucho incendio." When at last I realized the place

DUMFRIESHIRE
"That fine four-poster, the DUMFRIESHIRE, commanded by Captain McGibbon, came in before we left. Also the SCOTTISH LOCHS and the GLENALVON, Captain Frank Andrews, made port Iquique."

113

was on fire, it did not take me long to get out of my room! Out on the passage way I met big Frank Andrews, his underclothes tied round his neck for a scarf and his trousers just tucked into his boots. The place was all wood and well alight; it was built with a courtyard and a wide staircase. As we made our way through the smoke we met the British Consul coming up with a hose. The fire brigade consisted of amateurs, "What the hell? What in blazes are you fellows doing here?"

"Putting the fire out the same as you," we replied. One thing we did which should be put on the record—we saved the piano and with the aid of Chileans managed to get it out and down the street to a place of refuge, the circus!

The confusion was embellished when a shop containing guns and ammunition went alight and boxes of cartridges were continually going off—bang! bang! By this time, daylight was coming in. We thought it advisable to get off to our ships and clean ourselves up. Whenever a fire occurs in a Chilean port, they shove the person who owns the place in jail until he proves that he had nothing to do with the outbreak . . . not a bad idea.

That fine four-poster the DUMFRIE-SHIRE, commanded by Captain McGibbon, came in before we left. Also the SCOTTISH LOCHS and the GLENALVON, Captain Frank Andrews, made port in Iquique.

Whilst we were only about half-loaded, the POTOSI came in and my agents, Gildermeister & Co., informed me that if I didn't complete loading by a certain date I would have to wait until the big German was loaded. By engaging shore labour I just managed to do it. By the time the MICKY finished loading and was ready for sea, the POTOSI was ready also.

On March 24, 1897, late in the afternoon, both ships were towed to sea. The wind was then very light and southerly. The German P-ships had great reputations, especially on the West Coast which was a hotbed of Germans.

They were fine ships, well-manned and skippered, yet, there was a lot of it blow, frothy, like their beer. In their favour, they were "no time" on the Coast, thus did not get foul like other ships. Mostly they bought their own cargoes and had every help from their confreres ashore.

I was out to do my best with my lovely ship and wouldn't have had any anxiety about the issue—if only I had been clean. The MICRO-NESIA was now going on eighteen months out of drydock. We would still give them a run for their money. We kept in company for two days until the wind freshened and the big fellow[9] gradually left us. We had bent our heavy weather canvas before leaving and I was glad that I had done so as we had no doldrums.

As the wind came fair and the sea rose I noticed that quantities of growth (due to our foulness of bottom) came floating up and our sailing improved. We were in the Roaring Forties and a strong northwest gale was blowing, when one morning shortly after daybreak we made out a sail abaft our port beam. There to our delight was the big five-master POTOSI! He was swinging his upper t'gallant sails and four full courses. Our little ship was carrying fore and main t'gallant sails and courses.

As soon as I saw him I set the main royal, mizzen t'gallant sail and cro'jack. The wind had gradually hauled while we were making sail and was now west south west. It was blowing some. The MICKY was fairly jumping from sea to sea and it was taking two men at the wheel to hold her straight while the sweat rolled off them. The German did not gain any and presently he set his four royals. Seeing that, we set our fore and mizzen royals. For the rest of that day we kept together, neither altering our bearing to each other. I had an ensign hoisted to show that we recognized him but he would take no notice. He did not like it that our little full-rigger, and British at that, could hold his big ship—the pride of Germany. No doubt he suffered with overwhelming conceit (I did anyway). Before the passage was over we were able to show him some more of our stern.

[9] ed.note. Beavis uses a masculine reference to the German ship.

The weather was clear and sun was shining brilliantly. Although I had often seen ships at sea, both in fine and foul weather, yet such a sight as the POTOSI will never fade from memory.

As night fell and squalls became heavier, we took our royals in and our friend followed suit. We had a good moon and a moon is half the battle in dirty weather. All that night I kept on deck but at 4:00 a.m., when the mate came on deck, I had the main royal set with all hands. Before leaving the deck I had a good look at our big friend. Only his main and mizzen t'gallant sails were set and we had gained a bit. Evidently a bit of the blow and froth had gone: in Iquique he was going to show this blasted Britisher his "starn" and the way to carry sail! Well, he would have to get up earlier in the morning to best us.

I was young in those days and just loved a scrap. It was glorious to be alive and to feel the kick of my bonny ship—how I loved her. She responded to all I asked.

By noon the following day we had run 340 nautical miles in 24 hours. We were now

POTOSI

"Whilst we were only half loaded, the POTOSI came in and my agents, Gildermeister & Co., informed me that if I didn't complete loading by a certain date I would have to wait until the big German was loaded. By engaging shore labour I just managed to do it. By the time the MICKY finished loading and was ready for sea, the POTOSI was ready also.

"On March 24, 1897, late in the afternoon, both ships were towed to sea."

drawing near the Diego Ramirez Islands and at 4:00 p.m. we sighted them, fifteen and a half days from Iquique. It was a record. The squalls were growing heavier and reluctantly I had to take in the royals and mizzen t'gallant sails.

The last we saw of the POTOSI was just before midnight. The moon broke through for a few minutes and what a glorious sight it made. There she was, out on our port quarter, carrying her three t'gallant sails. The sea was rolling up astern, and she would lift her counter and bury herself to the knightheads. Then up, up, up again she would lift, showing her fore foot and the pink of her boot topping. We were keeping a little more to the north than she was, and next morning she was not to be seen.[1]

We had four runs of well over three hundred nautical miles before the wind began to sluff off. Our luck was still with us and we carried our fair wind right into the S.E. trades without any calms. At the equator I fell in with the INVERKIP (not one of Milne's barques). She had been with me in Newcastle. Captain Jones who commanded her spent the day with me and I was going to spend the following day on board his ship. We were both beating to windward, and although the wind was light, we were creeping up on him at night fall.

Coming on deck in the mate's watch, I found the ship was running off several points. I asked the mate what he meant, and he replied *he* wasn't jamming her into the wind. With that I sent him to his room. This had been brewing for a long time.

When the second mate came on deck I found that the mate had deliberately run the ship off so that the INVERKIP would not be near us in the morning. I decided to keep the mate's watch and appointed the senior apprentice third mate to keep it with me. I would not have the mate at table but instead sent his meals to his room. After keeping him there for over a week he came to me with apologies for his behavior. I told him to take charge of his watch again but that he would have to look for another ship when we reached port. I had had enough of this old grouser.

In the tail end of the northeast trades whilst I was at dinner, a little bit of a squall happened along and took the main royal and sky-sail mast out of the MICKY. The royal skysail had not been hauled down.[2] I was very annoyed and said quite a bit to the second mate for his carelessness. We were in 33 degrees north latitude. A day after, strong fair winds and thick misty weather came to us, so it did not matter except that it spoiled our trim appearance. We were more than a little proud of our good looks. All of us wondered where our opponent was and wished we had our skysail mast.

The wind still kept strong southwest and thick. I was beginning to get uneasy and not a little anxious running on dead reckoning. I felt I should reduce sail but was loath to do so. On the morning of the 67th day out, May 30, 1897, the wind shifted to the northwest and cleared. There was the Lizard on the port bow. "And what's that on the starboard beam?—by all the great sea gods, by all that's holy—It's the POTOSI!"

I had a good look at her; then called the steward. We must celebrate! It was "Grog O" at the cabin door; a welcome sound that, and my hard as nails crowd gathered around. To my astonishment, "Three cheers for our Captain" and three more for the gallant MICKY. It was too much for me. I told the steward to give them a second tot. Those horny handed rascals of mine knew how to get around me but they had been a willing crowd.

We kept away for Falmouth, England, and our rival stood up channel, a veritable cloud of sail. So the MICRONESIA had made a dead

---

[1] ed. note. Beavis switched back to the feminine gender in this lovely description of the POTOSI.

[2] *"In Australia during the long strikes, besides having reefs stuck into all three t'gallant sails, I had given the MICKY a main skysail. The old main t'gallant and royal mast was badly sprung. I was able to get a beautiful Oregon spar that was too long but I did not see the use of cutting it—hense, a skysail mast."* ed. note. This passage suggests that sailing vessels were not strictly rigged according to a master plan but in harmony with the resourcefulness of the captain and crew.

heat of it and a record passage. It never occurred to us to think it was to be her last.

After several days at Falmouth we received orders for Ostend, Belgium, leaving May 31st. Whilst in Falmouth my wife had joined me and was delighted with the thought of a trip to the Continent.

Leaving Falmouth with a very light southwest wind the weather became thick and finally a dense fog. This was not good, and I began to wish I had not brought my wife. We drifted up channel for a week; what wind there was was fair. There were also many scares from the ram-you-damn-you steamers. You could scarce hear our foghorn on the poop; it was one of those hurdy gurdy things you turned with a handle. I kept a number of rockets handy and was glad of it when several times steamers nearly crashed into me. It is wonderful what a rocket will do at close quarters, illuminating the fog besides giving off quite a noise.

After a week of this, the welcome sound of the Dungeness [England] foghorn was heard, still thick as mud. With the lead going I crept on[3] and suddenly out of the fog the chequer buoy at Dungeness loomed close aboard. It was a case of letting go the anchor in a hurry, then clewing up the sails. After lying at anchor for awhile, the London pilot cutter showed up through the fog—hailing me—coming alongside.

"Captain," he shouted, "You had a heart to come up in this fog." I began to think to myself: I was tired out, bleary-eyed—a whole week of it. A little later a Dutch tug, the PRESIDENT LUDVIG came alongside, and after a lot of bargaining agreed to tow me to Ostend for £40.

About 8:00 p.m. the fog lifted and we got underway. Everybody was joyful, all talking and yarning of what they were going to do. No one had guessed what was about to happen.

INVERNEIL
Beavis's notation says, *"passed by Micronesia on her last voyage."*

It is the INVERKIP, though, that he mentions in the text,

"... At the equator we fell in with the INVERKIP (not one of Milne's barques). She had been with me in Newcastle. Captain Jones who commanded her spent the day with me and I was going to spend the following day on board his ship. We were both beating to windward, and although the wind was light, we were creeping up on him at nightfall.

"... When the second mate came on deck I found that the mate had deliberately run the ship off so that the INVERKIP would not be near us in the morning."

---

[3] ed. note. Beavis was taking soundings with a lead and line to determine the depth of the water and the nature of the bottom.

CHAPTER XII

SHIP AFIRE

O' don't you hear our old man say
Leave her, bullies, leave her,
Tomorrow you will get your pay,
It's time for us to leave her.

The mate had the 12 p.m. to 4 a.m. watch. About 3:30 a.m. as the bo'sun was walking the quarterdeck he noticed a wisp of smoke coming up the main ventilator by the pumps. He called the mate. They lifted the ventilator and went down on the fresh water tanks but could see no fire. At that, the mate called me and I went down but, barring a little smoke, I could see nothing. I gave orders for all hands to be called and to lift the booby hatch. This was a heavy teakwood affair for the use of emigrants.[1] It was bolted down on top of the after hatch.

This being done and the hatches removed, the mate and I went down in the after 'tween decks—still no sign of fire. We had no choice but to take the 'tween deck hatches off and we both jumped down on top of the nitrate. What a sight, from right forward to the mainmast she was on fire with the blue flames leaping from bag to bag. Immediately I gave orders to batten the after-hatch down and return and bolt down the booby hatch. "Stop the tug and get him alongside!"

The tug, without letting go the tow rope, dropped down alongside, wondering what was the matter. I ordered all hands into the tug just as they stood, and then, after putting my very frightened but very brave wife aboard, jumped aboard myself. It was then and only then, that my collie dog came. He made one leap and landed on the sponson, giving a joyous bark.

It was a case of shearing off and not a moment too soon, for just then the fore and main hatches blew off with a roar. The flames leaped sky-high and set fire to the canvas aloft, whilst some of the wreckage of the hatches fell onto the tug.

The tow-rope was still fast and the tug tried to keep ahead of the ship, but she was shearing about wildly. Taking the mate with me, I went aboard again to try to steer the ship but we were driven out by the heat and the fearful smoke. We were forced to return to the tug.

It was shortly after this that a French fishing smack[2] went alongside and some of their crew went aboard. At once I had the tug sheer back to the ship, and jumping aboard, although she was burning fiercely, I was followed by my crew. I ordered those Frenchmen over the

MICRONESIA on the beach near Pegwell Bay after her fire in 1897.

[1] ed. note. Emigrants on sailing ships were usually housed for the trip in the "steerage," that portion of the ship where the steering mechanism is contained, generally under the helm at the stern of the ship. The hatch covers were often grated to allow air circulation for the passengers below.
[2] ed. note. A sloop-rigged coasting vessel with a well to keep fish alive.

119

side. They did not appear to be going so my own sailors, who were feeling pretty mad having lost everything except what they stood up in, just went for those frog-eating sons of guns. I tried to keep them from being too rough; one moment I saw my bo'sun haul off and down went a French skipper. With that my sailors just picked these would-be pirates up and dropped them, neck and crop into their smack and then cut her adrift. After that the smack kept away as did others.

The foremast was now toppling and the MICKY was one inferno from forward to aft so we dare not stay aboard. All this time we were trying to tow the ship around the South Sand Head into the Downs. The gun of the lightship kept booming over the waters as a distess signal and soon after, two lifeboats came off from the shore and numbers of Deal [England] boatmen. The ship was ablaze fore and aft, and the smoke was like a great black column. A Dutch man-of-war bore down with all his boats swung out, but seeing the crew was safely on the tug, including my wife, signalled and went on his way.

Presently the Ostend mail boat hove in sight on his way to Dover and coming close, stopped to hail us. The father of one of my apprentices was on board, having gone to Ostend to meet his boy. We had been drifting so long up the channel in the fog that he had had to leave. One can imagine his thoughts when he found out that it was the MICRO-NESIA that was burning. His son, the little nipper, was a first voyager and as black as the ace of spades. When he saw his father he began jumping about like mad yelling out, "All right, Dad, I'm all right, we're all right!" So the Ostend boat proceeded.

It was about this time that the hawser parted, burnt through, and the windlass crashed through the forecastle deck. The weather was perfect every moment, a flat calm, a lovely, cloudless day. It was the ideal Bank Holiday, this Whit Monday, June 7th, 1897.

The ship was now adrift from the tug so we boarded the old girl again, but this time right aft. We lashed the steel towrope around the mizzen mast and again lashing the wheel, we tried towing stern first.

As the day wore on excursion steamers came out from Ramsgate with crowds on board. All were anxious to see the burning ship. Jellyfish came up by the hundreds around the sizzling plates, attracted by the heat. The ship's pigeons had been released when the ship caught fire but were flying around trying to find a place to alight that would be out of the smoke.

Toward late afternoon the fire had burnt out somewhat at the fore end and the jib pennants of steel were hanging down from the tip of the bowsprit. The tug AUSTRALIA of London had come on the scene and was able to get under the bow of the ship. The bo'sun, climbing up one of these pennants, was able to get a tow rope fast to the end of the bowsprit. The AUSTRALIA then went ahead and commenced towing. Once again the mate and I with two volunteers went aboard the smoking ship to steer her. The second mate and some hands were towed astern of the MICRO-NESIA in the ship's gig to pick up those on board in case we were driven over the side or if the ship exploded. The Dutch tug made fast astern to help steer the ship. We proceeded past Deal pier which was thronged with thousands of sightseers. The pier owners were doing a great business charging double the price to gaze at the burning ship from the pier—it's an ill wind that blows nobody any good.

Pegwell Bay, east of Deal, was where we decided to beach the ship. I could not anchor because my chain cable had all fused together with the terrific heat. It was around 6 p.m. that the MICKY took the ground. Expecting to see her foremast go crashing over the side at any minute, it still stayed aloft, although hanging over to port at an angle of 45 degrees.

The fire continued to burn as I left the ship in the hands of the coast guard. The crew was landed on the beach at Deal. Everybody was looking the worse for wear, black with smoke and pretty hungry, having had nothing to eat for twenty-four hours. When the crew had had a meal, I sent them to the Sailor's Home at Dover in charge of the second mate. Taking the mate with me I went to the Royal Hotel at Deal where I found my wife already clean and rigged out in borrowed clothes. Everybody at the hotel asked for the honour to lend clothes to the shipwrecked mariners. I was so black that I had to have two baths and then, in borrowed clothes, I went down to dinner. The wife and I were the cynosure of all eyes.

The following day the shipowner, Colonel Goffey, arrived and also Captain Stewart from the London Salvage Association. Going off to the ship we found the fire had burnt out and the ship making no water. The next job was to get the foremast out of her since she could not go into any dock the way it was.

Captain Stewart arranged with Dover riggers to unbend two sails, the mizzen t'gallant sail and royal (the only two that were not burnt) and cut the foremast out of her. All of this for only £200—no cure, no pay. The riggers unbent the two sails and then jibbed at the job of getting the foremast out, finally chucking the work up. Stewart was in a nice fix and came to me.

"Well," I said, "You made the arrangements without consulting me, but if it still holds good, that is, the £200 for getting the foremast out, my mate and I will do it."

"My god, can you do it?"

"Sure," I said.

"All right, it's your job," he said.

It took us just two hours before c-r-a-s-h, the foremast went. It broke into two pieces. It was the easiest £200 I ever made; divided with the mate £100 each and the owner never knew—well, I ask you, why should he?

We had to wait for spring tides to get the MICKY off. I laid both anchors out on the quarter with 200 fathoms of beautiful steel wire, sent out from Bullivant's. Then when the top of the springs [tides] came, with the aid of two tugs, the MICKY once more was afloat. We went to the Tilbury docks to discharge the burnt out cargo which had by now formed another saleable chemical.[3] The mate

was paid off. I only saw him once after, but he had retrieved himself and, in the end had acted like a man.

The ship was going to be a considerable time in dry dock so I decided to take rooms in Gravesend. My dear wife was nothing loath as it was her native town.

Gravesend in those days was a pretty little town, 26 miles from London in the county of Kent. Tilbury, where the MICRONESIA was docked, was on the other side of the river in Essex. The River Thames flowed by—a veritable panorama of shipping. This was especially true when the flood tide made. Barges galore with their tanned sails; tugs puffing along with a string of barges; big steamers, little steamers, lordly liners crowded their way through the shipping lane. Occasionally a graceful and beautiful Sou-spainer with her towering spars would drift by. Cattle steamers and huge tankers all would pass up, stopping for a while for Customs and to change pilots.

Gravesend—with its shrimps and smelly little high street and the old "Three Daws Inn" at the very foot of it, was right against the town pier. In my mind it was a delightful spot for a sailor to let go anchor. Inshore up the hill there was a background of beautiful country, lovely lanes and a high road meandering towards Chatham.

So it came to pass that I settled here to live. My wife and I got to know one another. She rode a bicycle and I didn't, so to keep company with her, it was a case of chartering a dogcart (expensive at that). Often with a wave of her hand, she would go flying away from me, whip up the horse ever so much as I did. I determined a bicycle would have to be my mount. Had I not often ridden a more precarious mount when fisting a frozen, lurching, swaying t'gallant sail reeling one hundred-and-fifty feet in the air away down in the Roaring Forties? It took me just three days to learn the

---

[3] ed. note. Sodium nitrate (salt peter) was used in the manufacture of gunpowder.

bicycle after a number of falls and collisions with lamp posts and gates. Now I was able to escort my fair lady. Soon, like all women, she had a use for me; her nimble brain evolved a scheme in which I was to have the privilege of towing her by a line up the hills. No doubt her waterside education was coming to the fore. Not for naught had she seen those fussy little tugs puffing along with a barge or two in tow.

It was all right, except for the remarks passed by shrimpton ladies with big hats. "Oh look, ain't she got him on a bit of string, oh, la, la." Damn it all, and my dear wife would laugh.

All this time the MICRONESIA was slowly discharging her burnt-out cargo. I was employed by my owners and also the underwriters. As a matter of fact, the ship had been abandoned to the underwriters while on the beach at Pegwell Bay. There was also a salvage case brewing, brought by the Dutch tug.

I visited the ship every morning, just a nice little jaunt across the river in the ferryboats. We would spend the afternoons cycling through the pleasant lanes of Kent. The weather was gorgeous there in the summertime. Cobham, Chatham, Maidstone, sometimes Tunbridge Wells, Sevenoaks and Knowle Park were our destinations. We would stop at little country inns to have a meal of cold roast beef and salads, topped off with foaming Kentish ale served in deep tankards. My wife, dear girl, with a grunt of disapproval, would take tea or if the weather was very hot, iced lemonade.

Most weekends we would cycle to London and visit my wife's people. Going through Dartford, that long and dangerous hill, we would coast.

One eventful day, the MICKY had finished discharging and was dry-docking. What a sorry sight—my once proud ship was now a brig, desolate, grimy, filthy. The survey was held. Her keel and keelson were in seven pieces, yet she made no water. Such a tribute to the work put into her by her builders.

She was taken out of dock to an adjoining jetty to await her fate. I had a premonition what it would be, a constructive total loss. She was sold for £900 to ship breakers.

Sadly I watched her being towed across the river to Northfleet, and there on the mud flats, piece by piece, she disintegrated. My work was finished.

The Admiralty Court had awarded the tug a nice piece of salvage. The underwriters of the cargo sent me a nice cheque for not letting water get onto the nitrate. It was for my "resourcefulness", they said, though it was only common sense for I knew water wouldn't put out the nitrate fire.[4]

Now I had to think, indeed I had been thinking for some time what was best to do. My owners had no ship for me. Sail was then in deplorable condition. Ships were fast being sold foreign. My MICKY, if she had been repaired (the lowest bid was £16,800) would only have fetched around £5,000. The owners were lucky, she had been insured for £18,000.

Talking things over with my girl, I found she did not wish me to go again on these long voyages. In fact, we had grown very fond of one another; we had never had the time before. Much as I hated steam kettles, I decided there was nothing else to do.

---

[4] "Nitrate was worth about £7 per ton at the time. The burnt out nitrate fetched £4.10 per ton. There was some loss in weight no doubt, yet, if I had played water on it there would have been no nitrate, no ship, nothing left."

The mate is in the foreground. Captain Beavis, the owners and the underwriters are standing in a group near the cabin, aft.

MICRONESIA, burnt out on Whit Monday, 1897

123

CHAPTER XIII

MUCH AS I HATED STEAM KETTLES...

There came a day shortly before Christmas 1897 when I was offered the berth as third officer in a tramp steamer, the URSULA BRIGHT.[1] Packing a grip, I joined her in Havre. To my astonishment I found that the master was Frank Whitson. The last time I had seen him he was captain of that grand old four-masted ship the WENDUR.

There was trouble from the start. The crew was on six month articles and these were due to expire in a few days. They wanted to be paid off so they refused duty. Whitson was a bull-headed man and went to sea with the crew, sailors and firemen loafing in the fo'castle. They were put on bread and water but what did they care? My introduction to steam was not appealing.

We had bad weather all the way across; the crew did nothing. The engineers and officers helped fire the boilers. We put into Halifax for bunker coal. My God, I thought, give me back my old sailing ship—any old time. Arriving at Baltimore, all hands trooped up to the Consulate. There was a Court of Inquiry, and all those who had refused duty were heavily fined practically all their wages, and these were to be divided between the officers and engineers for working the vessel across. But it was not to be.

Havelock Wilson, the head of the Seaman's Union was in Baltimore and he took it up. The crew laid a charge of drunkeness against the captain, and I am sorry to say they had ample proof. Rather than face the charge, the captain paid all hands off in full. And we got nothing.

This was the first time I met the notable Havelock Wilson. He was then a comparatively young man, with a pleasing smile and a fine personality. He certainly got the best of Whitson.

We loaded a full cargo of grain and some general and left for Glasgow.

After a stormy passage we arrived at Glasgow and docked at the Queens Dock. Here more trouble developed with our crew, this time on deck. The mate, a very young man by the name of Leslie, was not very tactful. Neither was the second mate, an Irishman by the name of Jack Burns but a most delightful companion. I was only third mate, of no account, until a row started.

The men were not allowed ashore during working hours, but seemingly they had been ashore and had gotten some liquor. Seeing the mate and second mate in trouble, I barged into it. I was, in a gentle way, propelling a man along the deck, when all of a sudden, the wharf was alive with Glasgow longshoremen! What they were going to do to us was really terrifying, so much so that the chief engineer got the steam hose out and aimed it at them. At that a squad of Glasgow police appeared, great, big, hefty men, and they needed to be, to be able to handle a waterside crowd. They

[1] *"She was a ship of Bright's, a son of John Bright, the Quaker."*

ASTRAL

laid in, using their truncheons freely, so, with the steam hose emitting boiling steam the dock-side was soon cleared. Our own men slunk off to the fo'castle to sleep off the evil effect of Scottish liquor. Captain Whitson came up to me with compliments on the adequate way I had handled some of our crew. Whitson with all of his faults was a sterling seaman of the old breed. The first and second officers were young and had not been brought up in that hard school of sail. I was not so old myself but hard as nails and could ill brook a back answer.

My wife did not join me because we were only to be a short time in port. It was here that I first met the engineer superintendent, Mr. Sage. He had charge of both deck and engine room. Besides looking after Bright's ships he had a consulting business of his own in London. He and I became firm friends.

One night, and one only, I spent ashore in Glasgow with the two mates. After going to a music hall and wandering around the streets for a little while, both mates went off with girls. They tried hard (as also did an impudent little red-haired lassie) to make me wander from the path of virtue, but I wouldn't. I was in love with my wife. Good women have always kept me straight since my boyhood days. Not that I claim any virtue in that, but it always felt loathsome to me to think of being in company with such women and then to associate with sweet, pure and wholesome lassies, full of fun but with no evil thoughts. And now I was a grown man and happily married—the others were not.

Later in the evening the mates and I met again in a restaurant in Sauchiehall Street. They had had several drinks, and Burns, the Irish second mate, nearly got into a scrap with a hefty Scot. Always was the Scot eyeing me. Later, when peace reigned and I had a decent chance to ask him why, he replied, "Weel, I was sure I could lick the other two, but I nae sae sure about you."

We sailed for Philadelphia in ballast but stopped at Greenook, Scotland, to land the skipper's wife, a lady with tousled, blond hair,

evidently dyed. She was said to be of the theatrical profession. Whitson was very drunk; so was she. Mr. Sage, the overlooker, was in a terrible rage. He had come down the River Clyde with us. The last I saw of them the lady was embracing a ventilator in the tug and Mr. Sage was trying to look as if he did not know her or any of us. Whitson had to be put to bed.

What a life! Did I like steam? I was getting a great introduction. After the Old Man had recovered sufficiently, we headed north to Ireland. He decided to go north across the Banks for Cape Ray, [Newfoundland] a rather unwise decision with the time of the year, early spring.

A week or so later, I had the eight to twelve watch with thick, murky weather and fairly smooth water. Shortly before midnight, I saw a line of white right ahead. It looked like breakers. Ringing the engines "full astern", I whistled down the tube to the skipper. He came on deck just as she was stopped and close up to a field of ... ICE. What I thought had been broken water was ice.

Whitson, in a dressing gown and half drunk, rammed her full ahead and made some disparaging remarks about my abilities, etcetera.

"All right, sir," I said. "She's your ship, not mine."

Just then the second officer relieved me and I turned in with the sound of the ice scraping by. Turning out a little before eight in the morning, I found that we were stopped. Heavy ice was all around as far as the eye could see. The bows were holed and the forepeak was full of water.

We were jammed here for two whole days. Some of us who were more venturesome than others would go out for a short distance on the ice.

A gale of wind later sprang up and the ice began to break up and move. How ever the steamer stood it, I don't know. We proceeded at slow and half speed, even stopping at times. Heavy cakes of ice would crash and grind against her sides. Soon the No. 1 hold was leaking and the pumps had to be kept going.

After some hours we were able to get clear and proceeded at full speed with a crumpled bow and leaking badly. This taught me a lesson that I would never forget. When I was later in command in the North Atlantic trade, I never voluntarily entered an ice field. We had been lucky to survive the ordeal.

When we arrived at Philadelphia we found the dry dock occupied, so we went to Pt. Breeze and stuck her bow on the mud. There we built a coffer dam about her. Temporary repairs were affected and we loaded a general cargo for Rotterdam. Anchoring in the Delaware, we took aboard a deckload of cottonseed oil in barrels.

The URSULA BRIGHT was what we called a "three-island steamer," namely fo'castle head, bridge deck, and poop. So it was that we had both wells full of cargo.

Leaving port we encountered bad weather which later became worse. Soon the deck cargo broke adrift. We had to heave-to. Before the deck cargo went overboard a great deal of damage was done. Winches burst, hatch combings started and some of the bulwarks carried away. It was a miracle no one was injured.

Cottonseed oil is like butter and these greasy barrels would go careening back and forth, whilst we the crew watched in a frenzied state of mind. We would try to help these barrels over the side; the last few gave us the most trouble. Some of these had burst and the decks were slippery as hell. It was dangerous, yet comical to work. What a job we had to get rid of the grease on our persons; we stripped naked and poured hot water over one another. Our clothes had to be dumped.

Several of us had invested in phonographs in Philadelphia. They were very crude, some of the first on the market, but we used them to cheer our spirits with music.

Arriving in Rotterdam, Mr. Sage was again there, and a new master, Captain Coulthurst. Whitson and the mate, Leslie, were both discharged. I was promoted to mate and the poor second mate was rather disgruntled over it but soon his Irish nature came to the fore

and we were good friends. Whitson was in a deplorable way so we made a "tarpaulin-muster"[2] of officers and engineers to bid him goodbye on his way to London.

After discharging at Rotterdam we proceeded to Shields to drydock and effect permanent repairs. The repairs made in Philadelphia had not been good and our forepeak had filled a few days out. My wife joined me in Shields and we had several happy weeks together. Like the minx she was, she completely captivated old Mr. Sage, the overlooker. Whenever I wanted to find him, there he would be in my room, yarning away with my girl. He liked us both but I know who he liked the best, and so did she—the little wretch.

We were chartered to load a full cargo of coal for Funchal, Madeira, capital of the Islands. From there we were to proceed to Pensacola, Florida, to go on a time charter for twelve months in the timber trade.

Leaving Shields we had a fine run to Funchal and anchored close in. I had friends there in long standing; one of them was my father's oldest friend, Mr. Gordon of the firm of Cossart, Gordon & Co., wine merchants. Gordon had married a Portuguese lady, the Countess Torrobella, and after much pressure from his wife, Gordon surrendered and became the Count de Torrobella. Not so his eldest daughter Ella; she would have none of it. The Scottish Gordon was good ono' for her, and she always remained Ella Gordon.[3]

So it was that I sent a note ashore to the Count, and the dear old boy came off. We were enveloped in coal dust, a dirty British tramp. But it was all the same to him. I was the son of his old friend and he had known me as a little boy. He invited me to dinner that night with no excuses but I told him I had no fit clothes. That didn't matter a damn, come I

[2] ed. note. A collection of money.
[3] *"Her sister married a Portuguese and her brother Murray, who was about my age, was in the diplomatic service in Vienna."*

must. Then he went ashore. Such prestige we had because of it. All the launcheros and stevedores could not believe their eyes as the white haired old count with his hand on my shoulder was escorted to the gangway. It soon got abroad in the port and our agents were thunderstruck when they heard it. My skipper was also greatly pleased and immediately gave me shore leave.

But now the great difficulty was to dress me for the occasion. I had a rather dilapidated uniform that certainly was no good for a dinner. We combined what second mate Jack Burns had and what I possessed, and I soon found myself rigged out in whites. What a job to keep clean from the coal dust! Everybody took a curious interest in me. I was not to disgrace the flag—not if they could help it.

The Count's townhouse was a lovely old place in a side street, with great high walls and a heavy door, and inside a wonderful courtyard. He met me dressed in ordinary clothes, out of deference to me. The Countess was all the other way, but not so Ella Gordon. She was just the same dear woman she had always been, a few years my senior but oh, how sweet.

In the hallway and the drawing room there were a number of my father's paintings. How homelike that made it for me. Presently the guests arrived, all Portuguese in full evening dress. It was then that I realized how the Count had acted, why he had not dressed and why Ella had not. After a gorgeous dinner Ella played and sang Scottish ballads. Unbeknownst to me I was to spend the night. The old Count had arranged this with our agents; I was to be his guest in port.

The following day after breakfast the Countess, Ella and I went up the mountain in the little train. It took several hours and as we climbed we had a glorious view of the harbor and town, and the endless sea stretching away in the distance.

The Gordon's country home was away beyond the end of the railroad with vineyards all around. What a delightful place for our lunch. In the afternoon we returned on a sort of basket sleigh. I was rather alarmed but felt it would be terrible to show my blue funk with ladies around. They assured me there had never been an accident. The basket was a wide affair and I was wedged in with a lady on each side. The helmsman (for so I will call him), a native, stood in the runner with a pointed stick. Away we went—seemingly to destruction. The steep road was of cobblestone. Now a stone wall dead in front. With a swing we darted away, escaping death—at least I thought so—by mere feet. I could feel Ella giggling. She said I turned pale through my bronze. No doubt I did; I felt very pale all over. We came down in twenty minutes while it had taken us over three hours to go up.

The ladies took me home. They claimed I needed reviving; I think they were right. The old Count laughed.

Back down at the mole I went aboard and I never saw my dear good friends again. A delicious hamper of fruit and a case of Madeira wine were sent on board to me as a reminder of their high spirits and congeniality, dear friends of long ago.

Finishing discharging we left for Pensacola and made the long run in fine tropical conditions- "flying fish" weather. Passing through the Hole-In-The-Wall by the Great Abaco Islands [Bahamas] and then bucking the Gulf Stream, we skirted close along the reefs to try and catch the counter current. At last we arrived in Pensacola.

WENDUR

WENDUR.

Passing quarantine, the doctor was irate and would not board us until we put the accommodation ladder over. Not for him the flimsy pilot ladder.

We shifted to an anchorage off town. Here the charterers and stevedores took charge. They were in a devil of a hurry. After having some words and nearly coming to blows with them, things were arranged amicably. On a time charter they naturally wanted to get all they could out of her. We were quite agreeable to them, but at a price—filthy lucre. I made more money the twelve months we were on charter than I ever made as master in sail.

Both lifeboats were put in the water and hand winches brought off from the shore. Not a bit of steam would they use, these knights of Columbus. Half the labour was white, the other half black. One gang worked against the other, all singing ribald songs. As soon as a flag fell from a staff ashore they stopped working, put a chunk of rope in the cogs of the winch and left the log hanging. Tumbling into the lifeboats, off ashore they would go. Boats were left ashore to bring them off in the morning.

We were soon surrounded by rafts of timber. The time charter made a great deal of difference. There was a lot of stealing from the rafts, but not so with us since the timber all belonged to the charterers. I did not have to bother with the chains and dogs belonging to the rafts; that was up to the charterers, too.

On one occasion here, there were several other steamers loading. A big raft of logs broke adrift from a steamer not far away and came slowly drifting down. The mate of the steamer had sent his boat with a heavy hauling line but was unable to reach it. As it came closer, I sent my boat with a very light line, reached it and, taking the line to a steam winch, hove it alongside. I sent the second mate ashore, hell-for-leather for the poundmaster. The poundmaster paid a dollar a log for all logs collected.

Within minutes the captain of the tramp steamer came along and asked me for the logs; I told him he could have them if he paid me the same as the poundmaster. There were 475 logs.

"No, I won't!" he shouted at me. "I'll see you damned first."

"All right," said I, "the poundmaster is here and it'll cost you a dollar and a half once he gets them. You weren't very smart, my man. If you had put a man on the raft when you couldn't reach your logs to heave them back, I couldn't have touched them."

The captain went away swearing vengeance on me, hoping I would lose all my rafts. That didn't worry me a bit; we were on time charter.

The poundmaster handed me a cheque for $475 which I divided up with my officers and crew on a percentage basis. The captain of the tramp steamer talked with my skipper but got no satisfaction. Didn't he wish he had a smart mate, my skipper asked.

These were days of outsmarting the authorities, too. We used to carry huge deckloads and to evade the Merchant Shipping Act, when in winter months you were not allowed to enter a British port with a deckload, we used to go to the Continent. We would discharge our deckload there and then return to England. Sometimes, though, we paid the price for our misconduct. Several times during the winter months we lost a goodly portion of our deckload.

The time charter for twelve months allowed us to visit many ports both on the Continent and England during that period. My wife used to join me wherever we happened to be and travel around with the steamer until we finally sailed for Pensacola, Florida, or Mobile, Alabama.

On one voyage we were in the James Watt Dock, Greenock, Scotland, where the old CITY OF ROME always lay afloat. We lay just astern of her, discharging our timber when we signed a lot of her firemen. We called them packet rats. They were about the roughest, toughest specimens you ever came across. We had trouble with them the entire voyage but the climax came in Yarmouth, Nova Scotia. It was there that we landed them all in jail.

On the way over I had fallen on the deckload and broken the knuckles of my right hand. My hand had been set by the doctor and was healing all right until one afternoon when I missed the second mate, my Irish friend. I found Burns under the bridge deck having a scrap with a big, hulking fireman. My friend was getting considerably the worst of it. Knocking him down, the fireman was kicking him unmercifully when I happened along. That fireman never saw me and never knew who belted him. I hauled off and hit him under the chin; down he went but I had busted my knuckles again. He was unconscious for quite a while and I was terribly afraid I had killed him. There we were, the second mate and I, feeling his heart. Presently he groaned so we left him to his own misfortunes.

That night the fireman and his mates were in jail. I dared not appear in police court as a witness on account of my damaged hand. They all got six months' richly deserved hard labour.[4]

We made five round voyages to the Gulf ports. On one of these, just as we approached the Great Abaco and the Hole-In-the-Wall, I had the four-to-eight watch. It was just as I was having my morning coffee that a fearful racket occurred in the engine room and I thought the whole of the engines was going to pieces. A long silence followed until steam started to blow off. We had lost our propeller, the shaft had broken just inside the boss. Here we were, rolling silently in smooth water and fine weather. We set the trysails but she would not steer. I made a sea anchor with a

trysail and booms in an attempt to stop the drift. What a hopeless, mournful thing is a steamer when disabled.

We drifted around for three days, getting closer and closer to the Great Abaco reef. Not a vessel had we seen. We had no wireless. The evening came when we could see the great, white breakers, so we lowered the two lifeboats to the rail, provisioned them and gathered a few belongings but not many. As night fell we commenced firing rockets every half hour in the vain hope of attracting attention.

Suddenly there came an answering rocket from seaward, and to our great joy within minutes the many lights of a steamer appeared. She was a passenger vessel. We continued to fire rockets. It must have looked like a Chinese New Year. The rescue steamer stopped and I was sent off in the lifeboat to make arrangements with the captain to tow us to Nassau, Bahamas, about 100 miles away. The vessel was the SANTIAGO of the Ward Line of steamers from New York to the West Indies.

A towrope connected the passenger steamer and soon plucked us along at a faster clip than we could steam. It was none too soon, we were only about three or four miles off the reef with 90 fathoms of water right up alongside of it.

Just at daybreak the hawser parted and getting a towrope aboard the SANTIAGO, the work had to be repeated. It was all quite a thrill for the passengers taking their pre-breakfast walk to the stern to have a look at us. We were dropped late in the afternoon of that day in the outer anchorage of Nassau and the passenger steamer proceeded on her way.

No tugs were available at the port but a little coasting steamer recognized our plight. Getting up her steam she plucked us into the inner harbour. We anchored in such clear water that you could see the bottom, the cable and the anchor, also the sharks. We had a spare propeller and tail shaft on board so it was a job for the engineers and myself to tackle. To tip the ship we filled the forepeak and Number One hold with water. There was

[4] "We were told that that night in jail the police had to take their boots off as they were kicking the doors. They played cold water on them, not to quench their thirst but to stop their filthy noise. These were Greenock CITY OF ROME firemen and I never wanted to be shipmates with them again."

very little equipment to be had from shore. However, we did it—and in a week's time we were on our way to Pensacola again.[5]

At the conclusion of the time charter we found ourselves in Swansea, Wales. The ship had been sold to Freddy Woods and a new overlooker. Freddy Woods was a notorious character. Not nice. All of us decided to leave. A new captain came down from London. The overlooker wanted me to rewrite the ship's logbook and put in a lot of lies. Now it was my chance. "To Hell with you and old Freddie, do your own dirty work robbing the underwriters!" Needless to say I was leaving, we all left together. The captain, the other officers and I all travelled in the same train.

That afternoon we saw the old URSULA BRIGHT tied up in the basin. There was no crew, no one would sign on her. Seeing us all leave it got wind ashore that there was something wrong with her. The new captain came to me and asked that I make just one more trip in her, just to help things along. "Not on your life," was my answer. I was finished. They managed to get the vessel out of the dock and anchored in Swansea Roads. That was the last I saw of the URSULA BRIGHT.

My wife met me in London and I went home to our cottage in Gravesend. We had blossomed out to a modest home of our own with a maid of all work. My eye! weren't we becoming toffs! We celebrated with a dinner I was very fond of, beefsteak and kidney pudding and foaming Kentish ale. The pudding was steaming hot. Alas and alack there was a yell—and the pudding was on the floor. Our Yorkshire terrier, Roguey by name, had gone for the girl's feet. The dog got the pudding, hot as it was, and we dined on bread and cheese.

I got a berth as chief officer in the WAZZAN, one of Forwood's steamers trading to Gibraltar and the coast of Morocco, Canary Islands and Madeira. The WAZZAN was a pretty little thing carrying about 60 passengers and commonly called a banana boat. Forwood had a fleet of five steamers. The WAZZAN was only 664 tons net but we had a good turn of speed, about 14 knots. I made two

voyages in her; the pay was poor, only £8 per month and the accommodation vile.

Leaving London, the first port of call was Gibraltar, then sometimes Algiers. After that we headed down the coast of Morocco as far as Mogador [Essaouia, Morocco], then to Tenerife [Canary Islands] and finishing up with Funchal, Madeira. It was a rush all the time. Moorish passengers were carried between ports on deck.[6]

On one passage between ports we had some large cumbersome boxes with airholes in them. Each of these contained ladies of the harem. I think one had three. We used to try and peep through the holes.

I learned a lot about bananas and about London fresh eggs. The eggs were picked up at Morocco ports. They were packed in oblong cases about 8 feet long and 4 feet wide but only 2 feet deep. Many of them would crash against the ship's side in loading while rolling in a swell. Egg juice seeped down the ship's side. Officers were allowed a ration of bananas, eggs, new potatoes and tomatoes; also at Madeira the chief officer had a couple of demijohns of wine. On the way home we exchanged our bananas for those in the cargo and had a quartermaster candle our eggs.[7] Oh! we were adroit connoisseurs in the art of exchanging. The second officer had the worst of it. On the coast we generally shifted ports in his watch and we were ready to start discharging again when it was his watch below. He would have to look after his hold.

---

[5] "Months later when I had left the Company and was in another vessel, I received a cheque for two months pay. The underwriters awarded us all—all except the master. He had been ashore all of the time we repaired the ship, enjoying himself at the English Club. Some kind friend had notified the owners. Actually, he would only have been in my way; he was better ashore where he wasn't doing any harm. A sailor's luck."

[6] "They were an unholy lot, all trying to avoid paying for their passage. I would go along with the purser and when some villain of a Moor would say he could not pay—had no money, I administered a few cuts with a teaser (a nice little rope with a Matthew Walker knot on the end). Requisite fare was always forthcoming."

[7] ed. note. To test eggs by holding to the light.

From Madeira we would thrash through it at a gait of thirteen knots, one mass of spray, often-times keeping ahead of the Union Castle intermediate steamers—much to our pride. On arrival at the London docks, close to the Tower Bridge, the skipper would leave. As soon as he was gone the chief officer (myself) would disappear. By the time we arrived at our berth only the bo'sun would be left in charge. It was rather disgraceful. We were only two days in port and away again. This was the chief cause of our negligent behaviour and then of course this only occurred when we arrived after office hours.

Two voyages were quite enough for me. Neroutsos was chief officer of the TELDE, practically a sister ship of the WAZZAN. He did not seem to mind the duty but I did. I had an application in with the Norfolk and North American Steamship Co. Simpson, Spence & Young (Philadelphia Trans-Atlantic Line) which was building a fleet of cattle steamers. I went to see Captain Young, the junior partner, and was appointed chief officer of the CROWN POINT, building at Sunderland, but the CROWN POINT was not nearly ready so I would have to wait.

After a week or two at home with my wife at Gravesend I was appointed to fill a gap as second officer of the PINNERS POINT, 2518 net tons, 3908 gross tons. Going out in ballast to Philadelphia we had the usual Atlantic weather. The PINNERS POINT was a crank, ticklish vessel to handle in port. She nearly turned over at the grain elevator at Port Richmond, Philadelphia. She gave us the scare of our lives that night. The engineers were pumping the water ballast out and the ship had a lot of cargo in the tween decks with the lower holds half empty. Over she went, fortunately onto the dock. The longshoremen came climbing up and beat it for the shore, never stopping before they arrived at the nearest saloon. It took a lot of rye whisky to make them feel better. We had to run the ballast tanks up again, they should never have been started until the lower holds were full. A survey was held and the ship righted soon

after loading the lower holds. She was, however, very crank.

The S. S. HIGHLAND FLING was similar to the type of steamships operating during Beavis's career aboard them. This vessel is ashore at Cadgwith. Even though Beavis had many problems and incidents with which to contend, he always felt he was *"wonderfully free of accidents."*

Waters Company, San Francisco

CORMORANT

As early as the 1830s, steam vessels began to appear in the Pacific. Some were originally built like sailing ships with steam engines added. Others were converted sailing vessels. The broader beamed steam freighter and passenger liner became commonplace by the early 1900s. A few steamships were eventually re-rigged or converted to sail from steam, and the engines removed entirely or simply used for auxiliary power.

S. S. MONTAUK POINT

CHAPTER XIV

ATLANTIC TRADE

Arriving in London I was transfered to the CROWN POINT then completing in Sunderland. Captain Wall was the commander and was at that time Commodore of the fleet. I made five voyages as chief officer in the CROWN POINT between London and Philadelphia carrying cattle and general cargo, very little at that time was carried westbound.[1]

On arriving in Gravesend one eventful Saturday, a telegram was handed me. I had been appointed master of the MONTAUK POINT sailing that night for Philadelphia. I was instructed to report at once to the office. Captain Wall did not like letting me leave and was not particularly nice about it. But it was a promotion and I was now to be in command of an Atlantic liner.

It was a very quick turn round for me. I never saw my home that voyage and only a wee bit of my dear wife. I relieved Captain Robertson and as the MONTAUK POINT came out of the West India Docks I saw my old ship, the CROWN POINT going in. The MONTAUK POINT and the WEST POINT were sister ships, slightly smaller than the CROWN POINT.

We had very stormy weather across and before long we found we were practically running on our tank tops. Whenever the carpenter would sound the forward tanks the water would squirt up several feet from the sounding pipes. On arriving at Philadelphia I reported this to the management and after cabling London, the ship was placed in Cramps Dry Dock. Here we found the bottom

S. S. EAST POINT in 1903 in heavy seas

badly set up and many hundreds of rivets out. A number of plates had to be removed and faired[2] before replacing.

After the repairs had been made and we loaded cattle, we sailed for London. On arrival I was relieved of my command. I was said to have driven the ship unmercifully, this after making a long passage. I felt badly about it. The ship had been leaking the previous two voyages but Captain Robertson had never reported it.

I had good friends in the management in Philadelphia. After visiting at home for three enjoyable weeks, I was sent down to Sunderland to take command of the latest and

[1] ed. note. The dates here are indefinite but approximately early 1900s.
[2] ed. note. When the plates were "faired" the curves were corrected.

most up to date of the line's steamers, the EAST POINT. She was fitting out. It was only a temporary appointment because the Commodore, Captain Wall, was to take her if he arrived in time. He did not and I had the crack ship for close to ten years.

Leaving Sunderland February 15, 1901, we ran our trials in misty weather averaging 13 knots and then after the usual banquet, proceeded direct for Philadelphia. We headed north through the Pentland Firth, Scotland.

I was glad to see my friends in Philadelphia again.[3] I was the youngest skipper in the Line and commanded their finest ship. All of the steamers were built especially to carry cattle and a limited number of passengers. During the first few years the Line did very well but the depression soon undermined them and they had a hard time of it. The cattle trade was sadly curtailed owing to foot and mouth disease. It would soon be at an end.

We used to load our 450 to 500 head of cattle at the piers at Port Richmond, sailing as soon as they were on board. The cattlemen consisted of a cattle foreman and a few experienced hands. Still others served in any capacity at all and were called stiffs. In the summer months these stiffs might be very decent men, often college students working their way across for a trip to Europe. They had a free passage back again.

Cattlemen underwent the procedure of signing the ship's articles on board ship. The British Vice Consul would be at one end of the table with the cattle doctor at his side. At the other end was seated the Head of the Immigration Office.

Often times the cattlemen were drunk. On one occasion there was a drunken British ex-soldier, a regular he-man, having passed the Consul and the doctor, he was before the Immigration Officer who was making out his return pass. "Have you any tattoo marks?"

The fellow replied, "Yes" and showed some. He was asked if he had any more. Suddenly he pulled down his breeches and shoved his bare stern in the Immigration Officer's face. "How's that?" he grunted. Tattooed in broad letters he read, "A Merry Xmas to You."

Puff-puff-puff. "Take him away!" yelled the Immigration Officer. We at the other end of the table could not conceal our laughter. But that was not all. We had barely completed our inspection and signing of crew but could not resist a prank. Chief Immigration Officer Hughes returned to his office and his phone rang. "Is that you Hughes? Yes? Oh, a Merry Christmas to you." This went on for the rest of the day.

The next few years were spent thrashing my way across the North Atlantic, winter and summer. Some winters the Delaware River would be badly frozen, filled with ice. Other winters there was hardly a teacup of ice. It was not a bad life, healthy anyway. My principle hobby was photography and I had a nice dark room fitted up off my bathroom.[4]

On an east bound passage with 500 head of cattle we broke our rudder post. We were hundreds of miles out due south of Halifax. It was night, blowing a hard gale from the northwest and a dirty sea running. It was tough getting the rudder secured. The job was done by wrapping mooring chains around the stern and heaving them tight with the steam winches, thus binding the rudder hard over. The rudder trunk had to be cut through before we could locate the break. Aceteylene torches were in vogue but fortunately it was a long break and we were able to bind the broken rudder together with 13 derrick bands. This held and we proceeded at reduced speed. Only once did we stop to tighten wedges.

[3] *"The president of the Philadelphia Trans-Atlantic Line was Fred Taylor and his brother James was vice-president. They came of a good old Quaker family that had resided in Philadelphia many years. Both these gentlemen were good friends throughout the time I sailed between London and Philadelphia."*

[4] ed. note. Documents indicate that Captain Beavis had gathered the second largest collection of sailing ship photos in the world by 1931. He was the photographer of many of the views within the collection, but he also purchased and traded a great many, too. The collection remains intact under private control.

Since I had refused assistance and had a valuable cargo and cattle on board, I was not a little anxious. We were only a few days late and I arrived at Gravesend with all my cattle intact but with a very few bales of feed for them. The underwriters rewarded me with £500 and a pro rata division for the rest of the crew. It was really the engineers who did most of the work.[5]

I was reminded of the seaworthiness of my steamer EAST POINT on one of my eastbound passages aboard her. I came across a derelict, a wooden barquentine called the WHITE WINGS. She was lumber laden, her deck cargo was awash, a lamp was burning in the galley and one in the fore rigging. She had not been long abandoned. I sent the chief officer on board to examine her and on his return, sent him back with a barrel of oil. He had instructions to set her on fire but she would not burn. I had cattle on my ship so I reluctantly left her.

In all the years barging across the North Atlantic my old EAST POINT was wonderfully free of accidents. Fortunately, so was I in steam.

Captain Beavis aboard the EAST POINT with Chief Officer A. Mealin and Second Officer H. Young. Photo taken in 1902.

[5] "Our reward was owed to the generous spirits of Captain Young of Simpson, Spence & Young who was in charge of the London office. On arrival in London the master was required to report to the office; Young was in the directors' room. He was seated on the opposite side of a long, imposing table. He always shook hands and asked if everything was all right. If so, he would gruffly say, 'Go home, I'll send for you if I want you.'.

"Simpson was the Senior Partner and an entirely different scoundrel. He reminded me of a prosperous grocer but was reputed to be an inveterate smuggler. That is to say he always wanted the captains of the steamers to smuggle for him, much to the annoyance of Captain Young.

"I got to windward of him once. He had sent down quite a large parcel from Messrs Peter Robinson's, a very well known shop in Regent Street, London. It was addressed to Mrs. Simpson, care of me. We were sailing that night for Philadelphia. When I arrived at my ship there was a frantic wire awaiting me from Mr. Simpson. It directed me to open the parcel and separate the lady's underwear which was not for his good wife (but for somebody else??). I was on the point of sailing so I kept him on tender hooks all the passage over. A cable was awaiting me in Philadelphia, reply pre-paid, to which I laconically answered, 'DON'T WORRY I HAVE SEGREGATED THE LADY'S PANTS.' I don't think he ever forgave me.

"His son was then a youth, later to become the husband of the lady who aspired to become Queen of England—Wallis Simpson."

By The Lords of the Committee of Privy
Council for Trade.

Certificate of Competency

MASTER

OF A FOREIGN-GOING SHIP.

To *Lancelot Russel Walrond Beavis*

Whereas it has been reported to us that you have been found duly qualified to fulfil the duties of Master of a Foreign-going Ship in the Merchant Service, we do hereby, in pursuance of the Merchant Shipping Act, 1894, grant you this Certificate of Competency.

By Order of the Board of Trade,

this 25 day of June 1897.

Ingram B Walker { One of the Assist Secretaries to the Board of Trade.

Countersigned,

Registrar General.

Registered at the Office of the Registrar General of Shipping and Seamen.

(175c)

Master's Certificate for Captain L. R. W. Beavis, June
25, 1897

CHAPTER XV

TURNING TO THE EARTH

Around 1908 freights were low and the cattle trade had gone flat. The Company was in difficulties and Furness, the marine pawnbrokers, absorbed them. I left as did all my savings which I had in the Line. These amounted to over £2,000 in 1£ shares. After a long time I recovered 4½d or 9 cents for every pound share.

After being ashore some time, I decided to venture to Canada with a determination to start life afresh. I had been considerably influenced by being asked to deliver a new lake steamer to Messrs. Norcross in Montreal. This trip was followed by several trips up and down the Great Lakes.

In Toronto I decided to try farming and go West, dropping off at a little place called Dysart, Saskatchewan. When that train disappeared into the distance I felt pretty lonely as I watched the tail lights fade away. My wife and little girl[1] were in England and I had to make good for their sakes.

I hired out to a farmer named Bullivant (his named appealed to me being that of the great steel rope makers). This did not work out well. He made me move a barnyard of manure and then wanted it moved again. "Not on your life, you don't rub it in," and I went after him with a pitchfork. To make matters worse he gave me a phoney cheque—this after I had walked eight miles only to have it dishonored. I approached the magistrate who persuaded me to wait until the harvest came in when the farmer would be certain to pay me. At that time I came in with the rest of the creditors and of course lost out.[2]

From the farm I went stacking [wheat] and then to a harvesting outfit. *Never* did I go inside a caboose to sleep. I always slept in the open, nestling in the strawrick at night, bathing in the horse trough, back to nature's life. I was renewing my youth and I did not get lousy.[3] If you slept in a caboose you ran the hazard of this predicament but it was a carefree healthy life. I was over forty but becoming hard again. Most of the farmers that we thrashed for put up glorious meals. The farmers' daughters waited on us and saw to it that our innerman was well provided for.

Sometimes in the evenings there would be dancing. A harvesting outfit was a motley crowd, all sorts and conditions of men, some very decent, others—well, not so nice. Sometimes on a Saturday night the more riotous ones would take a wagon and team and drive to the nearest town. They would fill themselves to the brim with moonshine and driving back make the night hideous with their ribaldry.

Being a man of the sea my fellow workers found my yarns intriguing. I would spin them on those long summer nights with all the harvesting crew agape, also the farmer's wife and daughters.

At times we would work late, well on to dark, especially if there was a forecast for

---

[1] ed. note. Beavis's only child, a daughter, was born Peggy Elizabeth Beavis on November 15, 1902, in England.
[2] *"That damned farmer still owes me two months pay!"*
[3] *"The common report was that you could not go on a harvesting outfit without becoming verminous."*

frost. Then the day would come when it was wet and no work would be done. If you stood well in with the farmer's wife there were always a few chores to be done for her. These were paid for with a great hunk of pie and a pretty smile from the daughter.

Shifting from one farm to another was a voyage of discovery. Many was the stack of good wheat that would be thrown into the engine furnace as we meandered along, wondering what the next farm would be like, chiefly in the way of grub.

At last came a day in the late fall when a flurry or two of snow foretold winter. That made me pull out. Boarding a train for Edmonton, Alberta, I bade farewell to the Prairies.

Edmonton in 1909 was not a very large town. They were just installing water and sewage systems. At that time you bought your water by the barrel; I think ten barrels for a dollar. I rented a two room shack and prepared to put in the winter. I had to look for a job. There were none of any account so I tackled labouring and went digging ditches for the city to lay their water pipes. I had to buy my own shovel and pick. That purchase was much against the grain; the job was not at all to my liking and I gave myself the name of "Jack Burns".[4]

The first week was not too bad because we spent it filling the trenches that had already been dug. These were twelve feet deep and the width of a pick. But the next week was different, a case of hard digging now, and to make matters worse they set pace makers. I had a big lumbering Swede as mine who was soon three or four feet down. I was only scratching the frozen earth top. After a while I was having a rest and along came the foreman who began to blackguard "Jack Burns" for a lazy lout, all the time looking at me. Suddenly it dawned on me that it was me he was calling names. My blood boiled and hurling my

Wife and daughter bound for Canada

shovel at him with an awful flow of villainous curse words (every one I could remember from my early sea career), I demanded my time. I had completely forgotten my name. The foreman grinned, he was not a bad sort. "So, you had forgotten your name," he said. He gave me my time and told me to try the round house of the railway. "It will be easier for you."

The following day I was out at the Grand Trunk Pacific Railway yards to see the yard foreman. I landed a job at night watering the trains and cleaning windows. The overland came in every evening and went out the next morning. It was a twelve hour job and brought the princely sum of $3.10 per night.

I soon got a little promotion and was sort of a foreman over six or seven Poles. We started at seven at night but I was generally through by midnight. I would crawl into a mail sack in a heated car and have four hours to doze. One of my hoboes would call me at four when I would go through the train checking everything.

One vile night—snowing and sleeting—a special came in. We had just finished our own train. I had to water, charcoal and clean the windows of the second train, too.

This was bad enough but half a dozen black stewards and cooks inside the train doors kept ordering me to do this and that. The lid flew off and I cursed the blacks and the whole railroad system. I was interrupted by a voice say-

[4] ed.note. This was the name of his Irish second mate on the URSULA BRIGHT.

ing, "Man, man, don't curse so much!" It was Mr. Hayes, president of the Grand Trunk. This was his private car.

My men and I were wet and frozen. He called one of his stewards and told him to fetch some whisky and give each of us a hot toddy. That finished all the cursing but it proved worth it.

Hayes talked with me and got a little of my history. He gave me a letter for the Superintendent of the Round House providing for free passes for my wife and little girl and one for myself to meet them in Winnepeg. I never saw Mr. Hayes again but I often thought of him and I deeply regretted his untimely death in the TITANIC.

A few weeks later I met my wife and daughter and brought them along to Edmonton. It was a severe winter. Our water in an iron barrel alongside the stove froze often. I was fortunate to get on day work at the Round House. Being handy with a palm and needle, I had the job inside repairing canvas covers and tarpaulins.

My wife did not like these arrangements; there was no future in it. When the New Year came in, we packed up and made for the West Coast.[5]

[5] ed. note. Beavis's wife writes of their first dwelling in Edmonton in her diary:

"The first home in Canada was at 152 Henry St., a very dirty looking part of Edmonton and called a two room shack. When I first saw it I thought it was a shed for our baggage so you can have a little idea of how I felt when Lance said, 'Go in.' I was waiting outside to go on. I grabbed hold of Peggy [their daughter]—a job I had got used to, so did it in my dreams—and went in. The boards were thick with black mud and the stove seemed to fill the room and was red hot. The one bed was in an alcove round the corner, one old table and wooden boxes to sit on, just nothing for our use at all. I was to get furniture on the hire system the next day but believe me, what with being up all night to keep the fire going and crying all day, it was a week before I could see out of my eyes."

CHAPTER XVI

HYDROGRAPHIC SURVEY

Arriving in Vancouver, B.C. in the latter part of February, 1910, after leaving Edmonton with snow up to our knees, how lovely it felt to come into a city with mountains all around and the sea at its feet. A few sailing ships were left in the harbour at the Hastings Mill. How glorious the rain felt after we had been frozen up for months. I had not been in Vancouver since the time I left the TITANIA in 1889. It had become quite a city.

Taking temporary lodgings at Cadero Street I looked for a job on the waterfront. There was nothing offering so I crossed to Victoria by the night boat and called on the Canadian Pacific Railway Coast Lines office.

The Marine Superintendent eyed me curiously. I had already recognized him. "What can I do for you?" he asked. I told him I was out of a job and wanted one in the worst way.

"Where have I seen you before?" quizzed the Captain.

"In London years ago, sir, when you were mate on the TELDE and I was mate on the WAZZAN, two of Forwood's steamers in the Morocco trade."

"By gad, you are Beavis. Sit down."

He told me he could put me in the coast trade but it would only be temporary employment. There was a third mate's job in the RESTORER cable ship. That, too, would be only for a short time but there was an opening in the Chief Officer's berth in the Hydrographic Survey Naval Service of Canada. It was not much money but it would be permanent. He gave me a letter to the Chief Hydrographer, Captain P. Musgrave, and I was accepted.[1]

I hastened back to Vancouver and we moved to Victoria. How happy we were even though my salary was only $75 per month; it went further then. At first we took rooms in a house on Fort Street but after one season we moved to a house of our own in Esquimalt. We rented it from the Hudson's Bay Co. It was a very old cottage that had been the factor's house. It stood in grounds of about fifteen acres that sloped abruptly to the water. I could keep a boat in front of our home. The water supply was from a deep well and we pumped it into a tank in the house. It was a very pretty little place and I rented it for seven dollars a month. The garden alone was worth it. We could grow all our own vegetables and keep chickens. The view was not to be equalled. There was a nice dining room and a very cool cozy living room both with open fireplaces, a kitchen and three bedrooms. Just with a little outlay for repairs I had the dearest home possible. It was lit with lamps that were restful to the eyes even if they were a little trouble to trim. My ship was fast to a buoy only a short

[1] *"It was a political job and I had to join the Conservative Association and swear allegiance to Dicky McBryde. I liked McBryde. Sometimes he would visit us on board the LILLOOET and I took special care that he did not slip. Dicky certainly liked his drop."*

distance away and I could keep an eye on her all through the winter.

The Hydrographic season extended from about April 15 to November 1 when we generally made fast to a buoy for the winter. November and December were employed laying the ship up and doing odd repairs. The crew was then paid off and the quartermasters were retained as watchmen. The first of March heralded us fitting out again. I liked the work and it was a wonderful experience for me to learn about the coast and the inside passages.

We usually had six surveyors besides the Chief Hydrographer for the Pacific Coast and a crew of around forty. The LILLOOET was a twin screw vessel of about twelve knots speed and built specifically for survey work. She carried three launches, two whale boats, a cutter, a barge, and a number of dinghies. The sound machine for deep soundings was aft and we could get reliable soundings down to any depth.

I remember we were at Ocean Falls in the LILLOOET when we heard the news of the loss of the TITANIC.[2] Ocean Falls was only just beginning. Whilst I was in the LILLOOET we surveyed Masset Inlet. The month of August was generally allotted to deep sea sounding in Dixon's Entrance.

Once a month we would be in Prince Rupert for supplies. Our coal was arranged to be left on the Government Wharf at Prince Rupert, sufficient fuel for the entire season. The LILLOOET was not a handy vessel to coal. The bunkers were on each side of the stoke hold and boilers. Our procedure was to load

as much as possible on one side then take the ship out into the stream, turn round and come in with the other side to the dock. This gave the ship a great list and to counteract it as much as possible all the launches and boats were swung out on the off shore side, then swung in when we came around.

We were coaling one time in Prince Rupert with a strong wind blowing and all our boats swung out on the starboard side. Along came the PRINCESS MAY of the Canadian Pacific Coast Service to berth just ahead of us.[3] Captain McCleod of the PRINCESS MAY misjudged his distance just a little too shy and sheered off two launches, one whale boat, and all of our davits. It was blowing half a gale dead-on the dock. McCleod admitted he was to blame when the reports were sent to Ottawa. With great perspicuity Captain James Troup, general manager of the C.P.R. inland fleet, dug out the Canadian Shipping Act and revealed a rule that stated all vessels alongside a dock were supposed to have their boats swung in. The Canadian Government shouldered all the expense and the C.P.R. was cleared of all responsibility. Later we found out that "men of war" and vessels of the Naval Service were exempt from this ruling and all vessels when passing a Naval vessel should pass clear of the boat beams. Yet the Government paid for all of the damages and the delay to the Survey in this incident while wise old Captain Troup chuckled to think how he had put it over.

The hydrographic surveyors were mostly young men though there were some older such as a Parisian, a French Canadian, and Lt. R.N. Knight. Knight was one of the smartest and the most efficient surveyors we had. He was also a gentleman. He had been in the Navy from his youth and the Hydrographic Branch of the service. I admired the way he took his sextant angles without ever stopping his launch. None of the others were able to do this. There was nothing snobbish about Knight and I admired him for this, too.

Saturdays were always spent cleaning ship, holystoning decks, cement washing the

---

[2] ed. note. The S.S. TITANIC collided with an iceberg and sank in 1912; 1,513 lives were lost.

[3] ed.note. The PRINCESS MAY (Ex-NINGCHOW, of Cass, Arthur & Cass; Ex-HATING of the China Coast Service) was built by Hawthorn, Leslie & Co. in 1888. She was a 1,394 ton steel liner measuring 249 x 33.2 x 17.7; she was a twin-screw with a 15-knot speed and spacious stateroom accommodations for 164 passengers. She was renamed PRINCESS MAY by the C.P.R. Coast Service in 1902. After experiencing a spectacular stranding at Sentinel Island in 1910, she was converted to an oil-burner, repaired and placed on the Skagway, Alaska run.

PRINCESS MAY

scuppers and laying coconut matting. This was followed by the Chief Hydrographer's inspection, everything Naval style.

The starboard gangway was kept for officers' visitors and occasionally we had a few notable people aboard. The port gangway was for the crew. We had several one man dories that were handy for towing astern of the launches. Our crew consisted mostly of Newfoundlanders who were able to put a surveyor alongside a rock with his instruments and not ship a drop of water. Deep sea sailors were useless, not to be compared to these Newfoundland fishermen for boat work.

An amusing incident occurred once while we lay at anchor at Naden Harbour. The steward had come to me for a boat to take him ashore with a small parcel of laundry. I told the quartermaster to take him ashore in one of the dories. Overhearing a commotion a little later and looking aft, I saw the parcel of laundry floating away. Going to the gangway I found the steward dripping wet, half-drowned and the quartermaster was red with wrath. "It's the bloody MAURETANIA you want to go ashore in!" screamed the quartermaster at the steward. The steward had stepped on the gunwale of the dory and of course, capsized it. He and the quartermaster went over with it. The steward was not popular and was terribly ragged about the incident.

For a time we were moored at the dock of the whaling station at Naden Harbour. The Chief Hydrographer wanted to see the Chief Engineer about something but he was not to be found. It was fairly late at night and the quartermaster on watch could not locate him. I stepped ashore in the search. A whaling station is not a pleasant place. It is to say odoriferous. I found the Chief Engineer at long last fraternizing with the engineer of the whaling plant. They were both gloriously drunk holding on to one another and drinking whisky out of a filthy tin pannikin. They were trying to recite Robbie Burns' poetry from an equally dirty book. The stench of decomposed whales was all around. Hiccupping, they offered me a drink out of that pannikin. It was really more than my stomach could stand, what with the awful stench and the greater filth. I fled, beating a precipitate retreat to the ship without the engineer.

During the month of August we would go deep sea sounding in Dixon's Entrance, making Egeria Bay at the north end of the Queen Charlotte Islands our anchorage. The weather had to be sufficiently clear for us to see the mountain tops. This was necessary to getting a "fix" with sextant angles.

Days would pass when no sounding could be done from the ship. Altogether it was a pleasant and instructive life. As the season waned, particularly if October came in stormy, little work could be done. The end of October saw us back in Prince Rupert coaling for the run home. We took but little time on our way south. We were not supposed to run at night but we did so at our own risk. Had anything happened all of us would have been fired. By the first of November you found the LILLOOET at her buoy in Esquimalt Harbour.

During the summer of 1914 survey work was being carried out on the west coast of the Queen Charlotte Islands. Coming into Skiddegate from there at the beginning, we had no wireless on the LILLOOET, and we had been without news for some weeks. To our astonishment we found that the world was at war [World War I]. That night we left for Prince

Rupert. The survey was ended. All our younger surveyors left for Esquimalt. We were ordered to scout.

After filling our bunkers we went out to the north end of Stephens Island, making Qlawdzeet our anchorage. From there we would slip into Prince Rupert for weekends. During one of these periodical trips, August 18, 1914, a very thick fog had shut in. We were at anchor and most of the crew was ashore on leave when a wireless report came in from the PRINCE ALBERT—"A Grand Trunk steamer is ashore on the Butterworth Rocks. Requires immediate assistance."

The PRINCE JOHN was in port and proceeded to her assistance. We had orders to go as well, so after a lot of trouble, we rounded up our crew and got underway. The weather was dense, so thick that we anchored off the north end of Stephens Island in twenty fathoms of water. We were not sure exactly of our position. As daylight came, the fog was as dense as ever. After consultation with Captain Musgrave the Hydrographer, I arranged to take two launches with a whaler in tow of each, plenty of blankets and hot coffee in thermoses. I would try to get out to the Butterworth Rocks. Soon after leaving the ship the fog lifted and we could make out the Channel and our position.

The LILLOOET was anchored just off Qlawdzeet. She had crept into a safe anchorage in that dense fog.

As the fog lifted we suddenly saw the PRINCE ALBERT badly ashore on her beam ends and amongst the rocks of the Tree Knob group. She was many miles away from Butterworth Rocks. At once altering the course of the two launches, we sped to the rescue.

Captain Musgrave wanted to be first but I had the better launch and soon left him behind. With a cry of "Women and children first!" we bore down on the wreck.

The PRINCE ALBERT was hemmed in by rocks and with a tremendous list to starboard. Her boats were in the water, sheltered a little by the ship. They were full of passengers, cold and wet, smothered in black crude oil.

I took the lifeboat with women in it in tow. Chief Engineer Bell of the PRINCE RUPERT, an old friend of mine, said to me, "I was never so pleased in all my life when I saw your old mug loom out of the fog, Beavis." He knew then that they were all right and would be given good care. I think he was mostly glad that he did not have to pull that lifeboat.[4]

With the life boat in tow I made for the open sea. In the distance we could see the PRINCE JOHN. Captain Wearmouth (later a Vancouver pilot) was in command. Getting clear of the rocks I shifted the passengers into the whaler and gave them hot coffee. There was one fatality, a little baby. The mother had handed him to the father who had laid him in the bottom of the boat. The boat filled with water and the poor infant drowned.[5]

We made two trips from the wreck to the PRINCE JOHN. After all the passengers and crew were safely on board, the PRINCE JOHN proceeded to Prince Rupert. Those of us in the LILLOOET launches returned to the wreck with Captain Mackenzie of the PRINCE ALBERT.[6]

It was quite a job to board her. Everything—boats, falls and all were slippery with oil. One of my boats' crew managed to board at last and found a ladder to lower to us. I can see in my mind's eye the hydrographer Mus-

[4] "Bell was later chief engineer of the crack steamer PRINCE RUPERT. Afterward he left to become shore engineer of a cold storage plant at Prince Rupert. When this fizzled out he went to rum running. Living close to me in West Vancouver, we would often yarn of the old days. Poor Bell died a couple of years ago [mid-1930s]. Hard times had fallen upon him and he passed away broken-hearted. He was a very clever engineer, one of the best and always cheery."

[5] "The child's father was an Austrian and [due to the War] he did not have a pleasant time with the rest of the boat's occupants."

[6] ed. note. The PRINCE ALBERT [Ex-BRUNO] was an 841-ton steel vessel built at Hull in 1892 for the Hull-Antwerp passenger service. She was purchased by the Grand Trunk Railway of Canada at Hull from the Wilson Line for coastal service in British Columbia and was in service early in 1910 as the first of the "Prince" steamers, being renamed the PRINCE ALBERT. Following railway service, the PRINCE ALBERT was notorious as a rum runner during Prohibition, and her last service was as a steam tug, the J.R. MORGAN. She was broken up at Vancouver, B.C., in 1949.

146

"Prince Rupert" On The Rocks. Yes Sir. Snow Storm. Nr Prince Rupert. B.C. 23 Mar: 1917. No 576.

F. Button, Prince Rupert

grave perched up on the bridge of the wreck trying to take sextant angles to give an exact location of the wreck. The tide was out but would soon be flooding and everything would be destroyed.

Captain Mackenzie told us to help ourselves to the stores of the shipwreck and we did. Soon our launches were filled with tobacco, beer and whisky. Captain Musgrave returned with his launch to the LILLOOET but I remained for a while and then proceeded to Prince Rupert in my launch.

Once clear of the wreck and the rocks, we noticed a three-funnelled war vessel outside in Hecate Straits. She was apparently stopped, looking at her through the glasses. She conformed to the silhouettes we had of the LEIPSIG and NURNBERG. Certainly it was hazy but there was no doubt in my mind or that of the crew. At that discovery I returned to the LILLOOET and informed Captain Mus-

PRINCE RUPERT on the rocks
This steamer went aground March 23, 1917. Beavis was involved in a similar rescue.

"After filling our bunkers we went out to the north end of Stephens Island, making Qlawdzeet our anchorage. From there we would slip into Prince Rupert for weekends. During one of these periodical trips, August 18, 1914, a very thick fog had shut in. We were at anchor and most of the crew was ashore on leave when the wireless report came in from the PRINCE ALBERT—'A Grand Trunk steamer is ashore on the Butterworth Rocks. Requires immediate assistance.'."

grave. He at once ordered me to report in Prince Rupert.

We took out hell-for-leather in our fastest launch to notify the authorities. There was a great excitement in the town; all money was sent up country. The LILLOOET's coal was also sent up the line. Thirty-six hours later the RAINBOW, Captain Hose, showed up accompanied by the PRINCE GEORGE, a Grand Trunk steamer now converted to a hospital ship; also the SALVOR, the former DANUBE and a converted salvage ship, appeared in port.

The news was that the British Consulate at Seattle, Washington, had wired the Naval authorities at Esquimalt that a wooden steamer, the DELHI, had cleared from Seattle for Sulzer in Cordova Bay, Alaska, with 950 tons of coal.

Sulzer in all its history had never had more than ten tons of coal at any time. Suspicion was aroused. Captain Hose at once commandeered the LILLOOET and ordered us to seek around Sulzer and its numerous canneries. He would remain outside with the RAINBOW whilst our objective was to entice the NURNBERG to come out. They would not fire on a peaceful hydrographic vessel, so Hose told us, but I did not feel reassured of that.[7] However, it was a good policy on the part of Captain Hose. The only chance he had with the German ship was at close quarters.

Nosing around Sulzer and various canneries, they were quite hostile toward us. We came at last onto a deserted cannery wharf where evidently there had been quite a large amount of coal stacked recently. Inquiring, we found that the DELHI had landed it there. Well, nobody would say but we knew. The NURNBERG got that coal and proceeded south to Fanning Island where she destroyed the wireless station.

The RAINBOW remained north for a short time, cruising around the sound outside of Prince Rupert. She was stopping steamers coming down from the north. In the LILLOOET we went on with our scouting until finally ordered to return to Esquimalt in November 1914.

After a refit I was appointed Examination Officer and took the LILLOOET outside. It was a dreary job, steaming dead slow on a triangle run from Scroggs Rocks off Esquimalt to William Head, then back to Brotchie Ledge. We were not allowed to anchor except in a dense fog.

Stopping all shipping (and there was not much) we overhauled all crews and removed any Germans or Austrians. We were supposed to be relieved every 48 hours, but we in the LILLOOET were not popular with Admiral Story. Captain Musgrave had left the service and was strutting around ashore with a sword. He had had his commission returned to him. I wanted another officer because we were underway all the time but this the Admiral refused me. I pointed out that it was a lack of officers that had caused the RESTLESS to be badly damaged in collision. When I continued to be met with his opposition, I wired the Chief Hydrographer at Ottawa and we got another officer.[8]

I was transferred to the H.M.C.S. NADEN and ordered to take her to New Westminster to lay her up. If the Germans broke the blockade and came our way I had orders to hide the NADEN in one of the numerous inlets. I was to destroy her at once if the Germans discovered her. This never happened.

The NADEN had only recently been built for the Naval Service and was a very pretty little schooner without power. We towed from

---

[7] *"Some weeks later I read of the British sinking a German hydrographic ship. It left no doubt in my mind of what our fate would have been."*

[8] *"Incidently I was nearly put in the guard house, probably to be shot. Having had a few words with the Admiral, he threw his bunch of keys at me and before (or without) thinking I said, 'Bum shot.' He kept me outside for a whole month, Christmas and New Year, 1914-1915.*

"When I came in I was determined to get even with the Admiral so I took sick. Doctor Boake, the Naval doctor, was a very good friend of mine. He knew there was nothing the matter with me. The Admiral wanted me placed in the hospital but Boake would have none of it. He could attend to me better in my own home. 'But for god's sake be ready to jump into bed if anybody comes and don't go out except after dark.' I soon got well."

Esquimalt to New Westminster. My orders were to moor her in the north arm of the Fraser River inside of Poplar Island. This meant passing through a bridge with power wires overhcad. I mentioned this to my friend the Admiral; I doubted there was sufficient clearance for our masts. Quietly he snubbed me and knowing all about it, said there was any amount of clearance.

Going through, the bridge was opened. Our foremast was lower and cleared the wires but the main topmast fouled and came crashing down along with the power wires. A streak of flames shot down our backstays. My daughter was playing on the deck and seeing we were going to foul, I just managed to pick her up and drop her below. I was almost blinded by the flash. All the street car service to the island was out of commission for several days. And the Admiral knew all about it—well, so he did afterwards.

H. M. C. S. NADEN
"I was transfered to the H. M. C. S. NADEN and ordered to take her to New Westminster to lay her up. If the Germans broke the blockade and came our way, I had orders to hide the NADEN in one of the numerous inlets. I was to destroy her at once if the Germans discovered her."

After being in the Fraser River some months I was drafted for active service and given the rank of Chief Skipper. I was allotted to the RAINBOW in Esquimalt for gunnery drill and signalling.[9] Here I found Wingate, now in Pilotage, and he was No. 1. He ordered me to take his navigation classes and teach ex-policemen and others the rudiments. Some of them did not know one end of a ship from the other. My friend Wingate would sip nice little cold drinks and smoke cigarettes. Wingate had had command of Eaton's yacht at the outbreak of the War but smacking her through a southeast gale on the Grand Banks, they had lost several men overboard and damaged the yacht. Wingate was relieved of his command and sent west, out of the way.

One day Admiral Story came on board. He had me in mind, I don't know if it was for any good. Wingate talked with him.

"But where is Beavis?" asked the Admiral. "Taking a navigation class," was the reply. "Damn it, it's gunnery, gunnery, that I want him taught. He's forgotten more navigation than you'll ever learn." So that was that.

I was getting fed up with them all. I wanted to go overseas at once. Draft after draft went away but not I, so it happened one day that I was ordered to report to the SHEARWATER. I was not a commissioned officer, only of warrant rank. I was to be navigator but not on your life unless they found me a sextant. I refused to use my own and a warrant officer, according to the Articles of War, was entitled to that. A few days later I had an official document, my services were no longer required.

The following day I was master of the five-masted auxiliary schooner JANET CARRUTHERS. I passed Admiral Story close to on the the street and I was tickled to death not to salute him.

9 *"Just before joining the RAINBOW I was making munitions in New Westminster at a plant belonging to the B.C. Electric Co. I was doing so with the object of reducing my weight for active service. In this I was quite successful. I used to boil shells, 4.7.—being stripped to the waist and sweating as if in a Turkish bath. Generally we averaged from 1000 to 1100 shells a night. I was the only man amongst 100 girls (jolly pretty ones, too!). My age was the great factor I suppose but they had not thought about me being a sailor. The girls soon found out I was an easy mark. I boiled the shells in soda water, then washed them in boiling water and lifted them out onto the table. The sweet little minx nearest to me was supposed to take them then, but with a smile, she inveigled me into a second lift to her table. From there they were pushed down a long table, each girl doing something to them. At the end of the table they rolled onto a tray and were afterwards baked for several hours.*

"On the other side of the plant was another building where men worked. To keep them separate from the girls our supper hours were different. Evidently I was favoured. One time travelling on the street car with my wife a very engaging flapper came and sat alongside of me. Totally disregarding my wife, she started to talk to beat the band and as she left, she kissed her hand to me. My wife was much amused and asked, 'Who's your girlfriend?' "

PRINCE GEORGE in Johnston Strait
"She conformed to the silhouettes we had of the LEIP-
SIG and the NURNBERG. He at once ordered me to
report in Prince Rupert.

"We took out hell for leather in our fastest launch to
notify the authorities. There was a great excitement in
the town; all money was sent up country. The
LILLOOET's coal was also sent up the line. Thirty-six
hours later the RAINBOW, Captain Hose, showed up
accompanied by the PRINCE GEORGE, a Grand
Trunk steamer now converted to a hospital ship; also
the SALVOR, the former DANUBE and a converted
salvage ship appeared in port."

JANET CARRUTHERS at La Pointe Pier, Vancouver,
B. C.

CHAPTER XVII

BACK TO THE OPEN SEA

The JANET CARRUTHERS was an auxiliary twin screw motor schooner of the bald-headed type that is without topmasts. She had five masts. She was built of wood and measured 1253 tons net. She was fitting out at Wallace's yard,[1] North Vancouver, B.C. when I joined her as master. She was one of twelve schooners all of the same dimensions that were building for the Canada West Coast Navigation Co. Six of them were built in Victoria and the other six in Vancouver. They were sturdily built vessels but of green unseasoned timbers. They had Bolinder engines, oil internal combustion and not much was known about them at the time.

The JANET CARRUTHERS loaded a full cargo of logs at the La Pointe government docks. During this time I had three chief engineers. The first two threw their jobs up before we left. The third and last was an elderly man named Alfred Pepper who had been engineer in a tug and had never been with an internal combustion engine previously. However, the Bolinder expert from San Francisco and the Company marine superintendent certified him competent. So after taking on 16 feet of deck load, I sailed from Vancouver for Port Adelaide, South Australia, on the 20 August 1917. I had as pilot Captain Wearmouth although I did not require one. On board were the company's marine superintendent and the Bolinder expert.

The engines were not running satisfactorily and the pilot and I decided not to attempt Active Pass but go around East Point. Soon the Engineer Superintendent came to me saying we would have to put into Victoria for adjustments. I agreed without hesitation.

Later the two experts said everything was all right and *they thought*, mind you—they thought the chief engineer could handle the engines. After talking it over with the pilot, I told them that I would not stop the engines. I would slow them as much as possible but the experts and the pilot would have to make a leap for the pilot launch.

This was safely accomplished off Victoria and the JANET CARRUTHERS proceeded at full speed down the Strait of Juan de Fuca. Passing Race Rocks the weather set in foggy but we held on. Off Flattery it cleared, the wind came northwest and I gave her all the canvas. I had never been in a fore and aft craft before—always square rigged—but it did not take long to size things up.

My mate had been employed at the last moment and although a good roust- about-man, he knew nothing of schooners and very

---

[1] ed. note. Wallace Shipyards, Ltd., established some years prior to World War I by Alfred Wallace, received an order from the Canadian West Coast Navigation Co. for six five-masted, bald-headed auxiliary schooners of the type designed by J.H. Price. All were completed in 1917 and named for women in the families of the owners. The vessels were launched in this order: MABEL BROWN, GERALDINE WOLVIN, JESSIE NORCROSS, JANET CARRUTHERS, MABEL STEWART, and MARIE BERNARD. The last was launched in September 1917. The owners financed these vessels by a bond issue on the security of a 1916 British Columbia law which guaranteed their earnings. All of the vessels had passed into foreign ownership shortly after the end of World War I.

JANET CARRUTHERS at Honolulu, 1917

154

little of navigation. My second mate was a Swede and a good sailor, but no navigator. So it was up to me. That first night the wind came strong and fair from the northwest, so I ordered the port or lee engine shut down, keeping the starboard or weather one running.

The JANET CARRUTHERS made a good run of 256 miles the first 24 hours out from Flattery (also the *only* one she ever made). Toward evening of the next day the wind fell light and I ordered the port engine started. After many ineffective attempts, much coughing and spluttering toward dawn, and feeling much disgusted, I decided to turn in. I gave the mate his orders and went below. Barely had I taken off my coat when there was an awful explosion and the JANET rolled from side to side. All of the lights (electric) went out and complete darkness reigned. Going on deck I found the mate gazing down the engine room scuttle. Angrily I asked him what was the matter but he did not know. "Well then find out!" I shouted, "Get flash lights at once."

I followed the mate into the engine room and there we found the old chief engineer with blood streaming from him. The donkey man on watch with him was in the same shape, crouching behind the mast. The port engine was blown to smithereens and the starboard one had stopped.

We got both of them out and called the second engineer to look after the engine room. I repaired damages to the Chief. The donkeyman was not really hurt, only scared. The next couple of days were employed making repairs to the starboard engine whilst we jogged along under sail with a very light wind. Two days later the Chief reported the starboard engine as fit and I decided at that time to continue the voyage with one engine. Shortly after starting, however, there was another crash. The crankshaft was broken and we carried no spare parts. This was some how-do-you-do. What oh what had I done to be back in sail with a parish-rigged craft like this?

Rubbing my head, I cogitated. If I put into San Francisco (the nearest port) I would be deviating from my voyage. The whole bunch from Vancouver would be down and I would have no say in making the contracts. If I proceeded and put into Honolulu, I would be proceeding on the voyage and nobody could get there unless by sail. The mail steamers had ceased to run due to the war. I would have the handling of everything in Honolulu. Hawaii for me.

I found the JANET would not steer well. We had to be going a full six knots before the propellers would revolve and she would not stay. She would just come up to the wind and then fall off.

Finally the wind freshened and I fetched into Honolulu on the afternoon of 12 September 1917. Here I found the Inter-Island Steam Navigation Co. most helpful and I berthed the JANET CARRUTHERS alongside Pier 17. I cabled Vancouver, "BOTH ENGINES TOTALLY DISABLED, REPAIRS HERE IMPOSSIBLE WITHOUT LENGTHY DELAY. ADVISE PUTTING SHIP ON DRY DOCK, REMOVING PROPELLERS AND STRUTS, ALSO EXTRA CANVAS TO BE SUPPLIED IN SHAPE OF TOPSAILS AND SPINAKERS, OTHERWISE SEND ANOTHER MASTER."

This brought the speedy reply, "DO WHAT YOU THINK IS NECESSARY AND CONTINUE VOYAGE." After a survey, it was decided the ship must be drydocked. I wanted a goodly portion of the deck load discharged as I feared the weight would strain the ship. I notified the surveyors in writing but I was overruled by Lloyds. The ship went on the dry dock the twenty-first of September 1917. The dock was tipped as much as possible so as to keep the fore end afloat. The propeller shafts were drawn and the stern tubes plugged and the struts removed.

The vessel was floated out of dry dock at 8 a.m. on the twenty-second of September and returned to Pier 17. At once she started to take water at an alarming rate. Calling another survey I pressed upon them what I

Deckload on the JANET CARRUTHERS

had earlier said about straining the ship. The surveyors were badly frightened.

A centrifugal pump was installed between the wrecks of the two engines and a gas engine was placed to drive it. I paid off the chief engineer and the third engineer and sent them back to Vancouver, that is, whenever they could get there.

At last I was nearly ready for sea with a certificate of sea worthiness but now I was held up by the Naval Authorities. The SEEADLER was reported to be about.

On Wednesday, October 3, 1917, I towed to sea and at noon of that day the tug left me. The wind was very light and we were making barely two knots. That evening the Fanning Island steamer KESTREL, a small wooden steamer that had been built by Wallace of North Vancouver, B.C. for the Canadian Government for fishing protection services, overhauled me. She was built with a ram-bow and was noted for her slowness. In fact she was the laughing stock of the fish poachers.

The KESTREL was commanded by Captain Tait[2] and was used by the Cable Company. The KESTREL bore down on me and wished me luck. That was the last I ever saw of her.

The weather continued moderate with light trades for several days until picking up the southeast trades in 7'17" north latitude and 163'0" west longitude. I had received orders to run without lights of any sorts and all scuttles were screened. This made it very hot and stuffy below. Every night at sundown a hand was sent aloft to look for any sign of the SEEADLER. But not a vessel could be seen. We were alone on a strangely desolate ocean. Our best day's run was 162 miles on the twentieth of October. All this time we pumped periodically. It was for this pumping that I had kept the second engineer and the donkeyman, otherwise they too would have been sent back from Honolulu.

On Monday the twenty-second of October I was called by the mate in the early hours of the morning. The ship had listed badly to starboard and there was ten feet of water in the bilges and the water was over the gas engine in the engine room. My glorious second engineer had fallen asleep in his watch and only awakened by the water coming over his feet which he had conveniently placed on the gas engine. It was a case of immediately starting the gas engine and getting the Weir pumps to work, also the main hand pumps. The water was by now up to 12 feet amidships and the starboard rail was under water. It certainly looked ominous for us with a heavy list to starboard as the vessel became more and more sluggish. Whenever the hands had to leave the main pump to trim sail, the water would rise and we were unable to reduce it.

2 *"Later Port Warden for Vancouver."*

Then some of the crew fell ill with the exhaustion of continual pumping.

I was trying to fetch Samoa, if possible, but I was not sure as the wind was a bit south of east. The only chart I had was an American pilot chart and Samoa only looked like a fly spot on it. However, I had the latitude and the longitude out of Norey's. If I could not make Apia, there was nothing for it but to try and get to Suva in the Fiji Islands. This was a much farther distance and not a very pleasant prospect in a waterlogged vessel. We were having trouble with the hand pump now, too. The leather packing was continually giving out. Our coal supply on the donkey boiler was nearly finished and some hands had to be kept cutting up our deck cargo for fuel.

By the twenty-seventh of October things were becoming serious. We felt we would not mind meeting the German raider—it was an alternative to death on the open sea—perhaps. Just as it looked the blackest for us the wind faired and the sea became more moderate. We were able to lay our course, at last. The wind favoured and we sighted the island of Samoa at 4:30 a.m. on Monday, October 29.

The wind freshened and held fair while I skirted down the Coast looking for an opening in the reef. Soon we sighted several schooners at anchor, all flying the Stars and Stripes. Then the opening in the reef appeared. By this time the wind had freshened to half a gale and I had to reduce sail quickly. On hauling in with far too much weigh on, both anchors had to be let go by the run and we brought up with just a few fathoms to spare from the inner reef.

Not a soul was to be seen on any of the schooners, only the American ensign fluttering in the trade wind. Not a sign of life was on the water. Ashore there appeared to be some earthworks where the New Zealand flag was flying.

After being at anchor for about an hour, a boat was seen approaching from the shore. They were heavily armed. On getting within hailing distance, they shouted to me, but they were very leary about coming on board. At

long last they came abreast of the poop and the officer in charge (the Harbour Master) interrogated me. Then he came aboard. They had mistaken me for an American five-masted schooner that the SEEADLER was supposed to have captured. By this time the SEEADLER was a wreck at Mopelia, Society Islands, and they suspected that the Germans had manned the captive. As soon as all of the crews of the American schooners (three in number) saw me in the offing, they got in their boats and beat it for the shore, leaving their vessels to the protection of the Stars and Stripes gaily flaring in the breeze. These schooners were all commanded by Dutchmen, "squareheads" [sic] not by thoroughbred Americans.

I told my plight to the Harbour Master and went ashore with him to meet Colonel Logan who was in charge. "By gad, Sir, I was going to give you a hot reception. All the garrison was in the trenches with pom-poms trained on your vessel!"

I said, "Didn't you see the red duster flying and my schooner waterlogged and both life boats swung out?"

"Oh, yes. Camouflage, Sir."

Now they could not do enough for us. Soon I had the lighter alongside with shore pumps and a crowd of native labour. No diving outfit here but one could be procured at Pago Pago, American Samoa.

PASS OF BALMAHA (later the SEEADLER)

This was immediately sent for while I had dinner with Colonel Logan and heard all the news. The American ship masters and their crews sheepishly returned to their vessels crestfallen. I was able to replenish my stores and could always get fresh meat. This was not so for the American schooners with their Scandinavian crews. They had to be content to get whatever was left over.

The diver's outfit from Pago Pago arrived on Friday, November 2, and I proceeded to kedge the JANET CARRUTHERS inside the inner harbour or reef where the diver might work more easily. All this time the shore pumps on the lighter were going furiously and the ship's donkey was driving the Weir pumps. Slowly, ever so slowly, the ship uprighted.

On Monday, November 5, the diver reported finding a hole close to the bracket plugs on the starboard side. Under surveyors' orders, he plugged this up. Before he had completed his work and during the early hours of the following day, a heavy squall hit and the ship dragged her anchors. We were unable to pay out cable on account of the proximity of the reef and the ship took the ground with her heel. For a time it looked as if it was all up for the JANET, when as suddenly as it had breezed up, the wind and sea fell and we hove the ship off with both bowers having carried all the stern lines away.

American vessels at Apia, 1917

By the eighth of November the diver reported all patches finished and invited me to put on his helmet and go down to inspect them. He was quite naked but for the helmet. I refrained and said I would take his word for it and see the repairs in dry dock in Australia. (There were numerous sharks around these waters). I got a certificate of sea worthiness from Lloyds's surveyor and kedged the ship out to the outer harbour. Here I had to wait several days for the wind as there were no tugs, not even a launch.

Having some spare time, I took the opportunity to visit Robert Louis Stevenson's grave. [Robert Louis Stevenson died on the island in 1894.] It was quite a climb to the top of the mountain.

On the twelfth of November whilst I was ashore at the English Club, I felt a light air. Going off to the schooner immediately, we made all sail and got underway. This was a ticklish job. The entrance through the reef was very narrow and there were only a few feet to spare when I cleared the inner reef.[3] Was not I glad to get away and breathe a sigh of relief!

We had moderate weather for several days but on November 28 we experienced a strong northeast gale with very heavy squalls. What with the ship labouring and straining, she began to leak again badly. It was now that I realized she was evidently strained and had been built of green timber. Soon the pumping was continuous. Although we were able to hold the water with the centrifugal pump and gas engine, as yet we dare not cease pumping. Now also the starboard list increased which we had almost eliminated in Samoa. What a ship, what a hoodoo—

The weather continued to get worse. On the fifteenth of November I decided to put into Sydney, N.S.W. for coal and water and to over-

[3] "The bones of a German man-of-war are still to be seen there, a visable warning of the hurricane season. They were lost along with three American men-of-war in the March hurricane of 1889 when only the British warship CALLIOPE, Captain Henry Coey Kane, managed to get to sea."

haul the pumps. December 16 we anchored in Sydney Harbour in eight fathoms of water with 60 fathoms of cable on the starboard anchor. The ship was in Double Bay. I had the pumps overhauled and tested by the surveyors. The ship was recommended to be continued in her class by Lloyds's surveyor.[4]

Our hoodoo was not over. On Monday, December 31 at a little after noon whilst I was ashore clearing the ship, a terrific squall from the south struck the ship, causing her to drag her anchor. The second anchor was immediately let go and cable paid out on both, but before the anchors held, the JANET CARRUTHERS had dragged clean across the harbour and was right in the track of the shipping. The wind was blowing a terrific gale from the southeast and it took two tugs to hold the ship up to her anchors. Several hours later the wind moderated and we towed back to a fresh berth in Double Bay.

In letting go and heaving up, the windlass was badly damaged which necessitated repairs. When these were completed, I proceeded to sea—determined to get to Adelaide, Australia. Hoodoo or no hoodoo.

When I arrived in Sydney, I at once repaired to the owners' agents. They informed me in no uncertain terms that they were no longer the agents, showing me a cablegram to that affect. My ship had been sold to the French Government! I asked them to disburse me but they could not think of doing that. "Well, gentlemen," I said, "if that is so, my consignees, G.R. Wills, will." I bid them a good morning and turning to go, I casually remarked that I had fifty per cent of the freight to collect. At that they at once agreed to disburse me. "Like hell you will! Just a moment ago you said you wouldn't. Good day."

George R. Wills was only too willing to oblige. So on Thursday, January 3, 1918, with a light east southeasterly wind, I proceeded to sea in tow.

The ship still had a pronounced list to starboard but I had obtained a fresh certificate of sea worthiness. The tug left at eleven a.m. and we made all sail. I hoped our luck would now change but no, the ship commenced to leak again. At four p.m. she was leaking so badly that all pumps were operating constantly. Ominous though it looked, I was not going to put back. Just before nightfall, the tug KOPUTAI made an appearance and agreed to tow me on my way to Port Adelaide or as far as his coal would allow him. The tug was made fast ahead and we proceeded to tow and sail. We were pumping continuously. We passed Wilson's Promontory on the sixth of January, pumping for dear life while the pumps choked badly. On January 8 the tug left but promised to return after getting more coal.

So I sailed on, pumping for dear life, listing more and more to starboard. Would I be able to make it? Would the tug return? I couldn't refrain from wondering.

Off Warrnambol I had to shorten sail to a hard southeast gale—pump, pump, pump. Shortly, the tug turned up and we resumed towing. Now the wind came fair and we passed Cape Willoughby January 10, going through Backstairs Passage—pump, pump, pump. At eleven p.m. we anchored off the Semaphore, pumping all the time. By now we were able to reduce the water in her a little as

[4] *"During this stay in Sydney I renewed my friendship with my cousin Walter Beavis whom I had not seen for many years. I called his house on the phone, a new innovation in the days when no one dreamed of such contraptions. A woman's voice answered and I asked if it was the home of Walter Beavis. Her affirmative response prompted me to tell her I was his cousin. 'Father's out but I will call Mother.' (The last time I had seen Walter there was no wife.) Mrs. Beavis invited me to dinner but she did not seem too sure of me. I met his charming wife and two daughters but what a change I encountered. There was the same old boathouse at the bottom of the garden in which in far off years I had stowed the MICKY's gig. Walter Beavis was by then retired from head of the School Commission and we had a great deal of time to spend together. How we yarned...*

"I was loath to part from these cousins of mine. I met another old friend there, Captain McGibbon, the renowned master of Law's four poster DUMFRIESHIRE and whose wedding I had attended many years before. Mac was now snow white but his wife was just the same as I remembered her. His charming pretty daughter called her father 'Snowy'. His son was overseas in France.

"I also met my old friend Henmuir who had the CUTHONA during the Newcastle coal strike of 1896."

she was not straining. The following day, January 18, we docked at Port Adelaide at 5:00 p.m. It was another 36 hours after arrival before we cajoled our pumps into sucking and the ship was at last dry.

Here I received a cable from my late owners telling me to remit the balance of freight. Nothing doing. I consulted with George R. Wills and I decided to keep the balance of the freight money to disburse the ship. Previously they had cabled that they had sold the whole

COLONNA (ex-SIERRA COLONNA) at Port Adelaide Iron ship built in 1878 in four months at Stockton by Richardson & Co. for Thompson, Anderson of Liverpool. Measured 238′6″ x 38′ x 22′8″, 1591 tons gross, 1435 tons net.

fleet and had nothing to do with any of the ships any longer.

Whilst discharging cargo I had the topsides caulked and when the cargo was all out, I had planned to have the JANET hauled up at Fletcher's Marine Railway. Alas, Fletcher's was afraid they could not handle her so we lay a long time idle. Then I received orders to proceed to Sydney to load coal for Java and from there, sugar to Marseille. I would only take her as far as the nearest dry dock. That was Melbourne and it would be under tow all the way. I was fed up. My hair had turned white and I was far from well.

During the long stay at Port Adelaide I made several trips up Mount Lofty, a nice car ride. In the horse landaus of the old days, it took all day but now it could be done in the cool of the evening. What a glorious view one had of Adelaide coming down at nightfall with the twinkling lights like a sky of stars lying beneath you. The heat was terrific in Adelaide but up on Mount Lofty it was beautifully cool. Descending the mountain you noticed the difference in temperature and finally ran into a veritable hot blast.

I made a trip to Willunga Bay where the ill-fated STAR OF GREECE was wrecked. She would never have been lost but for too much liquor. If they had only put her on the other tack, "if,if," sums up the losses of many fine ships. I was greatly intriqued with the drive. Numerous flocks of parrots gay in colour would flash from one side to the other. Then at times wallabies would go romping away.

The principal street in Adelaide struck me as very fine. Named after King William, it was immensely wide and lined with beautiful trees.

Leaving Port Adelaide for Melbourne, we were still pumping but not quite so strenuously. I put the JANET CARRUTHERS in Dukes Dry Dock and had her thoroughly caulked. She needed it badly. Here I saw the patches the diver of Samoa had placed on her. They were wonderfully done.

5 ed. note. The Thwaite family was mentioned in Chapter IV.

One day a very pretty grey haired lady drove down to the ship in a handsome car. She was a former sweetheart of mine. She had been Ada Thwaite in those days and she used to come down to the ship in a dog cart with a fine trotting mare.[5] Now she was happily married with a grown up family. Pointing to her stalwart sons, she saucily remarked, "These might have been yours." I wonder!

She took me home to dinner—boy and girl sweethearts who were growing old. She was much concerned with my health. It dawned on me that this five-masted schooner had taken too much of a toll on my vitality. After a consultation with George R. Wills and Co., I decided to go home to Vancouver.

The Australian government would not allow the JANET CARRUTHERS to load coals. She would have to load wheat back to the Sound. Wheat in Australia was piled up in sheds and on the wharves without ships to move it.

The French government would not agree to the shipment. The ship was to be held indefinitely, certainly until all bills had been paid. The freight money was beginning to look scant. Though a little dubious of the mate's capabilities I put him in command.

Before I left Melbourne I was rather sorry. The mate visited me at my hotel very drunk. It was not a good beginning. Later he lost the JANET CARRUTHERS outside of Grays Harbor and drowned seven of the crew. It was

STAR OF PERSIA

Walter A. Scott, San Francisco

foggy weather but he had the engines and the whole of the Pacific outside of him.[6]

Taking a coastal steamer in preference to the train to Sydney I arrived there some three weeks before Easter, 1918. The town was full and all accommodations booked for the Easter week when horse racing would be in full swing. How the Australians love horse racing!

I stayed at Petty's hotel awaiting the mail boat for Vancouver. Just before Easter the management came to me requesting that I leave. They had booked my room. Insisting that they find me another place to stay, they boarded me in their house across the water at Mossman's Bay. Whilst in Sydney I came across a hansom cab and renewed my youth by many drives in it.

The first night at the boarding house I distinquished myself by having nightmares. In the early hours of the morn I was emitting weird and fearful noises, being finally aroused by people knocking at my door. Immediately I knew but I pretended to be in a sound sleep giving off a snore or two. I had heard the voices say, "He seems to be all right now, perhaps it will be as well not to disturb him." I smiled to myself.

At breakfast I noticed several of the guests eyeing me but I did not bat a lid—not even when the manager asked how I had slept. "Splendid," I replied. "It is such a peaceful atmosphere, such a lovely view." After that I took good care not to go to sleep on my back.

At last the MAKURA arrived and I departed. After clearing the Heads who should I barge into but Syd Philips, the captain. The last time I had met him he was a young second mate on the PORT JACKSON. I was in the MICRONESIA then. That was in 'Frisco in the early 80s. How we yarned.

We were a full ship and had a theatrical troupe, The Loftus, on board. Crossing the Tasman Sea a show was arranged in aid of the Red Cross, followed by a sort of auction. There were many wealthy people on board and the show was not going any too well in the way of subscriptions. Lots of pretty girls were soliciting. A charming little actress came my way

and brought me up all standing; I handed her a ten pound note. That did it. She jumped at me and gave me such a spanking kiss, singing out and waving the tenner, "Look at 'Canada'. Now then you Australians and New Zealanders—come across." For shame sakes they did. Soon a tidy sum had been collected but it was that ten pound and the kiss that did it.

We were two or three days in Auckland, a lovely city to be visited later on when I had more time to get to know it and enjoy it.

The war news was very depressing, not to say alarming. Every day we would scan the bulletin board and wonder. There were numerous passengers returning to the front. Amongst these was a group of young boys who had joined the air force. How many returned? Some I know did not.

Passing Mary Island we tried our gun out at a lonely palm tree. The MAKURA was armed with a solitary gun.

---

[6] ed. note. The JANET CARRUTHERS had been placed in service between Vancouver and Australia by the Canadian West Coast Navigation Co. The $150,000 power plant had disintegrated at Honolulu as Beavis described, and at Adelaide a $10,000 salvage claim was awarded against her. She finally reached her homeport in late 1918 and early the following year loaded lumber at Tacoma, Washington, departing that port January 20, to complete loading at Astoria, Oregon, for Shanghai. On the night of January 22, 1919, her master, Captain Cairny, mistook the Grays Harbor Light for the North Head Light marking the entrance to the Columbia River. Changing course inshore, the schooner was driven onto the beach four miles north of the Grays Harbor jetty. Six men attempted to leave the wreck in a lifeboat but they all drowned when the craft overturned. The remainder of the crew stayed aboard the JANET CARRUTHERS until low tide when they were able to walk ashore in complete safety. Efforts to salvage the schooner were abandoned when the Washington State Fisheries Department refused to allow the dumping of oil from the fuel tanks because they feared harm would come to the clam beds at Grays Harbor. The vessel gradually broke up, the remains of the engines were removed, and the hulk was eventually burned at low tide for the metal fittings. Before the vessel disappeared, motion picture film was taken aboard and reappeared as background scenes in numerous shipwreck episodes of sea dramas. [Information researched through *McCurdy's Marine History of the Pacific Northwest* by Gordon Newell, Superior Publications, (Seattle, 1966) p.311.]

Arriving at Honolulu, I found it had changed quite a lot since my departure in the JANET CARRUTHERS. America was now in the war. Prohibition was in force. The Club was shut down and you could not get a cocktail for love nor money. Although there was lots doing, everything was different.

We arrived at Victoria in the late afternoon and stayed some hours before proceeding on to Vancouver. Some of us went for a drive in Victoria but it was very cold. At least we thought it was after changing from a tropical climate in a few hours. Well, we called it frigid.

The rest onboard had done me good but I was not yet fully recovered. The thought of soon seeing my dear ones at Vancouver was exhilarating, though.

We arrived at the Canadian Pacific Railway docks in the early hours of the morning; soon we were all scattered to the four corners of the earth. I bid Sid Philips good-bye, never to see him again, also the friends I had made on the voyage. Some were soon entrained for the east. It was not likely that I should meet them again, such is life onboard ship.

Near Pier 17, Honolulu

Pier 17, Honolulu, 1917

Captain Philips, Tovetin, and Chief Engineer, all of MAKURA

R. M. S. MAKURA

SALVOR off Tahiti in 1918

CHAPTER XVIII

A SHORT SPELL ASHORE AND THEN?

It was a delightful reunion. We were living in New Westminster and our little girl was growing up. She was attending the Convent School there. Her great chum was Undine Howay, daughter of Judge F.W. Howay. She was a very clever little girl.[1]

I tried to find some signs of the Canadian West Coast Navigation Co. but they had departed lock, stock and barrel. Not a vestage was left; all had fled. When their ships were built, they had been subsidized by the Government, not to be sold out of Canada. Evidently there had been some underhanded work.

Now I thought it would be wise for us all to go up north to Prince Rupert and start out on my ranch on Stephens Island. I had two gas boats which I intended taking up myself.

One morning a young farmer and I strolled into the auction mart out on the green at New Westminster. Old man Trapp was selling a great deal of farm material. Just then a team of ponies with a brand new wagon and harness drove up. My farmer friend looked at the ponies. He returned quite excited saying they were just rising five and in splendid fettle. He would buy them but he did not have the money. The two of us wandered over to the ponies. When they were put up on the auction block, I bid casually—I did not want them. The bidding went on and the whole outfit— ponies, harness, wagon were knocked down to me for one hundred dollars. I was taken flat back. I expected the bidding to go on for say $150 to $200. Reluctantly Mr. Trapp took my cheque. Now what was I going to do?

I had no stable, no field.

I drove home and my little daughter ran to greet me. "Oh, Mother, look at Father!"

My dear wife only shook her head at me and sighed, "What on earth will you buy next?"

I had to rent a stable anyway, and then I bought some little pigs. I was becoming quite a farmer. I shipped all of the livestock to Prince Rupert. Later my wife and daughter headed north on the PRINCESS ALICE. I followed with my boats. I was a long time getting up there. I was misfortunate enough to be stranded in Blinkinsop Bay.

My wife was getting anxious when I was long overdue. Finally a Government launch spoke me and took word to my loved ones. When I at last arrived at the hotel in Prince Rupert where they were staying, they did not know me. I was tanned almost black and had a heavy beard.

All was going well. I had a scow chartered and loaded with lumber to build a shack and outhouses. Then the bolt struck. I had notice to report at once in Vancouver to take command of the S.S. SALVOR. She was bound for 'Frisco and New Zealand.

All ranching was knocked on the head. I put my ponies in the milk run in Prince Rupert and sold my lumber and pigs. I placed my wife and child in a house and sailed for Vancouver. The war still raged and there was

[1] "She has since passed to the great majority. I always fancied that she was over-educated."

167

SALVOR at Vancouver, B. C. in 1918
"I had notice to report at once in Vancouver to take command of the S. S. SALVOR. She was bound for 'Frisco and New Zealand."

a shortage of officers for the Mercantile Marine. It was my turn to serve.

Arriving in Vancouver, I found that a master had been engaged, an Australian. This action had been taken because I had arrived late. I had perforce to go as chief officer whether I liked it or not. The only advantage was that the pay was very good.

The SALVOR had originally been the old DANUBE, a Canadian Pacific Railway steamer, and before that a South African mail boat of the same name. She had been purchased from the salvage company by a Montreal man who did not know anything about ships. You might have bought her for $10,000 and glad to get it but the salvage company had recognized a sucker. They were paid £40,000 sterling for her, not dollars, and cash at that. She was over 50 years old and the original engines were in her.

At the time there were three men in the salvage company who went by the friendly sobriquet of the "Three Pirates of B.C.":

Billen had a shipyard (later called Yarrows); Logan was associated with London Salvage Association (he was the surveyor) and the third was Captain Troup of the C.P.R. It was a very good combination. Billen would do the repairs; Logan handled the surveying and Troup was very handy to loan you a tug.

Whilst fitting out the S.S. SALVOR, Chief Engineer Sammy Arbuthnott was nosing around aft. He drove his topmaul through the oxted plates on one side. At that he was mad and made a ferocious attack on the other side sending his topmaul handle and all through the oxted plates. Logan was furious. He wanted to have the chief fired but he dared not. They had a terrible time riveting on overhaul patches and filling them up with tons of cement. A long patch had been placed on each side between wind and water for about 40 feet, just level with the between decks. The plating was like brown paper.

Eventually we got away, calling at Victoria. Captain Watson was entirely unacquainted with these waters and I piloted the ship up the Inside Passage to Ocean Falls. Here we loaded a full cargo of paper for San Francisco and left on October 1, 1918, going outside via Cape Scott. A moderate southeast gale was blowing up and soon the SALVOR was in difficulties. The patches on her sides opened up and tons of water entered the 'tween decks. There had been scuppers leading below but these, too, had all been sealed with cement.

The captain turned in with a bottle of whisky and would not leave his bunk after sending out wireless distress signals. We were now off Flattery and the SALVOR was taking a heavy list to starboard, as much as 30 feet. We tried to bore holes in the 'tween decks to let the water go below. At last we found some lead pipes in the after end and cutting these through, the water got below to the engine room pumps. But for this, the ship would have undoubtedly foundered.

All this time the captain was in his bunk, although I had the boats swung out. Soon after the weather moderated and the old SALVOR limped into 'Frisco, and here the captain was relieved of his command. I expected to get the job but a young man by the name of Lappit[2] was sent down from Vancouver to assume command.

Influenza was raging in San Francisco and nearly all of our crew landed in the hospital. I discharged the paper which was in a terrible mess, water soaked and swollen. A lot of repairs needed attention in port but our new captain spent a lot of his time at a second rate hotel carousing.

We were to load a general cargo for New Zealand and in order to get more into the ship, the owner had all the permanent ballast removed. That consisted of some 100 tons of pig iron. The result was that just as we were completing loading, over goes the SALVOR but fortunately for us onto the wharf. This was a nice kettle of fish. We had to discharge nearly all of our cargo and take in the ballast again.

Prohibition was enforced in many regions in the United States and we had some three or four cases of Rye whisky in bond for New Zealand.[3] On boarding the first car we found it

Steamers in San Francisco Bay, 1918

had been neatly pillaged from the underneath and a great number of cases taken. Each car had been treated in this manner.

The NAVAU Union steamer of New Zealand left about three weeks ahead of us. We left several of our crew with the flu in the hospital and took on substitutes. We had to wear a nose and mouth mask, a filthy contraption, when ashore. If you were caught without it you were hauled off to the police court. Often on the street corners you would see a dozen or more people lined up under arrest.

Getting away at last in November we had to call at Tahiti for bunkers. Just before making the island we experienced a violent earthquake shock. We thought for a moment we had struck a reef but taking soundings all around there was nothing but deep water and the ship was not leaking.

A short while before arriving at the island we had news by wireless of the Armistice [November 11, 1918].

Arriving in the harbour at Papeete we were astonished to see the NAVAU at anchor with all her boats in the water. When the officials

[2] ed. note. Beavis indicated in the draft manuscript that he did not use this captain's real name in the text.
[3] ed. note. Twenty-four states voted against alcoholic beverages in 1916; the Prohibition Amendment (18th) to the U.S. Constitution was ratified January 16, 1919. The 21st Amendment repealed Prohibition in 1933.

boarded us we were told that the flu had been raging here for several weeks. They blamed the New Zealand steamer for bringing it. They were short of medical supplies so they commandeered all of ours.

The Governor was in his Palace and would not come out. Both of their wireless operators were dead so we loaned our one and only—a mere boy. There was no chance of getting bunkers for a while. Subsequently they commandeered my crew to dig graves but soon that, too, was impossible. They resorted to digging big trenches and burned the bodies. The roads and market place were strewn with dead bodies.

We got in touch with a French Man-of-War who was a long way off but was coming with medical supplies. The news from Samoa was equally alarming. Then we heard from New Zealand that it was raging there, too. On a little island in the harbour we found the captain of the NAVAU sick almost to death and in the adjoining room the second engineer was already dead. We made a box for the engineer and buried him. No one was allowed ashore from the NAVAU.

At last we received permission to bunker. They agreed to accept our tally and our crew put it aboard. As it was much too hot during the day for such labor, we worked at the coaling after sundown. All through this epidemic I gave our crew a liberal supply of Tahiti rum and limes and we had no recurrance of the flu. Whilst here I hardly ever saw our captain. He was no doubt off enjoying himself somewhere.

The principal club in Papeete was called the "Cercle Bougainville" and was much in demand by mariners. There was an old billard table off the balcony, the cloth of which was much patched up. A few French novels on a shelf and French papers, mostly of the naughty type, on one or two tables, comprised the literary reading selection. Here traders and masters of island schooners would congregate and sip cold drinks. There were several shell holes in the walls caused by the German fleet when they appeared here on their way south.

The other house of resort was the Tiare Hotel, not a great way off. It was owned and operated by "Lovaina" who was the best known woman in the South Seas. She died of the flu whilst we were here and I attended her burial. I had only met her a few times before she was taken ill. She was one of the first to die and was buried, not burnt.

Finishing bunkering we sailed for Wellington. We arrived there safely just a day or so before Christmas, 1918. We were nearly put into quarantine but being short of water and needing repairs it was finally waived.

Leaving Wellington in ballast for Auckland we had very bad weather just outside the heads. At this the old SALVOR did her best to turn over. We had a coast pilot on board, Captain Black, who had never in his life been sea sick but our ship did the trick for him.

Arriving in Auckland our skipper sent for his wife but in the meantime, he had gotten very friendly with another lady. When his wife came he arranged (and I still don't understand how he did it) for the other woman to accompany them on the voyage as his wife's companion. Picking up some cargo in Auckland we again proceeded to Wellington to complete loading. The cargo was tallow, called soap grease, for the Allies. We were bound for Genoa. Leaving Wellington for the Canal with barely enough coal, we had continual head winds and finally had to reduce speed and make for Acapulco, a world coaling station. We had not thought of the War but on arrival there to our dismay there was not a pound of coal. By then we had only about two tons left of our own. By wiring Salina Cruz it was possible in the course of time to get some. It was at least enough to take us to Panama but it meant further delay. It was just then that along came the American transport BULLMOUTH with some 15 to 20 submarine chasers. She had coal to spare and after wiring the American authorities at Washington and lubricating the Captain of the Transport with a case of absynthe and another of whisky, well, we got our coal. We also had a visit from the Governor ashore. He was a swarthy Mexican with two revolvers belted to his waist. He was looking for whisky, too.

Sometime previous to this the atmosphere on board had been decidedly sulphuric between the two ladies. One night one of the ladies threw most of the belongings of the other overboard. Two women and one man! The skipper was also becoming the worse for wear and drink was taking its toll.

Arriving at Panama we proceeded through the Canal. The skipper had now become so drunk that I had to take charge. The Canal Pilot came to me to say that if I didn't take command he would not take the ship through.

Arriving at Cristobal, Panama, one woman tried to commit suicide but for the wireless operator she would have done so. She had dashed down the deck and hurled herself over the end of the wharf into the water. The youngster swam in after her and brought her out. She was a pitiable sight. The other woman was terribly vindictive. It was not a pleasant job, taking her wet clothes off and rubbing her down with a crowd of men around. Lappit the skipper was idiotically drunk by this time and the other woman nearly so. Damn it all, this had to end.

I put them all ashore and several others of the crew also left. Once again I was in full charge. With most of the crew gone I shipped a crowd of negroes, U.S. ones. I made an Irishman quartermaster mate and a young Swede second. They were both without tickets, good sailors but no navigation. Had it not been war time or just after, I could not have done this. I still had the original chief engineer and the wireless boy.

Getting away, I headed for my next port, San Juan, for the bunkers. We arrived there late in the afternoon and bunkered, getting away by the next day. I stuck the SALVOR up north to get the westerlies. Rigging both booms out on the fore, I bent the trysails and went booming along wing and wing. The old SALVOR never reached such speed in her life before.

As we approached Horta in the Azores we were at first reported as a sailing ship. Here I received orders for Marseilles, later to be changed to Bordeaux. I began to wonder where I should fetch up.

Bunkering and ready to leave, I was held up. The coaling company would not accept my draft on the Montreal shipowner. Finally Bensaudes came to the rescue. Anyhow it was a pleasant delay and I had some lovely drives around the island. Before leaving I had instructions to steer for such and such at latitude and longitude, and then alter course for another position and then finally head for the mouth of the river—all this on account of the mine fields. It would not be very pleasant if the weather came thick. However, nothing happened, although I got the scare of my life when I passed a derelict floating mine.

Arriving in the river we anchored off Pauillac, France, because the dock in Bordeaux was full. Here we lay for two weeks.

One day whilst I was ashore at the agent's, I saw flags go up on the SALVOR. They wanted the police. Hastening off in the police boat, I found Flaherty, my Irish mate, and the wireless operator marooned on the bridge of the SALVOR with all the negroes clustered around them but afraid to be the first to storm the ladders. The chief engineer had also gotten the steam hose ready.

The mate had cracked one of the negroes on the head with a belaying pin for insubordination. I managed to get it smoothed over a bit

Papeete in 1918

171

but it cost Flaherty some twenty francs. These negroes were an impudent lot, not like the British West Indian variety. They were lazy and incompetent. We had had plenty of sugar on board and they had not been stinted. Now that the sugar was running short and they had to eat saccharine, they refused duty and went in a body to the British Consulate. This was after we had arrived in the docks at Bordeaux. I shall never forget the dressing down they got. "Sugar, you black scum! I have not tasted sugar for two years. Get back on board your ship and turn to ..."

They would not. They never went on board again. They were yanked aboard a French transport bound to Colon, Panama, at the point of a bayonet. I know they never got any sugar there. I paid their wages to the Consulate. They got nothing for the passage home.

We finished discharging and lay idle for some time. The ship was for sale. My youthful wireless operator was very good looking with blond hair and blue eyes. He was a great favourite with the French girls. They would come down in force with sufficient English at their command to call out, "We want Blondi, our boy." I went ashore once to send them away but, "No, not you. It's Blondi we want." I blushingly retreated and called Sparks.

"This has to stop. You are giving the ship a bad name."

"But Sir, there is nothing I can do," he replied.

This made me think back furiously to the days spent in Colon and around the Canal. The boy was right, it was not his fault. Finally I received orders that the ship had been sold to Spanish buyers and I was instructed to take her across the Bay of Biscay to Bilbao.

Arriving there I found there was no money to pay us off and cover our fares back to Vancouver. One good thing that the first captain had done—the articles read that we were to be paid off in Vancouver. I would not give the ship up. Don Menchaco, the Spanish buyer, wanted the ship badly. Finally he arranged for me to take my officers to a hotel and keep a watchman on board whilst the Spaniards

made alterations. The vessel was placed in dry dock and the tail shaft was drawn and replaced. It was the original tail shaft after 52 years of service. The SALVOR, Ex-DANUBE, had been well-built in Glasgow by John Elder. What builders they were in those days!

I had agreed with all my officers that we would accept an extra month's pay and a certain sum of money over and above for our passage home. In ordinary times we could have gotten home in two weeks but not then as troops were being moved. Time went on and our hotel bill was mounting. At last Don Menchaco came to the rescue and advanced the money. I paid everybody off, closed the articles and handed over the register.

Most of my men worked their way home. I went back to Bordeaux to settle up and then caught the flu. I was laid up for several weeks. Crossing to England I stopped off in Paris for a few days. The aftermath of the peace celebrations were on. What a sight the Champs Elysee was with the captured cannon.

I boarded the channel steamer at Boulogne. How I enjoyed the cold roast beef and foaming British ale. Arriving at Folkstone, I travelled in a Pullman with a Naval officer and his wife and daughter. We parted at Victoria Station. I drove by cab from hotel to hotel but there was no room anywhere. It was getting dusk. If I did not get in somewhere I was going to take the train to Gravesend. I felt sure that I could get in at the Clarendon, but just as I reached the Russell Hotel somebody was leaving and I got a small room. This was on a Thursday evening.

After dinner I went into the lounge for coffee—no sugar—we were all on rations. However, I had thought of this. There had been plenty of sugar in Spain so I had two kilos of loaf sugar in one of my bags in my room. Each lump was tastily done up in tissue paper. Getting several lumps, I returned to the lounge and selected a place near some very good looking girls. I sat down to smoke and dropped the lumps of sugar in my coffee. It was too much for them. "Oh please, please, do give us a lump of sugar." It takes an old sailor for finding a way to an introduction. (I took good care to keep away from the old dowagers.)

The next day was spent in visiting shipping offices to book a passage. I did not care which way I went, east or west. There were bonuses being offered in the papers for any sort of passage—in tankers or tramps.

There was no chance of getting a passage for six months. I could not afford to wait. Looking through the papers I saw that the transport MANXMAN was now in Cardiff bunkering. She was bound for Newport News, Virginia. I wired Captain Brooks explaining my plight. He replied at once that I should come along and get my passport visaed.

The passport office was in St. James Park and there were two long queues. At last I got to the little window and handed my passport across, only to wait. After a considerable time my name was called and I was told I would have to get a letter from the Canadian High Commissioner . That made me irate. "Why don't you put notices up to that effect?" I asked.

Jumping into a taxi, off I went. I got the letter and back I came just as they were going to close. This was Saturday. An argument ensued when they told me to return on Monday. Not on your life. I wanted my passport back. They were not going to let me have it but I made such a racket, and afterall, it was mine, issued to me by the Canadian Government. They gave it to me telling me I would never get over. "I am a sailor," I told them.

I took the train to Cardiff. Captain Brooks of the MANXMAN signed me on as fourth officer. It cost me nothing for my passage but the price of a small photo which had to be taken with a board and a number. But I was the Captain's guest all the way over.[4]

To my astonishment who should I find on board but the young wireless operator from the SALVOR. He had been sent down to her by the Marconi Company. The MANXMAN had previously been the CUFIC, a White Star cargo and cattle steamer. She was now getting on in years and all through the War had been

S. S. MANXMAN in 1919

[4] *"Whilst in Cardiff I came across the old SALVOR, renamed the NERVION. She had just arrived with a cargo of ore."* ed. note. A newspaper column from the *Vancouver Sun*, entitled "Over the Foreyard", by Ronald Kenvyn, dated January 30, 1937, states that Captain L.R.W. Beavis "was the last Canadian master of the SALVOR. She sailed from Ocean Falls in September, 1918, with a cargo of paper for San Francisco. There she had damage repairs and loaded a general cargo for New Zealand. Her next move was to Bordeaux, France."

Captain Beavis writes to the newspaper column, " *'She was then sold to Spanish owners, Menchaco & Co., and I delivered her at Bilbao, Spain, in July, 1919. Her name was changed to NERVION, which is the name of the river at Bilbao. She was put in the iron ore trade, a very exacting run and suicidal for an old vessel. She was built and engined by J. Elder & Co. of Glasgow in 1869, so was more than fifty years old when I delivered her to her new owners.' "* Responding to some stories told in previous articles of the same newspaper column, Beavis writes: " *'...I did not know that she ever carried a cargo of tea through the Suez Canal, but I do know she was one of the steamers that led the procession through that waterway at its opening. She also had the distinction of bringing Livingstone's bones home from Africa. She had had so many captains that there was hardly room for my name on the register. Some of the names were Hill, McCoskrie, John McLeod and Locke.' "*

carrying horses and mules. They had recently done away with all her temporary fittings and this left the decks exposed when they were already terribly thin from corrosion by the years. She was going to load a dead weight cargo of coals for the Italian Government. Winter was looming up and I strongly advised my young wireless operator of late that if he valued his life and could possibly manage it, he should get discharged. I did not consider the ship seaworthy. My young friend managed to get paid off in Newport News and years after came to see me. He thanked me for the advice. The MANXMAN had loaded a heavy cargo early that October for Italian ports and foundered in the North Atlantic off the Western Islands during very bad weather. Only a few Arab firemen were saved. Captain Brooks, all his officers, and the white crew perished.

We arrived in Newport News on Labor Day, 1919, and from there I went to New York. There it only took me ten minutes to get my passport visaed at the British Embassy. What a difference this was to the red tape and inefficiency in London.

Taking the train for Seattle, I stopped off for a day in Chicago to have a look around. I remember having dinner at a reputedly "high class" restaurant where there was a stage with a runway that extended between the diners' tables. Here a lot of nearly naked girls came dancing and prancing along almost touching you while you were eating. This was not at all conducive to enjoying your dinner, the smell of them was enough for me.

I was glad to renew my journey and it was still better when I got to Seattle and secured a passage on board the night boat for Vancouver. This was the PRINCESS CHARLOTTE under Captain Griffin. I had supper with him when he came down from the bridge and while yarning, heard all the home news.

The next night I was on my way north to Prince Rupert where I had left my wife and daughter. British Columbia certainly looked beautiful to me.

MANXMAN on Labor Day, 1919

"There was no chance of getting a passage for six months. I could not afford to wait. Looking through the papers I saw that the transport MANXMAN was now in Cardiff bunkering. She was bound for Newport News, Virginia.

"... My young friend managed to get paid off in Newport News and years later came to see me. He thanked me for the advice. The MANXMAN had loaded a heavy cargo early that October for Italian ports and foundered in the North Atlantic off the Western Islands during very bad weather. Only a few Arab firemen were saved. Captain Brooks, all his officers and the white crew perished."

CHAPTER XIX

INTERLUDE

I was not long at home before I had the opportunity to bring a small vessel from New Zealand to 'Frisco. We sold our home because my wife wanted to go to England to see her Mother who was getting on in years. The three of us travelled together to Vancouver in the PRINCE RUPERT. After seeing my loved ones off on the train, I waited for the S.S. MAKURA for a passage to New Zealand that arrived a few days later. Captain Philips had been relieved of his command, occuring this way:

The Captain had taken a short cut through prohibited waters. John Thomas Rolls, captain of the NIAGARA, had followed the same course but, the wiley Rolls was profuse in his apologies to the naval authorities and got off with only a caution. Not so, my friend Philips who was not as diplomatic. Being bluff, he consigned these naval authorities to a place where it never snows. He was relieved of his command as a result but immediately landed a shore job with the company.

Captain Crawford took Philip's place and was now in command. The ship was very crowded. At dinner I was at a small table for four (a stag party) and at an adjoining table there happened to be an Australian and his wife, both young but full of their importance. They were not popular. One night we smuggled an alarm clock into the dining saloon. Arriving a little before the others, we made it fast to the Australian's chair. Shortly after they arrived and whilst the soup was on, off

went the alarm. They were quite indignant—nobody knew who had done it. However, suspicion was pointed at our table. Most of the time our table was brim full of mirth and fun.

The ladies at the adjoining tables wanted to know our jokes. Some of these were impossible to reveal to them.

After leaving Suva we ran into rather dirty weather. One night going into dinner I bet that I could clear the dining saloon. The ship was lurching and rolling a bit. The soup was on and suddenly I appeared to be ill. Dashing out with my napkin to my mouth, I made my way to the deck. At that all the passengers that were left said it must be terribly rough if the Old Sea Captain was sick. Hurriedly, they all left the saloon. I was back in a hand's turn. Captain Crawford shook his fist at me; the saloon was nearly deserted. I won my bet and heartily enjoyed my dinner.

On the way south we had a fancy dress ball. One evidently wealthy lady had brought a most elaborate gown for the occasion. She won the first prize. This was hardly fair. One young woman had made a wonderful costume on board with pineapples for a covering. Some ladies came to my cabin and asked that I make up like Aunt Jemima. No! I would not. But with coaxing and numerous whisky sodas they had their way. They blacked my face, dolled me up in an old chequered dressing gown and placed carpet slippers on my feet. They handed me a frying pan with some awesome flap jacks that they had persuaded the cook to make. You did not go to your own table that evening but parked at anyone's. I won a prize

Suva

but what a time I had to get the black off my face. They had not greased me.

Arriving in Auckland I was met by friends whom I stayed with while there. Then I went on by train to Wellington. Here I had to wait for the vessel I was to take. One afternoon I went by motorcar to Featherstone over the Rimatakis. It rained and blew all the trip and when nearing the summit we met another car coming down . They strongly advised us to furl our hood. We did this but of course we were by then drenched. It was December 1919.

On my return in daylight I had a good look at the precipice. Never would I have made the journey had I known.

I had contracted for a lump sum to take a small vessel to San Francisco via the Tonga Group where I would pick up copra.[1] It was a most disastrous venture for me. The cargo was not ready and I wasted many weeks amongst the islands of the Tonga Group. When I arrived in San Francisco I was much out of pocket. Never again would you get me into a game of that sort.

[1] ed. note. Copra is dried coconut meat, a source of coconut oil.
[2] ed. note. Captain Cousins was close in age to Beavis, having been born in Maine in 1862. He received his first command in 1892 and eventually became master of first-class liners like the QUEEN, GOVERNOR, CONGRESS, and the RUTH ALEXANDER, as well as the PRESIDENT. His resourcefulness saved many lives aboard the QUEEN in 1904 and the CONGRESS in 1916. Cousins retired from the sea in 1926 and died in November 1930, at Seattle.
The PRESIDENT was added to the fleet of the Pacific Coast Steamship Co. in 1907, measuring 417' l.o.a., 391.9' between perpendiculars, 48.2' beam, 19.7' depth of hold, and 5,453 tons. She was a single-screw vessel with one funnel, equipped with a 5,000 horsepower triple expansion engine. The PRESIDENT was built by New York Shipbuilding Co. at Camden, New Jersey. She was an excellent passenger liner and an efficient cargo handler. The PRESIDENT and her sister ship GOVERNOR developed a heavy trade in citrus fruits between Southern California and Puget Sound.
[3] ed. note. The E.D. KINGSLEY, later renamed the coastal freighter SOUTHHOLM, was dismantled in 1950 by Union Steamship, operators of the Frank Waterhouse & Co. B.C. coastal freighters. Following the removal of the engines and equipment, the hull was used as a barge (renamed BULK CARRIER NO. 1 and later UNION NO. 1). The E.D. KINGSLEY had been built in 1919 for the Kingsley Navigation Company of Vancouver.

After delivering the vessel I travelled in the old PRESIDENT (Captain N.E. Cousins and his well known bulldog) back to Vancouver. Cousins nearly always took the PRESIDENT inside the Duncan rocks by Cape Flattery.[2]

There was not much doing in the shipping world in Vancouver in 1920. Knowing the manager of the West Vancouver Ferries I became master of the SONRISA. In fact I believe I was recorded as master of three of them, all at one time. These were the DON-CELLA, SONRISA and the NO. 5. I had been about a month or six weeks at this when I was appointed master of the E.D. KINGSLEY, a small coaster of about 1,000 tons. She was trading between Vancouver, Blubber Bay and San Francisco. With my appointment the route was extended to ports south of San Francisco, as far as Panama. This job lasted several months but it was not a paying proposition for the owners. When I returned to Vancouver they decided not to go below San Francisco. So the regular master rejoined the ship.[3]

I had hardly been ashore a day when there was a call for me to rejoin the West Vancouver Ferries as master. I remained with them all through the winter, having the extra boat, making two trips in the morning and two in the evening. It was a pleasant job and one got to know the passengers quite well.

All that winter of 1920 - 1921 it was very foggy but I never missed a trip and was never more than a few minutes late. I had a very likeable chap as mate but he often over imbibed in liquor. Sometimes there would be no mate. Waiting as long as I dared, we would pull out with only the engineer and myself on board. Once clear of the wharf, the engineer would take the wheel and I as master would collect the fares, punching the tickets with an old nail. It was a rather reprehensible thing altogether; one that I would not do in these days of greater traffic.

On one occasion a heavy easterly gale was blowing and most of my passengers were very sea sick. Headed west, we rolled almost as much as in days of old when running our east-

Loading coal in Papeete

ing down. Eastbound, I had to reduce speed. I have never since seen such a sea in the Narrows with an east wind. On my arrival in town, just as I was tying up for the night, I got a phone call from West Vancouver. The SONRISA had stove in her pilot house windows and the captain had been cut about the face. I had to take the run for the rest of the night. I was staying in town at the Patricia Hotel. When I got back to my hotel at midnight, I found my room wrecked. Both windows had blown in.

On one trip during this storm I had only one passenger. On arrival in West Vancouver she told me as she went ashore, "Not for a million dollars would I go again."

"Lady," I said, "if there happened to be that amount at stake you would. I would carry you on board whether you liked it or not."

When the spring came in, after putting in all the dirty weather of the winter, I was relieved by another man that happened to be a rate payer.[4] I was not.

[4] ed. note. One who pays rates or local taxes.

CHAPTER XX

SIBERIAN ADVENTURE

The Hudson's Bay Siberian Venture became my vocation not long after I was relieved from service on the ferries. The year was 1921. I joined the small motor vessel CASCO very deeply laden with supplies when it was leaving Vancouver in June. We were bound for Petropavlosk in Kamchatka. We had two forty-foot tunnel launches on board to be used in the rivers of Kamchatka. Prior to this voyage the Hudson's Bay Company had a representative in the territory gathering information and buying furs. The possibilities of trading loomed largely and the upshot of it was this voyage, this venture. Whoever the company had had in the Far East previously had not done too well and had rather let the company down. Mr. Elphick had been sent out from London to look the situation over and it was through his report that the Hudson's Bay Company decided to enter into the fur trade of Siberia.[1]

At this time the eastern portion of Siberia had broken away from the rest of Russia to form a republic, calling it the "Far Eastern Republic of Siberia." It was separate from the Soviet of Moscow, yet looked to them for support. Neither the United States of America, Canada, or Great Britain had any diplomatic relations with them. Nevertheless, the Hudson's Bay Company was willing to take the risk and it certainly was a considerable one.

They could expect no aid from their government if difficulties arose. No doubt the financial inducements were such, that if things were only reasonably quiet and favourable, the fur trade could be developed and was likely to yield handsome profits. This was due to its neglect during the long years of the Revolution. So it will be seen that in this enterprise this historically grand company was adhering to its traditions. It was a company of adventurers and gallant men.

If only Great Britain had lent a war vessel, a small crusier or even a gunboat, just to display the flag. This would have had a significant effect on the changeable governments, so much so that they would not have dared molest or place difficulties in the way. They undoubtedly did so with the Hudson's Bay officials, and the Company's flag might still be flying over the numerous posts erected in the four years of the Company's operations if the British Navy had had a presence here. All through this the Japanese had several destroyers and a cruiser in these waters. They were never molested and although they were thoroughly detested, in any dealings that the Bolsheviki had with the Japanese they held to their obligation. They dared not have done otherwise.

Before the Hudson's Bay Company came into the field there had been one or two American firms trading. The best known of these

CASCO loading at Vancouver, B. C., in 1921

[1] ed. note. The reader's attention is drawn to a change in writing style in this chapter. Beavis prepared a more scholarly treatise here than previous chapters. It has been left in its original form.

was Hibbard & Swenson. It was Mr. Swenson in one of his trading vessels who rescued the crew of the ill-fated KARLUK marooned on Wrangell Island in desperate straits.[2]

The CASCO was a diminutive twin screw motor vessel only 100 tons and was really much too small for our trading venture. This became evident when a lot of supplies had to be left in Vancouver and afterwards freighted up to Nome. There they had to be picked up by the CASCO which caused tremendous delay, a serious matter when the season was so short. The tunnel launches took up all the spare space on the forward deck reaching right up to the windlass. They had been placed on board with a floating crane. No one ever considered how they were to be taken off. Not one of the CASCO's executives even dreamed that they would have to do it. Fortunately the weather was very fine across the Pacific or I very much doubt if these launches would have arrived.

The Captain of the CASCO was a thick set Swede who had his wife, a rather attractive young woman, with him, as well as their young son. In such a small ship this was not conducive to the best of feeling with the head of the expedition.

During the first year Mr. Elphick was in charge of the expedition. He was accompanied by Mr. Hoogendyk, a Hollander who spoke Russian fluently—his only occupation in this venture. He was christened "Big Pig" by the traders and natives of Kamchatka. (He certainly resembled that animal in many respects.) There was also a younger man by the name of Skuce. Young Skuce showed great ability and was of genuine help to Mr. Elphick. The Hollander was just the opposite. We had shipped two gas engineers (Canadians) for the tunnel launches. Hoogendyk for unexplainable reasons took a violent dislike to both men.

On arriving at Petropavlosk there was a general disturbance amongst the authorities. Eventually, after they had investigated *everything* and had been well greased (and of course numerous taxes had been paid), then

Captain Beavis on motorship Casco

[2] ed. note. In 1912, veteran Siberian trader Olaf Swenson joined with Charles L. Hibbard, forming the Hibbard-Swenson Company of Seattle. In late summer 1913, while whaling and trading in the Arctic, and carrying supplies for the Stefansson expedition and the Herschel Island Post of the Northwest Mounted Police, Swenson and his crew of the BELVEDERE were caught in the ice at the island. Leaving the ship, Swenson and Captain C.T. Peterson *walked* from Herschel Island to Fairbanks, Alaska, crossing the Endicott Range and making one of the greatest forced marches on record in the Far North. The distance was covered in 26 days. They brought to the world news that Stefansson's steamship KARLUK had been trapped in the ice, carried northward and crushed in distant waters.

The next summer, news was broadcast that a number of survivors of the KARLUK had managed to find refuge on the isolated Wrangell Island and had survived the winter. Hearing of their plight, Swenson detoured his summer trading vessel KING & WINGE and saved the entire KARLUK party.

Hibbard retired from the company in 1922 and Swenson formed the Olaf Swenson & Company in Seattle. Swenson was president, treasurer and executive head of a corporation representing Japanese, American and Russian financial interests. In 1923 Olaf Swenson & Co. was said to be the world's largest dealer in costly furs, primarily sable.

the Hudson's Bay Company had the privilege to trade. Whilst all this was progressing, the captain and the crew of the CASCO were wondering how they were going to get the tunnel launches safely into the water. The masts and gear were totally inadequate and there was but little to be had from the shore. Here, again, the Company had to come to the rescue by purchasing spars and blocks which should have been supplied by the ship. Once the launches were in the water that Swede captain gave a sigh of relief and got gloriously drunk.

Petropavlosk, the metropolis of Kamchatka, is situated on Avacha Bay, a magnificent landlocked harbour surrounded by volcanoes snow-clad all year round. The town is on a hillside of the inner harbour and such as there is, is built on terraces. In 1854, during the Crimean War, a combined fleet of British and French, consisting of six vessels, made an unsuccessful attempt to capture the town. This was made as a frontal attack, up an almost precipitate hill. It failed. Later they realized their mistake and easily took the town from the rear.

The British portion of the defeated fleet, consisting of the PRESIDENT, PIQUE and VIRAGO, a paddlewheel steamer, returned to Esquimalt in August of that year. The total loss in the attack was 55 officers and men killed and 134 wounded, six of whom afterwards died. It was a rather deplorable incident in history as the place was quickly taken under the right plan. I believe the French admiral committed suicide a short while later, after they realized the futility of the frontal attack.

During the summer of 1921 I had been appointed nautical adviser to the expedition and also pilot for Siberian and British Columbian waters. I was also chief transportation officer for the Okhotsk Sea. This was quite a galaxy of appointments.

The Hudson's Bay Company was now using Petropavlosk as a base, establishing posts on both east and west coasts of Kamchatka. The coastline at Bolsheresk was low, stretching back for 50 miles to the mountains. On all of the west coast of Kamchatka a heavy surf prevailed most of the time; it was difficult and often dangerous to land. The Japanese were well established in the fishing business and one met hundreds of small Japanese schooners, mostly possessing auxiliary power. These vessels anchored every few miles along the coast from the Pass to abreast of Tigel. Most of the places where they anchored were mere salteries but there were some modern canneries, too. During our stay on this coast with the CASCO we caught a great number of cod and sole. The salmon as I found them were mostly the humpback and dog variety.

The weather on the coast was generally fair during May, June and July with occasional fierce winds. Often, however, there was a heavy swell during these months. After August one could expect anything in the nature of strong gales.

The Hudson's Bay Company post at Tigel was the farthest reached in 1921. Fort Tigel

Hudson's Bay Post, Port Ayan, Okhotsk Sea, 1922

was about 30 miles up the river of the same name. It had a population of about 300 natives and Russians. The settlement at the mouth of the river was very small and practically deserted during the winter. It was possible at spring tides for small vessels of light draft to go into the river and anchor off the settlement. We did this with the CASCO but the current on the ebb tide was very strong and it required very good ground tackle. The CASCO went ashore on leaving and narrowly escaped serious damage. There was a very good native pilot available there; it was due to neglect in obtaining him that the CASCO grounded. The only supplies we could secure at this settlement were fish and fresh water.

In 1922 the Hudson's Bay Company visited the northern shores of the Okhotsk Sea with a chartered Japanese vessel. The voyage was made difficult by ice and other obstructions. American trader Swenson had the MAZATLAN on this coast at the same time and did fairly well; but as I have said, he possessed the personality to win and hold the friendship of the natives. All trading was done from the ships and at a considerable distance from the villages. Nearly all the settlements were bar-bound, and the bars were hard to cross if there was a swell on.

At Ayan, on the southwest side of the Okhotsk Sea, Swenson and the Hudson's Bay Company established posts. This settlement had quite a nice little harbour, sheltered from everything but southerly winds. At one time during our stay there were no fewer than five steamers anchored in the bay. This fleet included the Hudson's Bay craft, Swenson's vessels and two Japanese vessels.

A trail entered Ayan from Yakutsk, and over this for centuries, pack trains of ponies and reindeer have brought down furs to trade for supplies. There were only a few inhabitants at this settlement, but at Okhotsk, some 240 miles east-north-east of Ayan was a community numbering several hundred, mostly Tunguses. During the summer of 1922 about 25 American miners went into the country from here and took up claims a few miles up the river. Owing however to the Bolsheveki, they had to pull out. There were indications of gold all along this coast, and nearly all natives, both men and women, carried their little pokes of gold dust. It would not surprise me to see Okhotsk a veritable second Klondike.

The principal fur trade at this point was squirrel. The sea of Okhotsk was first reached by the Cossacks in 1639 and since then has been open to hardy traders. By the year 1715, the post road from Moscow was a well-beaten track sharply defined by the bones of men and animals who had perished while trying to conquer its reaches. Away back in 1648 Deshnian had left Kolyma River on the Arctic with his frail craft tied together with reindeer thongs. He was the first man to double the northeast extremity of Asia and reach the Anadyr River. Later Captain Cook, at the end of August 1778, was off Cape North and, returning south, was the third to double it. Behring perished with most of his crew at the Komandorski Islands in 1741 and could not be considered to have doubled it. Cook spoke highly of Behring's charts, saying he had delineated the coast very well and fixed the latitude and longitude points better than could be expected considering his navigational methods. The Komandorski Islands are about 100 miles east of the Kamchatkan coast and are very bleak and barren. Some 600 natives, mostly half-breeds, live there. A considerable number of fox are on the islands, and reindeer have now been established.

Since the Bolshevik Revolution the natives have suffered severely, at times nearly dying of starvation. They had a school and a teacher but the pay was very small. While we were in Petropavlosk the young lady who had been teaching there returned to her homeland on a Japanese steamer, having thrown up her job. She was an attractive young woman wearing dainty patent leather pumps and well-cut riding breeches.

In 1922 the Vladivostok government was leasing out the fur trade to the highest bidder.

Whilst in Petropavlosk we often visited the

THERMOPYLAE

tiny graveyard at the back of the town where there were memorials to the fallen British, French and Russian officers and sailors. In the winter of 1921 the Bolsheveki broke the cross over the graves of the British. I found the brass tablet and brought it back to Vancouver. There was an interesting inscription on the plate stating that it had been erected by the H.M.S. EGERIA in 1878. That name alone made the Vancouver sector of spectators feel at home. The next year the British Admiralty replaced the old cross with a new one made of British Columbia fir and the plate was reattached. This was unveiled June 4 of that year after a religious ceremony held at the Russian church. It was attended by the Russian Governor and the Hudson's Bay officials. Another momento was also discovered, this time down on the wharf. Underneath the planks, on a piece of board nailed up, was the name "THERMOPYLAE, 1876." This was the famous clipper that put into Hong Kong on May 13, 1876, bound from Sydney to Petropavlosk where she refitted and proceeded on course. So the Russian Navy had had their coal brought to them by a very celebrated ship.

The Russian Governor, Bieritch by name, later resigned his office and returned to Vladivostok; but still later the Soviet secured power there, too, and he was killed. He was a very unassuming man and a civilian. I had the pleasure of meeting him, his wife and daughter. The latter was a very charming young lady who spoke English with ease. What the fate of this girl and her mother has been I do not know. One son stayed in Petropavlosk after his father left, publishing the newspaper there. He was in bad odor with his parents because he insisted on paying

Petropavlosk with Mount Avacha in the distance

attention to a beautiful but poor girl who was also said to be a native Kamchatkan. She may have been, in the sense that she was born in Petropavlosk but her parents were both Russians and not natives. Before I left Petropavlosk I attended their wedding. It was quite a lengthy affair but fascinating. The bride and groom drove away in the only carriage, or more properly speaking, cart, in the town. On several subsequent occasions I met them again, and they appeared devoted to one another. They were little more than children and I trust they have not suffered harm from the Bolsheviki.

The chief of police, a big, good-natured man, did not succeed in getting away when the Reds took control. After suffering unbelievable indignities, he was finally executed.

During my stay in Petropavlosk, I made several trips up the Avacha River for a distance of 20 miles. In some of its reaches it reminded me very much of the Thames above Reading. It was very beautiful in the fall of the year with the turning of the birch leaves. As one ascends the river, the current becomes stronger and the bends more frequent and pronounced. But it was not nearly as bad as our Dutch manager had described it to me. He said it was utterly terrible and almost impossible for a stranger to navigate. My first trip was made by night. I got within a half mile of the village to which we were bound when we ran aground and had to wait until daylight. Afterwards I experienced no trouble, so evidently it had been portrayed wrongly. There was quite a lot of wild hay growing along the shores and some of the people from Petropavlosk were cutting it.

The White Guard was in power there, having turned the Reds out in November of 1921. They were a remnant of Semenoff's Army who were out for loot. However, they did not last long; later the remainder of them sought refuge in Manila, seeking a home. On one occasion they were anxious to secure a launch to go on a punitive expedition up the coast. Three of the military turned me out one morning and demanded one of the Hudson's

Bay Company vessels. I refused and immediately had the boats disabled.

Later in the day they came again. As I still refused, they informed me I would be tried by court martial, all of my salary would be confiscated and I would be deported. I was only awaiting to go away so this did not worry me. Finally they left me alone. They commandeered our gas engineer to make a launch serviceable. That launch belonged to another trader called Wittenberg.

The Russian people in Petropavlosk were most hospitable and very polite. One had to be removing one's hat nearly all the time. It made me think of a semaphore hat.

When we were there the various government offices were decorated with portraits of the late Czar and Czarina, although the year before Lenin and Trotzky had graced the walls and are probably back again now [1938]. If Petropavlosk belonged to Canada or any other progressive country, it would long since have been a city of importance. Its harbour is generally clear of ice by April 25th and could be kept open the year round with ice breakers.

The possibilities of Siberia are immense. The potential of the south with regard to grain production is enormous, the future of fisheries and mineral development is tremendous. Japan has covetous eyes on Kamchatka and already practically controls the fisheries on the Okhotsk Sea and the Kamchatka coast. They hold the Kuril Islands which come within ten miles of the southern extremity of the peninsulas of Kamchatka and Sakhalin in the Okhotsk Sea. The Japanese port of Hakodate is but 1100 miles from Petropavlosk.

After leaving Avacha Bay and proceeding up the east coast, there were no safe harbours of any size until Anadyr. There were numerous bays and indentations all the way, but the coast was very rocky and mountainous. The principal place before reaching Anadyr was Ust Kamchatka at the mouth of the river of the same name. Here there were several canneries, but the bar to the river was very dangerous and every year there was loss of life in crossing it.

Anadyr was a small settlement on the river of that name. It was the last Russian wireless station. There was one each at Petropavlosk and Naiakhan at the far north end of the Okhotsk Sea, but the one at Okhotsk had been destroyed by the Bolsheviki. The conditions at Anadyr were bad; it was a bleak and barren place. It was here in 1921 that we met a Canadian lady named Miss Kelly. She and her relatives were living on a sternwheeler that they had built. They intended to use it in prospecting for gold when conditions were more favourable. Whilst we were there they were marking time at that god-forsaken place. The Hudson's Bay Company had a post there as did the Swenson interests.

Anniversary celebration of the Bolshevik Revolution Photo taken in 1920.

From Anadyr away north to the Behring Strait, there were a few settlements of Chuchis or Eskimo. Their villages were nearly always on headlands or capes. This was because the ice always clears away earlier from promontories than from indentations, and the inhabitants were therefore able to hunt walrus or fish earlier when they were residing in the out-thrust points. One of the best harbours in this section was Providence Bay. There was a safe anchorage for a vessel as large as the QUEEN MARY. Emma Harbour, an inner harbour of Providence Bay, was the home of an old settler named Billy Thompson. He had a store and a very small power schooner in which he freighted his supplies from Nome, Alaska. He was quite a character and called himself a Scotch-Russian. His father was a Scot, and his mother—well, a native.

All this coast was very mountainous and barren. The summer is short. At East Cape on Behring Strait there were three settlements. Mud Bay was on the southeast side, Whalen on the northwest, and there was a small village on the cliffs between them. There was a trader there named Charlie Carpendale, who I believe, originally came from Australia. He, too, was a character. One of his little girls had been taken away by the explorer Roald Amundsen to be educated. Now Amundsen has joined Scott, although their bones lie far apart.[3] (The little girl has grown up and returned to the frozen north.)

I am also reminded that when we were at South Head with the CASCO in 1921, two little Eskimo girls came off to see us. One of them was the true Eskimo type—flat face,

Japanese cannery not belonging to the Bolsheviks

black hair, small eyes and high cheeks. The other was a golden-haired, blue-eyed miss with a brown, intelligent and pretty face. Some of her forebears must have been of the Viking strain.

From East Cape to Kolyma River on the Arctic there were a few scattered villages. The most important of these was Serdjekamen and North Cape, but ice has always to be contended with in these waters. In 1922, a particularly bad season, no one passed through. One vessel was crushed and lost before it reached Serdjekamen.

In 1922 the venture was carried out by the BAYCHIMO, one of the Hudson's Bay Company's steamers. They also chartered a Japanese steamer, the KOYO MARU. Use was likewise made of the LADY KINDERSLY and an American power schooner, the RUBY. In 1922 the Company was exploiting in a big way. The BAYCHIMO came out to Vancouver from England and I met her at William Head. I did all of the British Columbia piloting besides attending to her loading and that of the RUBY. The Japanese steamer KOYO MARU joined the expedition at Petropavlosk and I took charge of her there, operating the Okhotsk Sea. She was an old dilapidated vessel chartered for the Company by the Russian manager named Marchinko. He apparently had been well-bribed by the Japanese; the vessel was not fit to encounter ice and was also very slow. I managed to do what was allotted, although at times it looked pretty

[3] ed note. Roald Amundsen was a Norwegian explorer who traversed the Northwest Passage in 1906 and determined the position of the magnetic North Pole; he reached the South Pole in 1911; Lincoln Ellsworth and Amundsen reached latitude 87 degrees 44 minutes N in two amphibious phases in 1925. Amundsen died in 1928 attempting to rescue the Italian explorer Nobile whose airship crashed in the Arctic. Robert Falcon Scott was an English Antarctic explorer born in 1868 who reached the South pole in 1912.

precarious. Marchinko was an absolute drunkard and none too honest. Hoogendyk was by now in charge of the expedition and had great faith in Marchinko. Birds of a feather?

Some 700 tons of freight that had not been landed was brought back to Vancouver, chiefly due to mismanagement. This after everything had been put up in parcels for the different ports. Hoogendyk would break into these parcels and disseminate them. The result was a fearful muddle.

On arrival back in Vancouver, this freight was discharged and had to be put in a bonded warehouse. The BAYCHIMO left for Eureka to load lumber for England. The management returned to England and I had to look after the freight that was left. This took several weeks. Much of it had to be destroyed, burning it in incinerators. Whilst this freight was at Evan's Coleman docks in Vancouver, I always had a large Canadian cheese on tap (ripened on the voyage) and a case of Japanese beer. This beer was far and ahead of the local stuff and was much appreciated.

In the following year of 1923 we had the BAYCHIMO once again but with another master. We also had the American power schooner RUBY. I was appointed to the RUBY for the Okhotsk sea district. We did practically all we set out to do, but the conditions were worsening all the time. The Soviet had ousted the White Guard and the taxes were heavier. Many more obstacles were put in the way. For instance, the Bolsheviki compelled us by force to take the RUBY to Gizika and Naiakapan at the far north end of the Okhotsk Sea. There we picked up their partisan army and wounded soldiers. We also transported some prisoners and the loot of their raid. The latter consisted of the debris of Boscaroff's army and all the fur the latter had collected during the previous winter.

Boscaroff was quite a young man, only 28, who had been made Governor of Gizika in May of 1922 by the White Guard. He had formerly served as an officer in the Russian volunteer fleet. He was killed by the Bolsheviks at Haiakapan on April 10, 1923, whilst fighting desperately to defend his post. His body was stripped and thrown into the sea after the head had been cut off. Later the body washed ashore and was again thrown into the sea. Once again it returned to land. This time they fed it to the dogs. This was their way of demonstrating hatred for an opponent who faced them bravely. We had some of his private letters and some photos of him that he had left for his wife on board the RUBY. Also in a sack stowed down below amongst the fur was his head which the soldiers were keeping as evidence that they had destroyed him. Whilst at Gizika I met his wife and young child, a girl of six. Madame Boscaroff was a tall, handsome woman who bore up with wonderful courage under her troubles. I did not tell her we had her dead husband's head in a sack on board our schooner bound for Petropavlosk.

After leaving Gizika we called at all of the ports on the west side of Kamchatka that had been visited going north. We were always crowded for if we dropped off any passengers there was a fresh lot to take their places. They slept anywhere, on deck, under and on top of the cabin tables and in the boats. Numberless dogs accompanied them and bunked in any open space.

It was a relief when we got to Petropavlosk and got rid of our passengers and their loot, not to mention the head. The sailors regarded it with awe and fear, believing it to be material bad luck, a Jonah, and a sure sign of misfortune. They were very loath to go below while the head was on board.

Later in the year we were returning from our second trip from Okhotsk and while passing through Lopatka Pass we noticed the volcanoes on the Kuril Islands erupting. While in Petropavlosk we felt the tremors of an earthquake which was coincident with the great tragedy in Tokyo and Yokahama.[4]

---

[4] ed. note. The centers of Tokyo and Yokohama were destroyed by this earthquake in 1923, leaving 120,000 dead.

We were about to leave for Vancouver when the Japanese steamer KOBE MARU was wrecked on Saghalien as a result of the earthquake. The RUBY was diverted to Oust Kamchatka with some freight that should have gone by the wrecked steamer.

On proceeding into the Gulf of Kamchatka, Mount Kluchi was erupting. It was a grand sight at night but not very comforting to the people thereabouts. While there we had a very hard blow from the northeast with a low barometer. We crossed the gulf for shelter to an anchorage that H.M.S. ALGERINE had used in former years. Here we held on for two days with a lot of passengers, women and children, that we were unable to land. We lost two koomgasses (sampans) with freight, one included the school outfit for the place. We watched the koomgasses drift away in the storm out into the Behring Sea. We were helpless to even attempt to recover them. We had all we could do to keep ourselves from following their example. As it was we were dragging slowly seaward. As the storm increased we double-reefed the foresail for we knew that if we ever dragged off the bank, away we would go. We had only enough fuel for the engine to last a couple of days. It was fortunate for us to have as passengers ten of the miners who had gone prospecting for gold around Okhotsk in 1922. Most of these men were sailors, husky men of brawn and willing helpers during the storm. Provisions were also low and we carried a number of shore officials of the Company as well as numerous passengers.

After two days the storm blew out and the sea moderated. We were then able to return to the mouth of the river and land our passengers and the remaining freight. The captain of the RUBY had gotten himself into a rather nasty mix-up with the authorities ashore and was denied his clearance. He would have been arrested had he not lifted anchor and made sail in a desperate hurry with an armed launch in pursuit. We soon out-distanced our pursuer. On arrival at Dutch Harbour the captain managed to get a protem for Seattle where we arrived late in October.

The following year, 1924, the Company sent the BAYCHIMO in again but such were the conditions in Kamchatka that it was not thought advisable to risk the BAYCHIMO and she remained in Japanese waters. So ended the Kamchatka venture. Personally, I think if Mr. Elphick's health had not broken down and he had been able to remain in charge that, with a little backing from the British government, the Hudson's Bay Company might have solved all its difficulties. Quien sabe..

Siberia always calls me. It is a wonderful land and has a great future, but it is no place for the tenderfoot. The virile and the strong thrive; there's a land for you, one to grow up with. And yet I once met a man wearing dancing pumps and puttees,[5] and another wearing spats. Both men were found within the Arctic circle. Everything else had gone but these; drink and the devil had done for the rest.

I can take Siberia year in and year out, the climate is much the same as Canada. I have experienced more extreme cold at Edmonton than has ever been recorded at Yakutz, but the Siberians claim that Yakutz is the coldest city in the world.

Petropavlosk, in the future, will probably be the home post of many small traders. The same can be said of Vladivostok. I heard a speech at the Hudson's Bay Company farewell dinner to the Siberian adventure when it was said, "We must eliminate the small trader." Well, it will take some doing. As the old Scotch proverb has it, "a weel-bred dog goes oot when he sees them preparing to kick him oot."

[5] ed. note. A cloth gaitor wrapped spirally from ankle to knee or a leather legging.

(upper) Petropavlosk in 1922 with the BAYCHIMO and
KOYO MARU

(lower, left to right) Mr. and Mrs. Wittenberg, Mr. Bar-
ker of the H.B.C., Captain Beavis, Captain Edmonds
of the BAYCHIMO, and Mr. Hoogendyk
*"This was the first moving camera to be seen in
Petropavlosk."*

193

E. D. KINGSLEY fire in the hold, at Astoria, Oregon.

CHAPTER XXI

COASTING

Whilst I was on the Siberian venture, my wife and daughter had returned to Vancouver from England. I had taken a furnished cottage out at Thorley Park, Jericho, and it was there that they joined me.

Shortly after the Hudson's Bay Company ceased command of its operations in Siberia, I received command of a small coaster, the E.D. KINGSLEY. We were trading between Vancouver and up-coast ports to San Francisco. This was the steamer I had previously commanded in 1920. Kingsley Navigation Company was a subsidiary company of Pacific Lime Company which had extensive lime kilns and quarries at Blubber Bay, Texada Island, British Columbia. They were now acquiring another steamer in the east called the ROCHELIE and becoming ambitious. R.F. Mather was the general manager; he later became vice president of both companies. He was most efficient and very popular in the shipping world of Vancouver. His death, which occurred some years later after my association with him, was greatly deplored. It left a gap in the company's affairs that they had difficulties filling.

Altogether, I had a very pleasant run. We journeyed as far south as San Pedro and San Diego. This in every twenty days kept one on the hop continuously. Very little time did we have in home port.

Quite a number of courtesy passengers were carried 'twixt ports. One time we had James Butterfield, columnist of the *Vancouver Province* whom we carried as far as San Francisco. At other times prominent shipping men were passengers, such as the Wallaces.[1] Mostly they were a thirsty crowd.

Once on a southbound passage, fire was discovered when we were some 70 miles south of the Columbia River Lightship. As far as we could locate it, it was in the Number 2 hold amongst shingles. As it was serious I immediately headed back for Astoria, only reaching there just in time. A dense fog had shut in around us. There, with all the firefighting force of the port enlisted, it was nearly 18 hours before we finally had the fire under control. The KINGSLEY was partially loaded with lime and if water had gotten to the lime, it would have been all up with us. She would have been a total loss; perhaps we would have been so, too.

This was one time when the underwriters were not appreciative of the good work of the crew. The only ones recognized were the longshoremen and the firefighting forces who all received new outfits. I rather think the Company would have liked her to have been a total loss. They probably did not put our services in too rosy a light. Yet, there was one exception, and I greatly appreciated this. Arriving in San Francisco after the fire (it was during prohibition) a special messenger came down to the ship from the Collector of the Port with a note to me and four bottles of Old Parr scotch whisky—the compliments of

---

[1] ed. note. These were the Wallaces of the Wallace Shipyard, Inc., in Vancouver whose yard had built the JANET CARRUTHERS and four sister ships. See Chapter 17.

the Collector and an intimation that he knew they had drunk me dry in Astoria. They had! Since then I have always had a soft spot in my heart for that Collector and also Old Parr.

In San Francisco we were continually shifting docks even for as little as 25 tons of freight. Such was competition. In the good old days this would have been an unheard of procedure, to go barging around for cargo. Then, too, latterly often the dry fruits would come right to the ship's side in a string of lorries with a motor lorry ahead and the driver half asleep. They had come all the way from Fresno County to Alameda, thus saving handling. About this time the C.G.M. [Canadian Government Merchant Marine] was running in vicious opposition to us. The Government was doing its best to do away with legitimate shipping. They generally left the same day but some six to ten hours earlier than we did. At that we nearly always passed them off Mendocino. We would be driving north in a perfect deluge of spray, whilst they were generally light and not so speedy.

As the years passed, more aids to navigation were established and it was possible to round Flattery in a dense fog in perfect safety and proceed up the Strait of Juan de Fuca by wireless bearings. What a difference to the years of long ago when I had passed in with the little TITANIA. I had always hoped to end my sea career without a stranding, but it was not to be.

I was leaving Blubber Bay one day in late summer and crossing to Powell River in a dense fog, one of the thickest on the Coast, accentuated by forest fires. We loaded paper

at Powell River with orders to call at Woodfibre, Howe Sound, for more cargo. The fog was as thick as ever. I managed to reach Woodfibre in safety, navigating entirely by echo.[2] There I picked up more cargo and left at 3:00 p.m. The fog had cleared as it often does high up Howe Sound. After passing Anvil Island it again shut down, a regular blanket of smoke and fog. Had I ignored all Bureau of Transportation Regulations and kept on full speed I might have been all right. But I reduced speed, and passing Bowyer Island a safe distance by echo, I was set inside the White Cliff Point. Even though I was allowing three-quarter's point for it, suddenly we saw the rocks on our starboard bow. Ramming the ship full speed astern with a desperate hope that she might not touch them, suddenly the trees loomed out of the fog ahead. Now she was barely moving—would she do it—*no*—she just touched and rested her forefoot on the beach. The tide was falling and realizing it was no good, I tried to avoid tearing the ship off and doing damage. I stopped the engines. All this time I had been receiving frantic messages from the Traffic Manager to "Hurry, hurry, make all haste." And you could not see ten feet in front of you.

I wirelessed my plight, saying I did not need assistance. The General Manager was away, however, and those left in charge completely lost their heads. A salvage outfit came

E. D. KINGSLEY

[2] ed. note. The echo system was a method frequently employed by Canadians and Americans on Puget Sound and through the islands and inlets near Vancouver Island. The captain of the ship sounds his whistle and counts the seconds that lapse before receiving the echo of that whistle. In this manner he may calculate the number of miles or feet his vessel is from land. In these waters where islands are numerous and heavy fogs are not uncommon, the echo system became the standard of navigation for pilots and skippers of the inland boats. It was a case that called for experience and technical skill in days predating radar devices.

Powell River, B. C.

Rod LeMay

up with Commander B.L. Johnson, Lloyds Agent. They would never have found me but for my very explicit sailing directions. (This was what Commander Johnson told me, anyway.) At that, they, too, got ashore.

My ship came off with the next tide while just warming the engines and turning them slowly over astern. We never even cracked the cement in the forepeak, never made a particle of water. Yet, I had been stranded. I was relieved of my command and perforce had to go as chief officer.

Not many months after, I noticed a nice cottage under construction at Blubber Bay—cumshaw from my stranding.[3] Such is life—up today, down tomorrow.

Later, the E.D. KINGSLEY was at the oil dock in Vancouver and the captain felt he was ill. No one believed that he was but he would not take her away from the dock. The Company would not give me command but sent Captain Tait, instead. He was a recent port warden who had been suspended by Ottawa. He did not arrive in time and we were ordered to leave the oil dock. No master. Over the phone I was ordered by the Manager to move the ship across the harbour to another berth. "Am I to have command?" I asked.

"No," was the firm reply.

"Then not on your life," I said. "If I'm not thought capable of taking her to sea, I'm not fit to move her in a crowded harbour. She can stay where she is for a thousand years for aught I care."

The Manager never forgave me but I still had some pride. The KINGSLEY stayed at the dock until Tait joined. He did not know the coast and asked me to do the piloting. This I did to help him; I liked poor Tait. He was his own enemy.

On a Christmas morning in 1928, we left Port Alice on Quatsino Sound bound for Vancouver. It was a lovely morning, a beautiful day sparkling with frost. Little did I think I was looking my last on Entrance Island. There had been vague rumours and I imagine Captain Uldall knew all about it. He had been posing as a pilot for British Columbian waters but as a matter of fact, only once had he piloted a steamer, of the McCormick Line. He had never been north to Prince Rupert. When we arrived we were told that the ship had been sold and we were all finished.

I was a qualified pilot and as such had been recognized by Lloyd's for the Hudson's Bay Company; only recently had the Government of Canada taken over the pilotage. I could have forced them to take me in but advancing years and knowing my limitations made me feel a distaste for boarding light steamers, swinging and swaying on a rope pilot ladder some thirty to forty feet from the water to the deck and often as not no spar would be lashed across it to keep it from taking a round turn out of itself. I decided—no pilotage career for me. So the end of my active sea career had arrived; I was 64 years old.

[3] ed. note. "Cumshaw" is a term used in Chinese ports meaning a present, a gratuity, a tip. In this case the property owner must have been paid well by the insurance agents as a result of the stranding.

Captain L. R. W. Beavis in 1927

CHAPTER XXII

FERRYBOAT DAYS AND THEN...

J was now well on in years but still undaunted when I joined the West Vancouver Ferries. Most of the time I was mate, although sometimes master. These little ferries were run on a nine hour shift which was not arduous except in foggy weather. Then it was decidedly harrassing, criminal if you like. Running full speed with numerous courses and more often than not, we had a very hot tide. The captain steered. It was a case of looking at the compass, looking ahead, blowing the whistle, looking at his watch and *listening* all of the time. The courses were all run on time. [This is also known as the echo system.] It was really wonderful how well they maintained the schedule and how free from accidents we were. The mate had to keep a look out as soon as he had collected the fares, which were taken on board. Hardly any of the passengers realized the risk they ran or the nerve-racking the skipper was going through. The ferries were owned by the municipality and the council did not care about operations. They were not sea-minded people and knew very little about it.

At times there were amusing incidents amongst some of the passengers. One lady (the lord forgive me for calling her such) hated to pay her fare. If she could not inveigle another passenger to give her a punch on his community ticket, she would head off for the ladies' room where she would stay until the ferry docked. Once an old lady remarked to me as I collected her fare, "Mrs. X is in the toilet and has been there a long time. She may be ill."

"Madame," I replied, "Not on your life do I collect fares in the ladies' toilet room."

At last Mrs. X became so notorious that we had orders to collect her fare before she boarded the ferry. And wasn't she abusive!

Saturday nights were the worst. On the last two trips from the City there would always be a lot of drunks. On one occasion a man would not pay his fare. That did not matter so much to me, except that his language grew abusive and then he struck me. That was enough. I just waded into him and left him lying on the floor of the SONRISA's smoke room. Heading for the pilot house I told the captain he had better go down and have a look at one of the passengers. "I think he wants first aid and he won't accept it from me."

Captain Smith returned with a broad grin. "Man, man," he said, "you may be old but you still have some punch."

Another time late at night, when I happened to be mate, there was a hefty Swede—very drunk. We were bound to West Vancouver. He would not pay his fare and would not leave the boat but instead, promptly made for the ladies' cabin to go to sleep. None of the ladies would go into the cabin. It was up to me to get that Swede out. Discreetly, the captain and the watchman stayed on the dock. He was much too big for me to tackle alone and years younger. I began to wonder; then a brainwave came to me—tackle him like the ancient Greeks did. Rushing him to the stairway, I grabbed him by the xxx and squeezed hard. Yah! Yah! he landed on deck with me and then took a flying jump to the wharf. It worked. The skipper and the watchman with the aid of the police were then able to handle their man.

And so the years passed. The only serious accident that happened to these ferries occurred after I had left them. In a dense fog, the West Vancouver No. 5 collided with the Canadian Pacific Railway's steamer PRINCESS ALICE inbound and sank. The ferry had been outbound to West Vancouver and had only a few passengers aboard. She had just safely landed a big crowd. If it had happened with the rush crowd there might have been a tremendous loss of life. As it was there was only one fatality, an elderly lady who was pinned by the wreckage in the lady's cabin. Captain Smith, the skipper, did his best to extricate her, leaving at last when the poor woman was already under water and the water then up to his neck as the ferry sank.

A year or so prior to this accident I had taken my superannuation [retirement or pension] and then shortly after I suffered a supreme sorrow in the loss of my wife. My daughter, who was in the telephone service, and I moved to a house right on the beach at West Vancouver. Here I could see the ships pass in and out through the Narrows and hear the lap of the tidal waters constantly pounding at our door. On the beach I used to cut wood and play around with the crosscut saw.

It was here that I met my goddaughter. She was Heaven-sent and gallantly helped this old sailor look at the bright side of life once again. Laughingly she would take the other end of the crosscut saw. This little lady had corn-coloured hair and sparkling blue eyes. I doff my hat to thee.

Looking back over the years that have slipped past rapidly, I feel that I have much for which to be thankful. There were many fine friends who gathered around when I was sick nigh unto death. I had passed through three operations at the Vancouver General Hospital with the skill of Doctor Lee Smith, the wondrous care of the staff and the unremitting thoughtfulness of my daughter. Coming out of the hospital a veritable wreck, most

of my friends thought this old sailor was bound for another port, but the Great Pilot had taught me to rerig my ship and to sail a little longer. It was to be in solitude. Shortly after, my daughter married and moved to Portland, Oregon. "Father, you did the same to Mother and I." I had selfishly thought she would always stay with me.

With my daughter gone, I was once again struck with wanderlust stirring in my blood. Vancouver was getting over-crowded, too noisy for me. Packing my belongings I boarded the CHELOHSIN of the Union Steamship Line. We were bound for that island that rejoices in the name of Lasqueti (last water) in the Gulf of Georgia some fifty miles westward of Vancouver. I hoped to find a comfortable anchorage but, arriving at False Bay around midnight, it looked as if most of the inhabitants of the island were

The author captain on Lasqueti Island

CHELOHSIN
"Packing my belongings I boarded the CHELOHSIN of the Union Steamship Line. We were bound for that island that rejoices in the name of Lasqueti in the Gulf of Georgia some fifty miles westward of Vancouver."

Built in 1911 at Dublin, Ireland, for the Union Steamship Company of British Columbia. The steamer measured 175.5 x 35.1 x 14. On November 4, 1949, the CHELOHSIN stranded off Siwash Rock. It was written off as a total loss. The steamer was sold to David Victor for $1500. To the amazement of everyone, he refloated her and the vessel was towed to North Vancouver in 1950. In 1951 the CHELOHSIN was sold to a San Francisco scrapper for $25,000.

down on the dock to greet the steamer and pick up the freight.[1]

It was a weird scene and I wondered how I was going to negotiate the seven or eight miles to my lonely ranch. Just then a youth surprised me by asking if I was Captain Beavis. "How did you know?" I asked with astonishment.

"By your beard, sir," he replied. How glad I was of my hirsute contraption.

Boarding a crazy old Ford truck loaded down with my freight and by no means forgetting my box of two Persian cats, we started off through the forest. The old Ford grunted and groaned, wheezed and coughed, then spluttered and hiccoughed again. At a snail's pace we crawled through the forest, dropping off one of our passengers and some sacks of food at a gateway on the road which was said to be a homestead. There was nary a light to be seen on this deserted highway at two in the morning.

We arrived safe and sound at what I thought must be the end of the world and no doubt my two felines thought so, too. I was met by the lady owner of the place, Mrs. Mabel Hawkshaw, who had gallantly come up a week ahead of me to put the place in order. I headed for bed after buttering my cats' paws.[2]

The solitude was immense. It could be felt all around.

The owner left the next day and I was alone. Two days passed and never a soul passed along that road.

I have longed for quiet. I am getting it with a vengeance.

Sometimes I feel like a shipwrecked sailor. When night falls it gets a wee bit creepy. One night, pitch dark, I was awakened by an awful noise on the verandah. "Clamp, clamp, clamp," and then through my open casement I saw the devil himself or so I thought. He put his head through the window; the cats were spitting and swearing. "Old sailor," I said to myself, "He has come at last for you." I was in a blue funk but on turning my eyes to the window, I saw that it was only an old horse. He was friendly at that and how he gazed at me in the morning. He had sorrowful looking eyes when I cussed him in no uncertain sailor language. It was my own fault for not closing the gate, even little children are taught to close gates. Horses, cows and sheep wander around the island at their own sweet will.

My place is close to the shores of a lake but in a hollow where Mount Trematon towers 1050 feet in the air quite close aboard. I am lonely. Mail day is the one great day of the week. How one looks forward to it.

The letters of my goddaughter have more than cheered my lonely way. They have been an inspiration to work, to do better, and still to hope. A little maid can soften an old sailor's heart and help him steer his barque from the stormy waters onto a safe course and smooth sea.

And so now in the sunset of my life I thank my Pilot for all those aids to heavenly navigation. With due humility I launch this small bark of reminiscences with many doubts as to whether it will reach a port of understanding. Yet, I hope with a sailor's philosophy that it will be of use to the younger generation now following the sea.

Then what care I.
Blow today and Blow tomorrow
Blow ye winds heigh ho.

[1] ed. note. Lasqueti, a tiny island often not appearing on maps, is near Texada Island. It has fewer than 300 permanent inhabitants as of 1986.

[2] ed.note. So they would not wander off. Old Wive's Tale.

203

INDEX

207

Photos are indicated with a p/ followed by
the page number. Information pertaining
to the subject may also appear on that
page.

210